Contents

Speech
Can Change
Your Life

Speech Can Change Your Life

TIPS ON SPEECH, CONVERSATION
AND SPEECHMAKING

Dorothy Sarnoff

A DELL BOOK

Published by
DELL PUBLISHING CO., INC.
1 Dag Hammarskjold Plaza
New York, New York 10017

ISBN: 0-440-18199-2

Reprinted by arrangement with
Doubleday & Company, Inc.
Garden City, New York

Printed in the United States of America
First Dell printing—August 1972
Eleventh Dell printing—February 1985

Author's Note

This book is for you who want to sound better (Part I) . . . be more interesting and at ease in conversation (Part II) . . . or speak more confidently and effectively—without the handicap of uncontrollable nervousness in formal presentations or speeches (Part III).

If you have speech problems, the hints that follow will help you correct them. If you speak well, they will help you speak still better.

Before reading the book, check the distractors you would like to eliminate:

- [ ] Nervousness
- [ ] Nasality
- [ ] Stridency or shrillness
- [ ] Speed, chop or slow talking
- [ ] Lack of projection
- [ ] Local or ethnic accents
- [ ] Mumbling
- [ ] Monotony
- [ ] Lisping

Check the categories in which you would like to improve:

- [ ] Public Speaking
- [ ] Impromptu speaking
- [ ] Conversation

- [ ] Capturing and holding attention
- [ ] Pacing . . . too fast? too slow?
- [ ] Convincing the listener
- [ ] Speaking with enthusiasm
- [ ] Using speech notes
- [ ] Listening and absorbing
- [ ] Communicating warmly
- [ ] Telling anecdotes and stories
- [ ] Handling panels and discussions
- [ ] Speaking with authority

In sum, this book can help you achieve the best possible overall speech picture for the business and social demands of your daily life.

Dorothy Sarnoff

Introduction

Let thy speech be better than silence;
Or be silent.   —DIONYSIUS

When Billy Rose heard a playback of his first radio broadcast, he clapped his hands to his ears and moaned, "Take it away! That's not me! It's an impostor! It sounds like a nail file scraping a cheese grater!"

Millions of men and women, ranging from business tycoons to housewives, would be dismayed to discover how they really sound to others. After a lecture on speech that I gave in Chicago, a woman approached me, smiling broadly, to say, "I ay-um so glay-ud I don't hay-uve the tway-ung my sister in Kay-unsus hay-us!" Poor woman! She had her sister's twang in spades, doubled and redoubled.

A student's initial talk in my classes is recorded on closed-circuit television and played back to him instantly. For the first time he sees and hears himself as others see and hear him as he makes a speech or presentation. He can hardly believe his own ears and eyes.

Madison Avenue warns us constantly of such social and business offenders as bad breath, body odor, and dingy teeth. We take steps to avoid these; but are our best friends telling us about our equally disenchanting speech habits?

You may not be aware of how you look and sound when you speak. But everyone else is.

DO YOU SOUND AS GOOD AS YOU LOOK?

Some time ago I attended an elegant dinner party at 21, one of the world's fine restaurants. The guests all wore their best. Jewels winked; shirtfronts gleamed.

The last woman to arrive outshone the rest of us as a peacock outshines sparrows. Her gown and grooming were the envy of every female at the table; her eyes sparkled; her skin was satin; her figure and carriage were superb.

Unfortunately, she not only caught the eye as a peacock does; when she opened her mouth, she turned out to have the ear-splitting sound of a peacock, too.

The man at my right, publisher of a fashion magazine, winced in dismay that was almost comical. I could not help leaning toward him and murmuring, "It's all your fault."

"*My* fault?" he exclaimed, astonished. "How do you figure that?"

"Because month after month, year after year, your magazine parades glamour aids before the eyes of women: gowns, perfume, makeup, false eyelashes, wigs.

"But you never tell them how much more attractive they would be if they paid the same attention to their speech that they do to their faces and figures.

"You give fashion advice to men, too. Why don't you point out that the impression a man makes depends far more on the quality of his speech and his ability to communicate than the cut of his jacket?"

"But can a grown man change his speech habits?" asked the publisher.

"Why," I said, "I could give our friend across the table a few simple tips that would soon have her sounding as lovely as she looks. There is no reason in the world why any normal person can't develop attractive speech."

"If it is really possible to help people that way, and you know how," said the publisher, "why don't you do it?"

"Do you know," I said, "I think I will."

That was the start of my courses in Speech Dynamics.
It was also the start of this book.

THE MAKING OF A SPEECH CONSULTANT

It was probably inevitable that I became a speech con-
sultant. The human voice, and how it communicates, has
fascinated me since, at the age of three, I stood before an
audience of parents at the Brooklyn Academy of Music
and sang "Little Sir Echo, how do you do?" I sang and
acted my way through high school and college. I went on
singing and acting professionally in opera, on Broadway,
and in supper clubs. And I seized greedily on every scrap
of information I could find about voice, speech, and speech
presentation.

Metropolitan Opera stars such as Florence Easton,
Queena Mario, and Giovanni Martinelli worked patiently
with me, teaching me how to use my breath, how to project my voice, how to add color and beauty to my speech,
how to protect my vocal cords.

I studied the stars with whom I played, emulated their
skills, unabashedly asked their advice and help. They were
unforgettably kind. Shirley Booth taught me to release
real tears at will on the stage. By watching Yul Brynner
I learned to black out every distraction while waiting for
the curtain to rise. Mary Martin taught me to trigger applause by punctuating songs with hand and body gestures.
Gertrude Lawrence showed me dozens of secrets of getting and holding attention.

All these bits of knowledge fell into place when, the very
day after that conversation at 21, I began developing the
study courses that are now known as Speech Dynamics.
Since then I have revealed the simple secrets of attractive
and effective speech to thousands of students here in New
York, to tens of thousands who attend my lectures na-
tionwide, and to millions of radio listeners and TV
viewers. I have redesigned and refurbished speech

habits, styles, and images for Americans of every size, shape, description, humor, purse, and origin. My students have ranged from septuagenarians to teen-agers; from executives to housewives; from stenographers, sales girls, clerks, and immigrants to brokers, lawyers, government officials, Arizona ranchers, and nurses.

I have seen—and heard—improvements in speech that seemed almost miraculous even to me. And again and again I have seen even modest improvements in my students' speech pictures effect Cinderella-like transformations in their lives.

YOU CAN HAVE THE SPEECH YOU WANT

Each day I receive thank-you messages. Some come from men and women whose names you may have heard. More are from persons who, like most of us, are known only to a few friends and to God.

A clerk in a shipping company, who had lived for years in the shadow of a dismissal notice, wrote exultantly that after improving his speech picture he had become a junior executive with "no ceiling on my future." A woman who had long been the forgotten member of her civics club learned to speak so eloquently that she was asked to represent her organization at its world convention. A young man won the girl who earlier had refused to take him seriously. The head of a brokerage firm, formerly the victim of stage fright whenever he had to give a talk, learned to command both his nerves and his audiences. "At last," he now says proudly, "I really feel like the head of my own company."

These men and women have discovered that attractive oral communication does much more than simply cover defective personalities with pancake makeup. It lets their truer, better personalities emerge. If a woman speaks more winningly, she will become more winning in other ways. A man who learns to speak with confidence and authority will begin to act with confidence and authority.

On the stage, an amber gelatin placed over the spotlight will make a presentable woman look downright homely. A pink gelatin, on the other hand, will give her face the soft glow of a Renoir painting. In light rehearsal, before *The King and I* opened on Broadway, I saw Gertrude Lawrence take the mirror from her handbag and check every square foot of the stage to make sure she would not work in amber light.

Your speech can alter your image as drastically as the spotlight gelatin alters an actor's. Make it not amber-drab, but Renoir-pink. Speech can reveal the gold in a personality that had seemed gray. It can make a moderately intelligent man appear brilliant, and a moderately engaging woman irresistible.

Mme. de Staël, a famous hostess of Napoleonic France, was a far from handsome woman; but when she spoke, men could not take their ears off her.

BE A PRINCE, NOT A FROG!

Are you a prince to look at, but a frog to listen to? A tiger to see, but a mouse to hear? Is your voice whiney? Nasal? Strident? Are you a whisper talker? A mumbler? Do you mispronounce? Do you draw out your words like taffy, or rattle them out like popping corn?

Are you uncomfortable in conversation? Do your acquaintances seem to be thinking about something else when you talk? Do they interrupt, or drift away? At parties, are you out of it?

Do business interviews, presentations, conferences, and speeches unnerve you? Do you feel inadequate when you conduct a meeting?

If you suffer from any of these common communication ailments, this book is for you. Unless your problem reflects some physical defect requiring therapy, you can turn your speech from gray to gold by following suggestions in the following chapters. You will find that they require a minimum of effort, and are enjoyable as well.

They will take less time each day than you spend on shaving (if you are a man) or making up your face (if you are a woman). In fact, as you do either you can put some of them into practice. In six weeks your speech will not be just as good as new; it will be much better.

Take advantage of the hints and shortcuts in this book and your speech will become clear . . . colorful . . . captivating . . . convincing. People will listen when you speak. And they will enjoy listening.

Don't wait until an emergency arises: until you are about to be interviewed for a promising new job, or make a speech for your favorite political candidate, or have your first date with your favorite example of the opposite sex.

The time to start is now. Read the following pages with care. Take the suggestions to heart. Don't skip; the part you miss may be the very one you need most. This book can dramatically change your speech, your conversation, your speechmaking—and your life.

PART I

SOUND
AS GOOD AS
YOU LOOK

1. Make Your Speech Work for You

Speech is a mirror of the soul;
As a man speaks, so is he.
—PUBLILIUS SYRUS

Most of the frictions of daily life, said novelist Arnold Bennett, are caused by irritating sounds and habits of voice and speech. Speech deficiencies can result in lost jobs and canceled business deals. They can torpedo international conferences, and break up homes. Your speech image helps people decide whether they want you to run their business, be their doctor, represent them in Congress. It helps them make up their minds whether they would buy a used car from you, or invite you to the house to become better acquainted.

You are not immune to the perils of speech distractors even if your thoughts shine like stars, if your ideas for increasing your company's profits work as well as J. Paul Getty's, if you are bursting with fascinating facts about art or sports, airplanes or mineralogy, concerts or computers. Few will hear you out unless you can engage their attention and then communicate warmly and compellingly. You have little chance of attaining your goals if yours is one of the chorus of dreary voices that only a mother could love.

Marshall McLuhan's famous assertion that "the medium is the message" may not apply to all forms of communication, but it certainly does to speech.

Speech distractors and ineffectiveness can sell you short.

They can tell unkind lies about you. They can distort your image.

Some speech mannerisms, like physical disfigurements, cry out for plastic surgery. Others need minor alterations, like last year's clothes. Still others need firming up, like a sagging midriff. Some speech needs tuning, as your automobile may; or, like your car's springs, needs to have the squeaks oiled away. A few voices, like little boys' smudged faces, could do with a good scrub in warm, soapy water.

IT'S NOT WHAT YOU SAY—IT'S THE WAY YOU SAY IT

Just as fingers were made before forks, so grunts, squeaks, howls, coos, and giggles antedate words. The Neanderthal man never had to parse a sentence, but by varying the tone of his voice he could either terrify enemies or soften the hearts of Neanderthal maidens.

Since human beings developed language, speech has changed the destinies of nations. By the force of his eloquence, Savonarola turned fifteenth-century Florence from a profligate into a puritanical city. The speeches of Peter the Hermit sent tens of thousands of men and women— yes, and small children—pouring into the Middle East in a vain and bloody crusade to snatch Jerusalem from the Moslems.

It is a pity that the voices of the great orators of the past have not come down to us along with their words. Suppose you could have heard Cicero insist to the Roman Senate, "Carthage must be destroyed!" Or Patrick Henry cry, "As for me, give me liberty, or give me death!" Or Abraham Lincoln, "This nation, under God, shall have a new birth of freedom!" Or William Jennings Bryan, "You shall not press down upon the brow of labor this crown of thorns; you shall not crucify mankind upon a cross of gold!"

Reduced to paper, these words are still jewel-like; but they are jewels without their settings. The speaker's *there-*

ness, his personality, his beat and drive and urgency—all these are gone forever.

If you doubt how dependent words are on utterance, go sometime to see a second-rater play Hamlet.

BLACK PLAGUE IN HOLLYWOOD

We take for granted today that attractive speech is an essential part of any actor's equipment. In motion pictures this was not always so.

When sound movies arrived in the late 1920s, a whole generation of motion picture actors was wiped out with a sweep of the scythe, as if a black plague had swept through Hollywood.

There had been no need for the stars of silent pictures to speak well. After all, their fans could not hear them. Sound caught these cinematic dinosaurs unprepared. One promising star, for the first time hearing her recorded voice, took an overdose of sleeping pills. Corinne Griffith, dream girl of a generation of motion picture goers, retired permanently after reading *Time's* unkind comment: "Pretty Corinne Griffith talks through her nose."

Just before sound tracks and motion picture film were wedded, John Gilbert, successor of Rudolph Valentino as the Casanova of the silver screen, signed a four-year contract at a million dollars a year. In his first picture under the new arrangement, Gilbert's thin, reedy tenor evoked snickers of derision from the same moviegoers who had cheered his passionate lovemaking only a year before. The ear picture canceled out the eye picture, and brought a great career to an end.

HOW DO YOU SOUND AT HOME?

If you are single, your speech may decide whether you will ever marry. If you are married, it may decide whether you stay that way.

A still-handsome woman sobbed to me that after thirty-five years of marriage her husband was insisting on divorce. There was no other woman, he assured her; he simply wanted to be alone.

Whatever else may have been wrong with that marriage, one handicap leaped to the ear. If I had lived with her convulsive giggle and mosquito-like voice for years, I would have wanted to be alone too.

It was not difficult to clear up the giggle. Unfortunately, it was too late to clear up the marriage.

So if your husband winces when you speak, or your wife never seems to listen to what you have to say, you could do worse than to take a look at your own speech.

THE KEY TO YOUR CAREER

Ability to speak confidently, concisely, and convincingly is essential to anyone who is ambitious for business success. The first thing a businessman has to sell is himself. From the interview that gets him his first job to the day he becomes Chairman Emeritus, he has to persuade others. If you are in business, your speech image—which includes the way you look as well as how you sound—will determine how far you rise.

Today, more than ever, the business speaker is seen as well as heard. Where once he might have talked to his associates in other cities by means of a telephone conference, he is now increasingly likely to use closed-circuit television. Even intra-office meetings may become television sessions in which none of the participants leaves his own desk.

Your ability to project yourself on television may be the key to your business success, whether or not you ever appear on a public broadcast. (It may be the key to your social success as well a few years hence, when the picture-phone will be as common as the telephone is today.)

"MY SPEECH IS KILLING ME!"

A friend of my husband's recently lost an important proxy fight though all the best arguments were on his side. "I suddenly realized," he told us ruefully, "that my speech was killing me. My stockholders could not be convinced by anything I said, because they were bothered by the way I said it."

He was right. Born abroad, he had retained the guttural Germanic "r," and had never bothered to master the American pronunciation of "th." A "w" for him was a "v." The cadence of his speech, too, was European.

Aware of his speech inadequacies, he made matters worse by talking apologetically. He mumbled; he failed to meet the eyes of his audience. The medium, for them, was the message; and both medium and message were negative.

A positive speech image can help you as much as a negative one can hurt you. Advertising tycoon Mary Wells, who took Madison Avenue by storm, is unexcelled at creating fresh, effective advertising campaigns; but her rise would not have been so meteoric were it not, as columnist Eugenia Sheppard remarked, that "Her soft, thrilling voice makes the maddest ideas seem perfectly possible."

Your speech image can be your greatest asset—or your worst liability. Make it work for you, not against you.

SOUND LIKE THE BEST POSSIBLE YOU

Your husband does not expect you to be a Julie Andrews in your speech. Your wife does not expect you to be a Richard Burton. You should sound like you—but the best possible you. Your speech should meet your real needs, and do justice to the kind of person you really are.

A bright young Bronx attorney asked me to give him the speech of an Oxford graduate. I refused. With a British accent, he would have been as out of place among his clients as H. Rap Brown at a meeting of the Ku Klux Klan. But I gladly helped him to rid himself of the tough-sounding intonations and speech mannerisms that belied the cultivated person he really was.

William Bendix's raspy voice would have shortened the life of any speech teacher; yet it served him well in the entertainment world. It was right for the parts he played. Similarly, the Hungarian accents of the Gabor sisters only enhance their exotic appeal. You probably would not want to sound like Mae West, but the Mae West voice is an inseparable and invaluable part of the Mae West legend.

Speech that distracts, however, cannot help you; it only gets in your way. You may be able to compensate for it, as a one-armed golfer may conceivably play in the eighties, or a wooden-legged man dance the twist; but why should you handicap yourself when you don't have to? Would you advise a sprinter to carry a fifty-pound weight in each hand? He might win the race, but not many people would bet on it.

To eliminate those speech distractors, you must first be able to identify them. The next chapter tells you how.

REMEMBER:

- ◄   People judge you by your speech.
- ◄   Poor speech handicaps you in every aspect of your social life . . . business life . . . and love life.
- ◄   Attractive speech habits open the door to success.
- ◄   You can sound like the best possible you!

2. Help, I'm Being Taped!

Ah, would some power the giftie gie us
To see ourselves, as ithers see us.
—ROBERT BURNS

How can you pinpoint the speech blemishes that destroy
or shatter an otherwise appealing image . . . rob you of
power, authority, and persuasion if you are a man . . . of
femininity and allure if you are a woman . . . lessen your
impact . . . keep you from being lovable at first listen?

If your face has a blemish, you see it in a mirror. You
go to a drugstore or cosmetic counter and buy something
to cure, cover, or camouflage it. If it is bad enough, you
go to a plastic surgeon and have it eliminated.

Speech blemishes can detract just as much—but how
do you know they are there? Before you can cure or
eliminate them, you have to recognize them.

A mirror can tell you a little something about your
speech picture. It can tell you, for instance, whether you
are using your hands too much . . . contracting the sides
of your mouth, and so making your speech as well as your
face ugly . . . being aloof, stiff, and tense . . . forcing your
voice . . . talking without moving your lips.

But the best reporter of speech is the tape recorder.
Many small, lightweight recorders are on the market at a
price any family can afford; if you have a mirror in your
home, you should have a tape recorder too. It won't be
long before you can buy an inexpensive video-corder for
instant TV playback, so that you can check yourself visu-
ally and aurally at the same time. Meanwhile, do get the

tape recorder. It will enable you, in privacy, to hear exactly how you sound. You can learn your defects and shortcomings, and check the results of the easily followed suggestions in this book.

In business, a tape recorder for your speech is an indispensable aid to success. You can use it to review your ideas aloud, to edit and practice speeches and presentations, to rehearse interviews, to check your speech and conversation habits in action by recording yourself on the telephone.

The tape recorder can provide a permanent vocal record of your children's lives, from the first goo to the loving "I do." It can be a Baby Book in sound. If yours is a family that likes to read aloud (as I hope it is), the tape recorder will preserve those relaxed moments and keep you abreast of the development in your children's speech.

If you have no recorder, you can learn a little something about your voice through either of two very simple procedures:

1. Say something with your nose almost against the middle of a large, half-opened magazine. You will hear a considerably magnified sound.

2. Face a corner of a room, as close as you can sit or stand to where the walls meet. Cup your hands lightly over your ears, and speak in your usual fashion. The sound will bounce back, amplified. And you may be surprised at what you hear! (Two thousand years ago, Horace told the Roman patricians they should recite while in the bathing pavilion. "The closeness of the place," he said, "gives melody to the voice." Actually, I suspect he should have given the credit to the marble walls. On concert tours, I did not vocalize in my hotel room, where the walls and carpet absorbed sound, but rather in the bathroom, where the porcelain and the tiles seemed to give my voice added brilliance and luster.)

What are the speech blemishes you should guard against? How can you recognize them?

ARE YOU A NOSE TALKER?

(Nasality)

This blemish is particularly common and disfiguring. When you talk through your nose, you twang. Clasp your nose between thumb and forefinger, so as to close your nostrils. Then say: "She sang seventeen songs and swooned." Your fingers will pick up the vibration caused in your nose by "m," "n," and "ng." These are the only three legitimate nasal sounds in our language.

For contrast, hold your nostrils the same way and say, "Woe, oh woe, oh woe, oh woe!" The sound should come entirely from your mouth. If you buzz, even on those "o" vowels, you are a nose talker. In the theater, the actor who wants to play a complaining and disagreeable character is apt to adopt a nasal speech pattern.

You cannot be lovable at first listen if you talk through your nose. You will be whining, lifeless, and negative. Yet your voice has to come out through your nose if your mouth does not open enough when you talk. Look into your mirror, and say, "Hi, you handsome, wonderful, lovable creature!" There should be almost a half-inch strip of darkness between your teeth throughout a good part of that self-admiring sentence.

If, instead, your teeth are fitted together like two rows of corn on a cob, or if, even worse, your lips are virtually closed, like those of a ventriloquist, you almost certainly speak nasally.

Nasality mars a woman's image even more than a man's. Have you ever heard a woman whose nasal twang was alluring? Of course not! If you want to be as persuasive as advertising tycoon Mary Wells, or as seductive as Brigitte Bardot, bring your resonance not from your nose but from your chest. There is more sex to the chest than two bumps.

The tight, clenched jaw was once considered the "society" way of talking. "Don't move a muscle; don't let animation show in your face; avoid laughter—it makes wrinkles." I for one, am all for those laugh lines. If you lack them, perhaps you don't laugh enough; and in our problem-laden world, we need all the laughter we can get. The animation in our faces is one way of reaching out to each other.

The clenched-jaw speaker emanates tenseness and strain. This prevented a woman I know from fulfilling a long-held and altruistic dream of recording books for the blind. Blind readers could not see her, but they could *hear* the tightness in her voice.

My husband says that the clenched jaw, sometimes described as "Locust Valley lockjaw" or "Massachusetts malocclusion," is an expression of agony carried over from the days of tight high-button shoes, tight celluloid collars, and tight corsets.

Anti-Nasality Hints: Pages 12, 43, 47, 53, 58

ARE YOU A SHRIEKER?

(Stridency, shrillness, screeching)

Do you screech even when you are not angry? Do you force your voice even when you are not calling the children? Women, particularly, often do, perhaps because of the million irritants which sting them each day. If you are a wife with a strident voice, your husband's teeth are set on edge every time you speak. Stridency and shrillness are even more disagreeable than nasality. I can think of only one politician—the late Mayor Fiorello LaGuardia of New York—who won and kept the affection of his constituency despite a shrill, strident voice. When LaGuardia read the Sunday comics over the radio, the whole city chuckled—because they loved the Little Flower, despite his voice.

This is another blemish that shows up in your mirror. Does your neck look taut? Do the veins and cords stand out like ropes? Are the muscles around your chin tight to the eye and the touch? If they are, you probably sound as strident as a seagull.

Try talking with a ribbon tied snugly around your neck. If you strain or force your voice, you will feel the ribbon choking you as you approach the end of each sentence.

Anti-Stridency Tips: Pages 37, 42, 43, 47, 48, 53

ARE YOU THERE?

(Lack of projection: the whisperer, the fader)

Do you usually sound weary and depressed? Does your voice have wrinkles in it? Does it lack vitality, vigor, energy, enthusiasm, intensity? Are you constantly asked to repeat because people do not hear you? The reason may be that you lack proper breath support. You are failing to project.

Whispering is for telling secrets and making love. There is only one time when you are justified in whispering in public. That is when you stand at the altar, and say, "I do." Even if nobody can hear you, everybody will know what you said.

What is a whisper? It is the ghost of a sound—one from which most of the tone and resonance are missing. A breeze whispers until it has something to vibrate against. As soon as it runs into a leaf, it rustles.

To recognize whisper talk, first put a finger against your Adam's apple and say "Zzzzzzz." You feel a vibration; "Zzzzzzz" cannot be said in a true whisper. It is a voiced tone. Now say "Sssssss." Your larynx does not vibrate. "Sssssss" is the unvoiced whispered counterpart of "Zzzzzzz."

Next, your finger still on your larynx, make some such remark in your normal voice as "I wonder whether I'll feel a vibration." If the telltale buzz is missing, you are a whisper speaker.

Do not confuse whisper speaking with soft but supported speaking. Your voice needs support even at its lowest volume. You should have at your command projection ranging from the very quiet to the very strong with infinite gradations of volume in between.

If you whisper for effect, as Marilyn Monroe did, and still manage to make yourself heard, you are not really whispering at all—you are stage whispering, an entirely different thing. The stage whisper is supported by almost as much air pressure as a declamation. In the theater, it can be heard from the nearest seat in the orchestra to the farthest row in the balcony. In his army days, General James M. Gavin was known for his low voice, but no one had trouble understanding him; he stage whispered. (Besides, if you are serving under a general as forceful as Gavin, you'd *better* understand him!)

The unprojected speaker, by contrast, is almost inaudible. Jackie Kennedy Onassis is one of these. Sometimes it was a strain to make out what she was saying on her famous television tour of the White House.

An instructor for a corporation which provided classified electronic information to navy men came to me for help because his voice was so low that his students beyond the first row could barely make out what he was saying. He kept his classified information classified even from his class. I am happy to say that now he projects so well that an enemy agent could hear him out in the hall.

Some people who are perfectly audible in one situation are whisper talkers in another. I know a chain store magnate who always whisper talks when he is out socially with his wife; yet he makes himself heard at board meetings. My suspicion is that he is trying, perhaps subconsciously, to tell his wife that she should moderate both the volume and the quantity of her conversation. If so, she has yet to get the message—which shows that whisper talking is no way to drive home a point.

Women may think that inaudibility demonstrates their feminine delicacy. Actually, they are substituting a meretricious femininity for the real thing. Whispering, like fainting, may have been an acceptable part of the culture in the days of Queen Victoria. If you are a girl with your eye on a man today, I don't advise you to try to win his heart by fainting. He may be sympathetic enough to call an ambulance, but I doubt whether he will bother to visit you in the hospital. By the same token, don't try to win him by faint murmurings. If your transmitter is so weak that it is a strain to hear you, he will simply turn to another station.

A woman once told me proudly, "My friends say my voice is *so* soothing that it puts them to sleep." The poor creature thought she was being complimented. Her friends were really trying to tell her that she was failing to keep them awake.

A not too distant relative of the whisper speaker is the fader. His voice comes and goes as if he were a crystal radio in a thunderstorm. A sentence may start perfectly well, on a flowing current of breath support through which the words swim as gracefully as fishes; but toward the end the current dries up, leaving the last words to expire, flapping a little, on the wet sand. Just when the sound should be strongest, it collapses like a fallen souffle.

Beware the unprojected voice if your purpose is to communicate. The only person an overquiet speaker can communicate with effectively is a professional lip reader.

Projection Promoters: Page 37

LAZY LIPS

(Mumbling)

Even a lip reader may not be able to make out a mumbler, because the mumbler's lips often do not move enough to be read.

The flock of a parish priest complained, "Six days a week he is invisible, and on the seventh he is inaudible." He was a mumbler.

A mumbler, like a whisperer, manages to keep secrets

even when he is trying to reveal them. His lips are lazy, and he fails to project. He runs his words together, sometimes omitting whole syllables.

Speak into the mirror once more. If your lips barely move, you are mumbling. To quote Ogden Nash:

I believe that people before they graduate or even matriculate,
They should learn to speak up, to speak out, to articulate.
It befuddles my sense acoustic
To be mumbled at through a potato, be it from Idaho or Aroostook.

This word-swallowing, these muffled mutes and slovenly slurrings
Can lead to calamitous misunderstands and errings . . .
It's easy to be manly and still make your meaning plain, whether in accents of Mt. Ida, Cathay or Boston, of Des Moines or of the deepest South
. . . Just take that towel out of your mouth.

My prescription, more prosaic than Mr. Nash's, is this: speak with *lively* not lazy lips.

Anti-Mumbling Secrets: Pages 59, 234, 235

ARE YOU A FOGHORN?

(Hoarseness and rasping)

Faulty breath support may show up not in whispering or mumbling, but in strain. An unsupported voice is like a Model T Ford trying to climb a steep hill in high gear. It moves slower and slower, starts to jerk, and finally stalls altogether. Excessive speechmaking with an unsupported voice cannot but produce hoarseness. Millions of television viewers of the Republican and Democratic National Conventions in 1968 heard platform officials force their voices (and sometimes their audiences) almost beyond endurance. Representative Carl Albert, permanent chairman for the Democrats, could scarcely speak at all by the time the convention ended. The Model T had barely made it up the hill. For unforced, focused, effective speech, you must know how to feed the gas and adjust the gears.

If your throat tires quickly when you talk . . . if you constantly clear it . . . if you are chronically hoarse, though you haven't a cold, don't smoke, and are told by the doctor that there is nothing organically wrong with your throat —then you are not using your breath properly to support your voice. The result is likely to be a fuzzy, foggy, grating sound that irritates the listener's throat as well as your own.

Projection Practice: Pages 40, 49

DO YOU COLOR IT GRAY?

(Monotony of pitch)

The average voice runs a scale of twelve to twenty notes. (A professional actor's or singer's may span thirty-six.) Some unfortunates have a speaking range of only five notes. If you are one of these, your voice has all the fascination of a faucet with a worn-out washer—you drip, drip, drip. Or, like a metronome, you tick, tick, tick. As you drone, others doze. You are a Johnny or Jenny One-Note.

Businessmen sometimes come to me with a complaint like this: "When I talk, people get a sort of glazed, sleepy look." Why wouldn't they, if they have to listen to that endless drip, drip, drip, tick, tick, tick? Even the hundred eyes of Argos, the monster of Greek legend, could not have stayed open. No variety of pitch. No color. Drab, drab, drab.

To check your voice for monotony, listen to yourself as you read aloud from a newspaper. Do you vary the pitch, the pacing, the emphasis according to the sense? Is there life, color, melody in your voice? Or does every sentence sound wooden—like the one before? Do they all end on the same note?

A tape recorder provides an accurate voice picture. Read into it and listen to the playback, pretending you are listening to someone on the radio. Decide whether you really enjoy hearing him speak.

Color Additives: Pages 60, 65, 273

DOES YOUR SPEEDOMETER NEED ADJUSTING?

(Speed talk; chop talk, slow talk)

President Kennedy, in most respects a fine speaker, sometimes raced so fast that some listeners had a hard time keeping up with him. President Johnson, on the other hand, used to dawdle so that a new international crisis could have arisen before he finished briefing the country on the current one.

If you talk too fast, you will not be understood—and you may leave your listeners breathless. If you talk too slowly, they will stop listening. Acceptable speaking rates vary between 120 and 160 words a minute. We read aloud a little faster than we talk. The rate should never be constant, because thought and emotion should alter pacing. Pauses for effect and changes of speed provide needed variety.

Read the following quotation aloud. (It is from the speech by the late Stephen S. Wise.) Time yourself by the sweep hand of your watch. Stop at the end of sixty seconds, and mark the last word you speak:

In his lifetime Lincoln was maligned and traduced, but detraction during a man's lifetime affords no test of his life's value nor offers any forecast of history's verdict. It would almost seem as if the glory of immor-

tality were anticipated in the life of the great by detraction and denial whilst yet they lived. When a
Lincoln-like man arises, let us recognize and fitly
honor him. There could be no poorer way of honor-
ing the memory of Lincoln than to assume, as we
sometimes do, that the race of Lincolns has perished
from the earth, and that we shall never look on his
like again. One way to ensure the passing of the Lincolns is to assume that another Lincoln can nevermore
arise. Would we find Lincoln today, we must not seek
him in the guise of a rail-splitter, nor as a wielder of
the backwoodsman's axe, but as a mighty smiter of
wrong in high places and low.

Lincoln has become for us the test of human worth,
and we honor men in the measure in which they approach the absolute standard of Abraham Lincoln.
Other men may resemble and approach him; he remains the standard whereby all other men are measured and appraised.

If you did not reach the phrase "Lincoln can nevermore arise" in the sixty-second period, you were reading
too slowly. If you got into the second paragraph, you were
beginning to rat-a-tat-tat. The faster you go, too, the more
surely you will chop-talk, losing smoothness and flow,
sounding like the Morse Code tapped out on a telegraph
key or a 33⅓ r.p.m. record played back at a 78 r.p.m.
speed.

If, on the other hand, you spoke at less than 110 words
a minute, your best bet is to hire out as a baby-sitter. You
can count on putting your listeners to sleep.

Points for Pacing: Pages 75, 232, 233, 234

DO YOU HAVE A SPEECH TIC?

(Padding)

Do you know people who say, "You know, you know," until you bite your lips to keep from screaming? Or, "That is"? Or, "He says, I says"? There are dozens of varieties of speech tics. I once monitored a Hubert Humphrey TV interview for a magazine article, and counted thirty-one "I b'lieve's" in forty minutes. That's a lot of b'lieving.

Meaningless grunts like "uh" and "ur," too, can recur as remorselessly as a tic. Bear in mind the warning of the elder Oliver Wendell Holmes:

> . . . And when you stick on conversation's burrs,
> Don't strew your pathway with those dreadful *urs!*

If you have a tape recorder, let it run while you are talking on the telephone. The playback will reveal whether you are a padder. Once you become aware of these tics, you will notice them in yourself and others. You will realize how irritating—and unattractive—they are.

Stop Signs for Padding: Page 158

DO YOU UPSTAGE YOURSELF?

(Visual distractors)

Fidgeting; frowning; raising the eyebrows; nose twitching; lifting one side of the mouth; pulling the ear or chin; biting the lips; fussing with hair, beads, pencil, fingers, or tie; swinging a leg—these are only a few of the common distractors which may be upstaging what you are trying to say.

When Senator Eugene McCarthy ran for the Democratic Presidential nomination in 1968, the camera usually focused on his head and shoulders, showing an expression as tranquil as a saint's. Occasionally, however, the shot took in his whole body, and you would see his hands in constant action, nervously worrying his ring. The viewer's attention was drawn to that gesture and distracted from his message.

A businessman I know arranges for his secretary to be in the audience whenever he gives a talk. If he gestures too much, she signals him by putting a pencil behind her ear. You may not be fortunate enough to have a signaling secretary, but if you watch yourself you can quickly tell whether attention-thieves are robbing you of impact when you talk.

Stop Signs for Visual Distractors: Pages 83, 155

EYE-EYE-EYE!

When you clasp someone's hand in greeting, you establish a physical contact. An "eye clasp" forms just as vital a contact. You set up a connection with another human being.

Our radios, our TV sets, are silent boxes until we make a connection by turning on the electrical current. With your eyes, you can turn on the switch and make a very real connection.

Not only do your eyes *send* messages; they *receive* impressions from others' eyes. "How interesting"; "I'm bored"; "I understand"; "I'm confused"; "I am ready to end this"; "I am content to listen more"; "You irritate me."

When you speak, do your eyes talk too? Or do you avoid direct eye contact because it makes you feel uncomfortable? Does your gaze take refuge on the walls or ceilings? Do you look at your feet instead of the audience? Do you see people as blobs instead of individuals? There is no surer way to lose an audience!

Eye Contact: Pages 85, 86, 121

HAVE YOU A SPEECH MUSTACHE?

(Mispronunciations)

One of the trademarks of Salvador Dali, the painter, is an oversized, black, waxed mustache with exaggerated points, like horns. I once asked him if he wore it to attract attention.

"Oh, no," he replied, in fragmented Dali English, "I am really quite shy; I don't *want* attention. I don't wear this mustache to attract, but to distract. People look at it instead of *me*."

Since attention is mother's milk to Dali, I did not take his disclaimer seriously; but it does seem to me that speech problems are something like an unwanted, untidy mustache. They distract from what you are trying to say. Your speech should be clean shaven.

Mispronunciations (discussed in detail in Chapter 10) are one such speech mustache. Some of these result from sloppiness or laziness: "Govment" or "gumment" for "government," "gonna" for "going to," "idear" for "idea," "Sadday" for "Saturday."

Mispronounced consonants. Lisping and the sibilant "s". The "s" is more frequently distorted than any other consonant. At one extreme, it becomes a "th"; at the other, a piercing whistle.

The lithp is found everywhere in the world, from humble homes to haughty salons and executive suites. A giant-sized, important executive does not stay giant-sized very long if he is afflicted with a baby-sized lisp.

Often the lithp ith tho thlight that itth owner doethn't know he hath it. It is easy to check. Simply say, slowly and distinctly, a phrase containing a number of "s" sounds:

"Essential hospital nursing services" will do very well. Where was the tip of your tongue as you spoke? If it touched your teeth or gum ridges on those "s's" you were lithping, whether or not your ear caught the "th."

The sibilant "s" often occurs because of a gap between two front teeth, either upper or lower. It is like the whistling sound of a teakettle announcing that the water has come to a boil, but it brings irritation instead of pleasure to the listener. Take that kettle off the stove!

Exorcisors for Lisping and the Sibilant "S":
Pages 96, 97, 264

Other mispronounced consonants. Consonants are subject to a Pandora's boxful of abuses.

The exploding "t" was made famous by Mae West: "Come up *ta* see me some *time*." When addressed by a practitioner of the exploding "t", keep your distance—you may be sprayed.

Some people substitute a "d" for "th" ("doze" for "those"). Many of us associate this sound with old-time movie gangsters.

A familiar consonant defect is the lolling "l", as in "wowwipop"—another baby sound. Some people even make an "l" of an "n," at least according to this story:

A woman asked the butcher for kidleys. After she had repeated the word several times, he exclaimed, "Oh, you mean kidneys!" To which she rejoined indignantly: "I *said* kidleys, diddle I?"

Some New Yorkers turn the soft "ng" in "Long Island" to a hard one: "Long Guy-land." Below the Mason-Dixon line, quite the other way, the final "g" of "ng" may vanish altogether: "Fussin', feudin', fightin'."

The Kennedy brothers, Boston born and Harvard bred, added the unwelcome "r" to words ending in vowels ("idear," "lawr," "Indianer," "sawr"), and dropped the "r" if it was really there ("papah" for "paper").

For Cleaning up Consonants: Pages 94, 236

Tarnished vowels and diphthongs. Without vowels, speech would be all snap, crackle, and pop. If you try to leave them out when you speak, you will be unintelligible. You will also sound as if you were strangling.

The vowels give your speech sheen and richness. Consonants are the pizzicato piccolo; vowels the 'cello notes. Reader, bow that 'cello!

On paper, there are only five true vowels—a, e, i, o, and u. "Y" sometimes stands in for "i." Orally, however, these turn into several times as many distinguishable sounds.

These sounds vary from region to region. In New York City, the sentences "I brought coffee to the office for the boss" is likely to come out, "Awee braw-wt caw-wffee to the aw-w-ffice for the baw-wss." In Texas, "you" becomes yawl"; "word," "ward"; "red hair," "ray-ud high-ah." This last is an example of a vowel that has become a diphthong.

Also, one vowel may turn into a quite different one. Some southerners say what registers on ears as "Thin he lint me the pin" when they mean "Then he lent me the pen."

In a diphthong, one vowel sound leads into another, with the stress on the first and just a dash of the second added, like the dash of vermouth in a martini. A pure vowel is iced gin, with no vermouth at all. "I" is properly pronounced as a diphthong—"ah-ee." In the South, an "I" is likely to lose its dash of vermouth. "I tried to buy pie on Friday ("Ah-ee trah-eed to bah-ee pah-ee on Frah-eeday") becomes "Ah trahd to bah pah on Frahday." "Wire" becomes "war," "down" becomes "day-oon" instead of "daoon."

Regionalisms like these are ordinarily acceptable in one's home town. To learn whether your vowels and diphthongs are distorted beyond normal acceptability and even understanding (unless some friend or relative is brave enough to tell you), compare your speech with that of some national (not local) newscaster such as Chet Huntley or Walter Cronkite.

Guide to Vowel Pronunciation: Pages 97, 98, 235

REMEMBER:

- ◄ Use a tape recorder to identify your speech problems.
- ◄ If your nose buzzes whenever you talk, you sound nasal.
- ◄ If your neck grows taut when you speak, you are probably strident.
- ◄ Don't whisper unless you are telling a secret.
- ◄ Speak with lively, not lazy, lips.
- ◄ Read aloud to check your voice for monotony.
- ◄ Check how many words a minute you speak.
- ◄ Watch out for speech tics.
- ◄ Don't upstage yourself with visual distractors.
- ◄ Contact your listeners with eye clasp.
- ◄ Check your pronunciation.

3. Getting to Know You

Speech can soar to the loftiest heights, but its source, as my father never ceased to remind me, is still the human body.

My father, a surgeon and professor of anatomy, dreamed that I might follow in his Hippocratic footsteps. He believed deeply in the value of anatomy films for the teaching of medical students; he made over six hundred of them, which were used all over the world. Often he asked us children to help him edit them. I could hardly bear to look at them, and, whenever possible, kept my eyes closed. I could not stand the sight of blood. There may be those who enjoy watching the extraordinary carryings-on of the human interior, but I am not one of them. No doubt Dad was right when he referred reverently to the human body as a temple of miracles; but I was not interested in examining the miracles too closely.

I did not want to be a doctor. I wanted to be a singer and actress. The idea that there was anything in my father's films that would help me in a stage career seemed absurd.

There was, though. If I had paid more attention to his picture studies of the muscle systems which cooperate for breathing, I might not have come within an ace of losing my voice altogether.

My early teachers kept repeating: "Dorothy, you've got

to remember there is a body beneath the tone." But I did
not understand well enough what they were saying.

The result was catastrophe. When preparing for my first
professional engagement, I continued practicing despite a
heavy cold—and without proper breath support. The cold
turned into laryngitis, and before the end of my first week
with the St. Louis Municipal Opera Company, I lost my
voice completely. I was rushed to the Philadelphia office of
a noted throat specialist, who focused his narrow light on
my vocal cords while asking me to say, "Ahhh." I could
not. He shook his head. "Your cords have hemorrhaged,
and you have huge nodes besides, young lady," he said.
"We will have to operate. You may never sing again."

I managed to persuade him (writing out the words) to
let me see if absolute silence would do the job. At the end
of three weeks, the cords had improved so that he canceled the operation. For another three and a half months
I did not utter one sound, communicating by writing on a
pad. At the end of that time, to the doctor's frank astonish-
ment, my vocal cords were again in mint condition. Several weeks later I was a finalist in the Metropolitan Opera
auditions, and my singing career at last was under way.

From then on, you can be sure I gave my voice the
breath support and projection all voices require. And
though I have sung in hundreds of smoke-filled supper
clubs, I have never had laryngitis since.

ADVICE FROM MARTINELLI

I loved all my voice teachers; but I remember Giovanni
Martinelli with particular gratitude. There have been few
singers who could support their voices as well as he, or
explain the principles of breath support so cogently.

If a man can be beautiful without losing masculinity,
Giovanni was a beautiful man. With his white mane, like
a frozen waterfall, and his barrel chest, he looked as
majestic as a lion. And as the roar of a lion shakes the
jungle, so Martinelli's magnificent voice would set the very

rafters of the old Metropolitan Opera House to trembling. His voice burst from the great sounding board of his chest, crashed against the wall, and bounced back with the force of Cassius Clay's fist. I do not know whether it is true that Enrico Caruso could crack a glass with the vibrations of his voice; but if he could, then Giovanni could have cracked two glasses.

Martinelli not only proved to me how indispensable breath control was to great singing, but also gave me an image that you may find helpful in understanding how breath control works.

Think, he would say, of a pingpong ball bobbing on the crest of a fountain. Imagine that the ball is your voice, and the fountain is the breath supporting it. If the support remains undiminished, the pingpong ball will bob there indefinitely. But if the support slackens, the ball drops away.

Without breath support, he went on, you will not be heard. Your voice will sound tired and old. You will be a constant candidate for hoarseness, sore throat, and laryngitis.

Breath support must be controlled and constant. No great energy is required: the breath needed to utter a word amounts to less than a fiftieth of a million of one horsepower. If all the three and a half billion people on earth were to say the same sentence at the same time ("Things are tough all over," is one possibility), the total energy created by their breaths would be too trifling to run a six-cylinder automobile across a street intersection.

When not talking, we breathe through the nose whether we are asleep or awake. When talking, however, we breathe through the mouth. When we are not talking, the abdomen area balloons out, unchecked. In speech, it should be kept tucked in, contracted, ready, like a spring, to give support as required.

DON'T BE A BLOWHARD

Proper breath control is not a matter of how much air you take in, but of how you support it on the way out. A sip of air is all you need to speak a long phrase or sentence—and, unlike a deep inhalation, it will not make you tense. Singers have no time during their long musical phrases to pause for a deep breath even if they want to. They take repeated "catch" breaths through the mouth as they sing. These sips are as quick and delicate as a sudden, silent intake of surprise.

A single exhalation is sufficient to carry you through eight or more lines of any jingle that comes to mind. Try this one:

> Sing a song of sixpence,
>   A pocket full of rye;
> Four and twenty blackbirds
>   Baked in a pie.

> When the pie was opened,
>   The birds began to sing;
> Was not that a dainty dish
>   To set before the king?

Muscle support, not deep breathing, is the prerequisite, the very philosopher's stone, of a clear, projected lovely voice, and I shall discuss it in detail in the next chapter.

A DRIVER'S MANUAL

Part I of this book, "Sound as Good as You Look," is not a mechanic's guide to your voice; it is simply a driver's manual. Even a Sunday driver should have some notion of what makes his car work. (If your automobile has ever rolled to a remorseless halt in the midst of expressway traffic, as mine once did, you know why I say this.) I had to learn at least the rudiments of speech production before I could attain the full potential of my voice. If you are truly interested in improving yours, you too should understand the principles behind *breathing, resonating,* and *articulating*—the three systems that make up speech.

So bear with me, before we begin corrective measures for specific speech blemishes, while I summarize for you:

- ◄ How your outgoing breath carries and supports your voice;
- ◄ How your voice box turns exhalations into sound;
- ◄ How the sound is amplified in your chest, throat, and nasal passages;
- ◄ How your mouth, in all its various parts, shapes the sounds into words.

A VOICE IS BORN

When you refer to someone's conversation as a lot of hot air, you probably have in mind the burden of the remarks rather than the quality of the voice. Yet it is true that voice is simply air—resonated, amplified, shifted in pitch, and finally shaped into the sounds we call words. An extraordinary number of organs and muscles are involved in the process.

Their interworking is as close as that described in a song you may have sung at campfires when you were growing up: "The headbone is connected to the neckbone, the neckbone is connected to the backbone, the backbone is connected to the hipbone," and so on. You could not utter an intelligible word without the active or passive cooperation of your diaphragm, chest muscles, lungs, windpipe, voice box, throat, nasal passages, sinuses, mouth, and jaw.

Your diaphragm sets the whole operation in motion. It is an almost horizontal muscle, a little lower behind than

before, that lies under your lungs like a bedboard under
a mattress, separating your chest cavity from that of your
abdomen. When you have hiccups it is because your
diaphragm has gone into spasmodic contractions. You cannot see it; you cannot even feel it; but it is down there
right now, working away morning, noon, and night, like
the operating end of a bellows.

Each time you breathe your diaphragm lowers, and
your chest muscles automatically move your ribs outward,
thus distending your lungs. (Your lungs lead an easy life;
all their breathing-in work is done for them by the
muscles.) Air rushes in. Then your diaphragm comes up
like an elevator, pushing the air in the lungs above it into
the windpipe; your rib cage contracts; and out rushes the
air.

This inhalation and exhalation takes place a dozen or so
times a minute from the instant your doctor first spanks
your red baby bottom until, a lifetime later, your hands
are finally folded across your too-quiet chest.

HOW SPEECH BEGINS

Speech starts on an exhalation (you can't speak in-
telligibly while inhaling) and the exhalation is the work
of your diaphragm and the great surrounding chest and
upper abdominal muscles—your vital or dynamic center,
or "girdle of breath support."

To produce speech, these muscles start a current of air
up your windpipe from your lungs. The air passes through
your voice box, along your throat, into your nasal passages
and sinuses, back to your mouth, and, finally, out into the
open as spoken words.

Along the way, a number of amazing events take place.

The first way-station is your larynx, which sits on the
top of your windpipe the way a factory whistle is sometimes seen sitting on top of a steamstack. Your larynx is
the hard bump in your throat, more noticeable in men

than women, that joggles when you swallow. It is called the Adam's apple because a piece of the apple which Adam ate in the Garden of Eden is supposed to have stuck there. Just behind your Adam's apple is your voice box, which is hung with two curtain-like membranes called vocal cords. As the current glides or rushes through, the cords vibrate, causing a sympathetic vibration in the upward-moving air. This vibration is what registers on your ear as sound. The faster your vocal cords vibrate, the higher is the pitch of your voice.

When a boy's voice changes at about the age of fifteen, the reason is that his vocal cords have lengthened, dropping his register a full octave. A girl's vocal cords lengthen at the same age, but so slightly that the drop in her register is all but imperceptible. Mr. Jones's voice is deeper than Mrs. Jones's because his vocal cords are about a third longer—six tenths of an inch as compared with less than four and a half tenths of an inch. The longer the cords, the slower the vibration and, therefore, the lower the tone.

The range of your voice is probably less than two octaves. A professional singer must be able to span a full two octaves, and many achieve three. There is a case on record of a singer with the incredible span of five octaves.

RESONANCE BEGINS

Before the air even leaves your windpipe, it has begun to resonate, using your chest as a sounding board. Resonance is a reverberation that follows the principal tone in a series of almost instant echoes. It can occur only in an enclosed space. The vibrations of violin strings, for instance, reverberate in the violin box, gaining richness and fullness with each bounce. The amplifiers of your hi-fi set work the same way.

After the vibrations of your voice box determine the pitch, resonance determines the quality of the tone. If your primary resonance is in your nose, you will twang.

If you resonate from the chest, you will command more respectful attention if you are a man—and more gallant attention if you are a woman.

On its way to utterance, the current of air that carries the sound of your voice passes through a whole series of amplifiers: the throat, the nose, the sinus cavities. Among them, they raise the level of audibility by as much as twenty times.

ARTICULATION

On its upward passage the current of air has become sound. It has acquired pitch from your vocal cords, and tone from your resonators. Its audibility has been multiplied manyfold. Its quality as sound has been determined. The sound may be as pure as a church bell, or as ear-shattering as an ambulance siren. It may be as dead and dry as driftwood. But it still has not been turned into words, or even syllables. It is like a piece of cloth about to be cut into a suit. Some of the vowel sounds are there, or are at least foreshadowed, but your mouth still has to shape them and add the consonants and the punctuation.

What a lively time it has doing that! Everything in and around your mouth that can move goes into action. Whatever cannot move backstops the rest. Your tongue, lips, teeth, cheeks, palate—even the uvula that hangs like a tiny fleshy tongue above the entrance to your throat—all go after that current of air like a pack of hounds after a rabbit. They tear it to pieces—and then put it together again. They chop, butt, slice, add, modify, enlarge, narrow, lengthen. Your tongue darts, furrows, spreads, curls, pushes, pulls. Your lips wriggle, squeeze, pout, stretch, relax.

Consider for a moment the versatility of your tongue. Say "ah," and it lies limp as a pancake. Say "a" as in cat, and it humps its back. Say "oh," and it furrows. Say "oo," and it furrows even more. All the while it is jumping up, down, and around like a madman. For a "t," its tip touches the upper gum ridge with feathery lightness; for a trilled "r," its side touches your side teeth, while its tip rustles like a flag in a breeze. For some sounds, such as "ee," your tongue widens; for others, such as "ss," it narrows and retreats. And all this is just the forepart, which you can see easily with the help of your mirror. If you want to know what happens farther back, I believe the American Telephone and Telegraph Company has a film that can show you all you want to know. Call their Public Relations Department.

Your lips are almost as lively. Say "p" (the sound, not the letter), and they pop. Say "mmm"; they automatically press together, so that the sound comes out your nose. Say "f" or "v," and your upper teeth almost bite your lower lips.

All these mouth movements take place at a breakneck rate, as hard to follow as the movements of a one-man band who kicks the cymbals, pounds the drum, blows the harmonica, and scrapes the fiddle all at the same time. It is not surprising in either case that the resulting sound is not always heavenly music.

So there we are—first the breath, then the sound, then the resonance, then the articulation.

The following chapter deals with breath support and projection. It consists primarily of a series of simple hints. You can follow them in your own home—some even in a crowded elevator, in the subway, or on the street, without attracting attention.

Follow these hints for ten minutes or so a day, and you will have taken the first essential step toward a voice that can win multitudes and move mountains—or, if your ambitions are more modest, a voice that will give pleasure to anyone—friend, lover, business associate, or stranger—who may be fortunate enough to hear you speak.

REMEMBER:

◄ Proper breath support is the foundation of a good voice.
◄ Your diaphragm supports your breath; your breath supports your voice.

◄ The way you exhale is what counts.
◄ Your larynx gives your voice its pitch; your resonance
    gives your voice its quality.
◄ Your mouth turns sound into words . . . and your
    tongue does most of the work.

4. A Better Voice Is Just a Breath Away

The word were better wordless, if the ear
perceive it not. Speak out, that all may hear!
—ANON.

The first step toward proper breathing is proper posture. The fact that proper posture makes you look ten years younger and twice as handsome is a side benefit. If round shoulders and a drooping midriff helped you speak better, I would be gung ho for round shoulders and a drooping midriff. It happens, though, that an upright carriage, naturally held, puts the muscles of your vital center in the best possible position to provide the steady exhalation of air that you need to support an attractive voice. Follow the old Quaker adage:

Head up, also chin;
Chest out, stomach in.

Incidentally, the one group to whom this adage does not apply is children. If you have a child under nine, don't scold him because he fails to throw back his shoulders and tuck in his tummy. He cannot. He has to be pot-bellied, simply because his pelvic structure is not yet big enough to hold his abdomen.

THE IMPORTANCE OF POSTURE

But you are past nine; or if you are not, you should be out playing instead of reading this book. So from now on you are to hold your head a little higher and your back a little straighter. That is Executive Posture. It will help your soul as well as your voice. "Grief," Shakespeare said, "is proud, and makes his owner stoop." If you refuse to stoop, you will be one up on grief.

Are you slouching as you sit reading this, with your upper spine leaning against your chair back? Then your dynamic center has gone slack. Touch your middle; does it feel flabby? Your waistline is sagging. You are tensing your torso and neck—and insuring the most unreliable sort of breath support for your voice.

For your slouch, substitute Executive Posture. It is nothing mysterious—it is simply the carriage described in that Quaker adage.

One of my recent pupils was a vice president who handled mergers for his company. He came to me because he was not effective in conferences and discussions. He lacked authority. His problem started the moment he walked into the conference room. His shoulders were narrow to begin with, and their drooping made them seem narrower still. His posture said "timid" instead of "powerful." Executive Posture made him another man. His shoulders seemed broader; his whole personality was more self-possessed. His voice was deeper, more commanding, fell more happily on the ear. He had thrown off his milquetoast image simply by throwing back his shoulders and sitting erect.

The problem of another of my clients, a young woman, began lower down. She always sat sidewise in her chair, with one leg over the other, slouching. Her focal feature was the cheek of her right buttock, pushing under a wrinkled, high-riding skirt. The position made her look a mess. In addition, her crossed legs cramped her dynamic center, so that her voice emerged in subsiding puffs, like steam from a kettle that is beginning to cool. It was the work of a few minutes to show her how to sit straight, and of a few lessons to keep her sitting straight out of habit. Under my eyes, she became a poised and engaging young lady. Her whine began to disappear as a result of improved posture even before she took her first anti-nasality exercise.

Another student's voice was soft and appealing—until she became excited. Then it turned to a screech. I persuaded her to divert her inner tension from her throat by pressing her lower spine against her chair back, or even digging the nail of one hand into the palm of the other. My ultimate goal was to remove her tension altogether, but this could not happen overnight. Meanwhile, by diverting her tension she was able to keep her voice relaxed and her face serene. She put her tension where it did not show.

SIMPLE RULES FOR GOOD POSTURE

So if you plan to speak before a group of people—or simply to talk to a friend—follow the old Quaker rules:

◄ Keep your chest up. Keep your stomach in.

If you are standing, add one more rule:

◄ Keep your weight almost evenly distributed, on the balls of your feet.

If you are sitting:

◄ Place your feet squarely on the floor. *Never* cross your legs. (Crossed legs also impede circulation.)
◄ Make a double L (as seen from the side)—one L of your feet and lower legs, and another of your upper legs and torso.
◄ To help the bellows of your abdomen, touch the

the back of your chair with your lower (but not
your upper) spine, almost pushing against it. Feel
that vital center tighten! No more flab!

When a sizable voice thrust is needed, some people
modify the last rule. I once knew a choir leader who
made all his singers sit on the forward side of a tape which
marked off the eight front inches of the chair. He said
that sitting on the chair edge while maintaining the "L"
position helped them to cannonade the audience with their
voices; if he let them sit back, they might relax so much
that the cannon would turn into a popgun.

The rules of posture, like the rules for proper breathing
that follow, can sometimes be broken without penalty—
if you master the rules first. Having heard that Maria
Jeritza sang the aria from *Tosca* lying flat on her stomach,
I decided to sing the aria from *Pagliacci* lying flat on my
back. It worked—but only because I had learned how to
use my support muscles. In a lying posture, these muscles
had to work many times as hard. (To get an idea of the
effort involved, lie supine, and bring yourself first to a
sitting and then a standing position without help from
your hands.) The principle is the same as the one that
permits a poet to write in free verse once he has mastered
prosody. He knows what he is doing. If a Picasso drawing outrages your notions of artistic correctness, bear in
mind that Picasso is the most expert and talented drafts-
man alive.

So sometimes one can get away with breaking a rule.
But the moral remains: never break a rule unless you have
mastered it. If you do break it, try to break it with style.

BREATHING

As an old preacher said, "You can put your mind into a
speech, and you can put your heart into it, but if you
don't put your diaphragm into it you've got no speech."

How do you put your diaphragm into it?

Let me tell you about a system that has worked for me, and that I think is bound to work for you.

To locate the muscles of the vital center that we have been talking about—the ones that provide the energy, vitality and power you will need for dynamic speech—sit in a double "L" position, the lower part of your spine touching the back of the chair, the palm of your hand pressing flat on the area about three inches above your navel and at the bottom of your rib cage. Now stand up. Sit down. Go through the same performance again. And again. And again. Each time, you will feel the muscles under your hand tighten. Doctors call the vital center the "abdominis rectus and oblique supporting muscles." Singers call it the abdominal brain.

Here are four ways to understand your vital center and help it provide solid support for your speaking voice:

1. Put your palms against a wall, standing one leg in advance of the other as if you were fencing, and try to push the wall down on a slow count of four. (This is another way to pinpoint the girdle of breath support.) You will feel your mid-muscles tightening and the flab fleeing.

2. Clench one hand into a fist. Pretend it is a balloon, and try to blow it up on a single slow thin thread of exhalation. Keep the other hand pressed against your upper abdominal muscles, spanning the area where the rib cage separates. Feel them harden and contract as you blow, pulling in toward your back, flattening out your middle.

3. Stand naked before a mirror. If your posture is poor, your abdomen will show a melon shape, and excess fat will droop over your hips. Now assume the Executive Posture, and again pretend to blow up a balloon. Once more, see how your muscles tighten and contract, as though something back around your spine were pulling them in. You look younger, more alert, more positive, more slender. If you are a man, this posture can let you wear your belt two inches tighter.

4. Pretend to push a grand piano—to pull a full bucket from a well—to haul up an anchor—to return a tennis serve backhand—to throw a knockout punch. Ex-

hale slowly and steadily with each action, and notice once
more the effect on your girdle of breath support.

PROJECTION

Even when you are speaking most quietly, your diaphragm and the muscles around it are supporting every
word. Or they should be. Proper posture, giving those
muscles complete freedom of action, is therefore the No.
1 requisite for projection.

When you have to project your voice to catch the attention of someone across the room, or to hold the attention of an audience, your muscle support digs deeper and
tautens. You tap the same muscles a rider uses when he
grips the barrel of a horse with his legs.

Projection is not shouting. Political candidates, addressing large crowds; sports coaches; fans at outdoor games;
foremen; supervisors; teachers; cocktail partiers—all these
often shout wildly instead of taking advantage of the
maximum carrying power developed by the vital center.
As a result they become painfully hoarse, as Hubert
Humphrey did in the 1968 Presidential campaign; or even
lose their voices altogether, as Wendell Willkie did in 1940.
At cocktail parties, guests often force their voices and
scream at each other, instead of simply projecting to make
themselves heard. The noise goes from loud, to *Loud,* to
LOUDER, to L O U D E S T . It is a crescendo, with
mounting throat tension. Voices should not be forced;
the force should be put into *supporting* them. Even in a
fairly crowded, noisy room your voice should carry fifteen
feet without strain—but you may have to make backup
muscles work harder.

In the last chapter I mentioned Giovanni Martinelli's
image of the voice in conversation as a pingpong ball bobbing on a steady fountain of air. To project at greater dis-
tances, change the image from a fountain to a hose. By adjusting the nozzle you can water the bushes at your feet, the

privet hedge a dozen feet away, or the Japanese cherry tree at the far end of the garden.

TO BREATHE FOR PROJECTION

Any of the following simple routines, carried out consistently for five minutes at a time, four or five times a day, will soon strengthen your support muscles and have you projecting easily, with no voice strain. (Remember, do these exercises standing, chest up, stomach in. *Do not* take a deep breath.)

R:
1. *Steam kettle*

Take a short sip of breath and, as you exhale slowly, hiss, in a fine thin stream, through your teeth. H – i – s – s – s – s – s. Count to yourself, and see how long you can make the hissing last. Don't push your breath; LET it come out. You should be able to get to thirty the first time around, and to seventy later on. Feel your girdle of breath support pulling in, getting tighter, tighter, tighter.

R:
2. *Numbers*

Take a short sip of breath, and count aloud on a long single exhalation, as fast as you can. The first time, try for forty by tens (one – two – three – four – five – six – seven – eight – nine – ten, one – two – three – four – five – six – seven – eight – nine – twenty, etc.) How far can you count—80, 100, 120? (This is the only time you will be permitted to mumble, so take advantage of it. We are not concerned here with the sound you make, but only with your breath support.) As before, you will find that each day you can go a little further. (This principle of adding a little each day applies to almost any of these disciplines. Swimming last summer at Lake Placid I discovered that by adding gradually to my first limit of forty breast strokes, I was finally able to reach a hundred and twenty-five. And for me, I assure you, that was an accomplishment.) In a few days you should be comfortable at a count of a hundred, and eventually you should reach 130. You will be getting thirty miles a gallon from your breath instead of ten. Keep it up, and you will have no further worry about breath support.

℞:
3. *Professor Higgins's candle*

Remember the scene in *My Fair Lady* where Professor Higgins shows Eliza how to blow a finely rationed thread of breath at a candle so that it flickered but never went out?

a   Pretend your index finger is a candle. Hold it about ten inches from your face, and direct your breath gently at it in a thin stream, keeping your mouth in a whistling position. If you are uncertain whether your breath is touching your finger, use a sailor's trick; wet your finger, and the evaporation of the moisture will sensitize it to the passing air.

Once more, monitor the bottom of your rib cage with your other hand, and feel the contraction there. This is how your vital center should feel when you speak on the telephone or to someone less than ten feet away.

b   Next, hold your finger at a distance of about eighteen inches, and aim the same delicate stream of air at it. You will find the muscle tension going lower and the support deepening, as it would if you were speaking to someone fifteen or more feet away.

The farther off your finger is, the deeper the support must go to project your breath. To make the candle flicker at arm's length, you use muscles in your groin, your thigh, your buttocks, behind your knees, perhaps even at the back of your calves. They are all backing up your diaphragm to provide that extra projection.

℞:
4. *Big Bass Drum*

Locate your dynamic center once more by coughing or laughing, with your hand at the lower edge of your rib cage. Now start to count aloud, preceding each number by a light grunt: "Uh-*one!* Uh-*two!* Uh-*three!*" Emphasize the numbers, not the grunts. Don't separate the "uh" from the "one"; connect them. With no break in your breath, dig into each number, trying to boom like a big bass drum struck by a drumstick. You will find your breath support seems to go right down to the groin.

EXTRA DIVIDENDS

a   When you are out for a walk, see how far you can go on a single slow exhalation. A third of a block? A half? I once recommended this to an Irish nun, who practiced it until she could walk a whole short city block on a single exhalation. As an added bonus, she found that she no longer minded cold weather. She was able to resume long winter walks, which she had abandoned because her nun's habit was not particularly resistant to chill and wind.

(Incidentally, she came to me in the first place with a request to remove her Irish accent. It was a delightful lilt, and I refused. "I will not," I said, "rob the world of anything as charming and lovable as that accent." I only take accents away when they distract others or rob you of comprehensibility.)

b   (If you are a homemaker and are constantly climbing steps, you will be grateful for this one.) Make a practice of climbing as far as you can on a single exhalation. You will soon find that you no longer reach the top of the stairs exhausted and out of breath. If you are a golfer, use the same technique going up a hill. My husband and I regularly do this at our golf club when approaching the sixteenth tee, which is at the top of a sharp rise. I think we are the only members who reach the tee breathing normally.

c   There are side benefits to making an exhalation go on and on. It often works like magic, for instance, against nausea. A doctor told me this is because pulling in the muscles inhibits reverse peristalsis, which is one of the causes of air and sea sickness. When a plane I am in enters an area of turbulence and the pilot says, "Fasten your seat belts," I tighten my breath support as well.

d You will find, too, that a constant, long, slow exhalation decreases your nervousness while you wait to speak in public or to undergo a trying interview. It can do much more than that. It can actually hold down panic and even reduce pain. Pregnant women practice it to help them in natural childbirth.

e A beautiful Swedish woman, whom I had long admired for her radiant complexion and unfailing energy, one day confided the secret of her glow to me. "I take a catch-breath," she said, "and pop into a tub of icy water. Then I count aloud at least to sixty on a single exhalation, take another catch-breath, and repeat. That is enough. I jump out, and miraculously I am not shivering but tingling and invigorated."

I have tried it—and it is a better pickup than a martini. (This is not for you though, if you have even a hint of a heart problem.)

REMEMBER:

◄ Executive Posture means more effective speech.
◄ Your vital center should always tuck in as you speak, supporting your breath.
◄ *Project* your voice—don't shout.
◄ Select the breathing routines most useful to you, and follow them five or ten minutes a day, wherever and whenever convenient.

5. Is Your Voice as Alive as You Are?

The Devil hath not, in all his quiver's choice,
An arrow for the heart like a sweet voice.
                              —LORD BYRON

Your voice can tell the best or the worst of lies about you.
It can say "vigorous" when you are tired. It can say
"young" when you are over seventy. But watch out if it
says "fatigued" when you are rested; "weak" when you
are strong; "frustrated" when you are fulfilled; "old" when
you are still young!

Sooner or later we all grow older. Some day today's
Miss America will appreciate what Gypsy Rose Lee meant
when she said that her figure was as good as ever—just a
couple of inches lower. We sag here, we wrinkle there, we
thicken or we grow scrawny, we give up horseback riding,
we don't enjoy staying up till all hours the way we used
to.

Don't let your voice give away your age—unless that is,
you are still on the diaper side of the generation gap.
Franklin D. Roosevelt managed to sound young and vibrant
even in his last speeches, when he was already mortally
ill. Winston Churchill's voice remained the same long
after his shoulders had rounded and his step become a
shuffle.

Don't give someone else voice fatigue. If you recharge
your own voice instead, he may very well pick up your
vitality. Voices are contagious.

You know what sagging stockings do to a woman's
image. A sagging voice is worse. Here are some vocal pro-

jection secrets that will keep your voice as snug as a fashion model's panty hose. *For voice vitality and vigor,* first follow the hints for breathing on the previous pages. Next, do the following—with energy and thrust:

Say each of the verbs below twice—quietly for the lower-case version in the left-hand column, and emphatically for the capitalized version at the right. The lower-case words should be spoken as if to someone ten feet away; the capitalized ones as if to someone at a distance of about twenty-five feet. Pretend all the while that you are on a balcony projecting *down* to the other end of the room. This will help you to resist the temptation to raise your pitch. Each time you say a word, stay two beats on the vowel of the accented syllable: ru-un, pu-ush,

run	RUN!	don't	DON'T!
quiet	QUIET!	do it	DO IT!
ready	READY!	try	TRY!
look	LOOK!	come in	COME IN!
shoot	SHOOT!	climb	CLIMB!
fire	FIRE!	stand up	STAND UP!
no	NO!	bravo	BRAVO!
go	GO!	go home	GO HOME!
rush	RUSH!	leave	LEAVE!
pull	PULL!	drive on	DRIVE ON!
hit	HIT!	stay here	STAY HERE!
push	PUSH!	move on	MOVE ON!

When you are speaking emotionally—in anger, outrage, defiance, command—your support muscles work harder. Or they should. What you should *not* do is let your pitch rise. Do you have a tendency to grow shrill in emotional situations? Then practice a few sentences like the following, remembering to give extra support from your vital center to each word you wish to stress. If you have trouble being emphatic, pound the table! Speak several ways: with strong conviction . . . defiance . . . anger . . . boredom . . . hilarity . . . authority . . . command.

1. I was born an American, I shall live an American, I shall die an American!

2. As a citizen of this great country, you must count your blessings—and demand your rights!

3. A situation like this demands strong minds, courageous hearts, abiding faith, and ready hands!

4. We are fighting by ourselves alone, but we are not fighting for ourselves alone.

5. We need dreamers, thinkers, doers—we need you!

6. I am ready to act now, and for my action I am ready to answer to my conscience, my country, and my God.

More Helps in the Appendix

HOARSENESS

Does your work require you to talk continuously on the telephone? Must you sometimes keep your listeners' attention despite competing noises—from a boiler factory, perhaps, or a discothèque? (The boiler factory is quieter.) If so, hoarseness is bound to set in unless you know how to protect your voice.

A number of common irritants contribute to hoarseness and laryngitis. One of these is strain—caused often by irritation, or by attempting to make yourself heard above noises.

Cigarette smoke, either yours or someone else's, is another irritant to your vocal cords. Emotional tension can cause you to strain your throat. So can strenuous coughing, loud laughter, and constant throat-clearing. Far from really clearing your throat, hruumping actually abuses the vocal cords. If you could look down your throat while these irritants are at work on it, you would see the normally pale cords turn an angry red. You are scratching one against the other.

Avoid clearing your throat to ease irritation. (Many professional singers strike beer and milk from their diets because they create extra mucus. If you find you have a tendency toward phlegm, you too should avoid drinking beer and milk for several hours before giving a talk.) Instead of clearing your throat, chew lightly on your tongue (this will produce saliva) and swallow.

Better still, simply pant and then swallow.

℞:

Panting puppy

You have often seen a dog stretched out on the rug, his jaw loose, his tongue hanging limply as he pants. Pretend you are such a dog. First yawn, until you feel an open throat. With mouth lax and tongue limp, pant low and slow in your throat. Inhale and exhale audibly but smoothly through the mouth. In and out, in and out. Feel the cool air moving over the tongue, down the windpipe and then back up again. Feel the air brushing and massaging the phlegm off your vocal cords. This exercise tends to dry your throat, so swallow after it. Breathe this way seven or eight times, swallow, and repeat the process ten times over. Then rest, and start again an hour later, if necessary. Each time make yourself sound like an old-fashioned steam locomotive idling in the station.

If there is really something the matter with your throat, though, you don't need a speech teacher—you need a throat specialist. If you have acute laryngitis, he will tell you to stop talking. And by the way, he will probably tell you also what Dr. Max Som, a distinguished throat specialist, advises: "For laryngitis," he says, "it is not enough just to stop talking. You should not whisper either." Whispering without breath support—and that is the usual kind—can only add to your voice strain.

He adds one more thing: Whatever the temptation, don't smoke.

To avoid the onset of laryngitis, speak as little as possible whenever a serious cold descends from your nose to your throat or chest. If you strain your voice at that point, you may well invite polyps or nodes.

Had I known before I lost my voice in St. Louis what I know now about breath support, projection, and panting, I might have avoided the hemorrhaging of my cords that almost cost me my career.

The rule of silence is even more golden when nodes have been removed by surgery. Tragically, many men and women must live with permanently damaged vocal cords —because they failed to take seriously their doctors' orders to observe *complete* silence for a number of weeks after the operation.

To prevent laryngitis, follow the advice for breath support I have given you. You will find that hoarseness and sore throat become as rare as May flies in December.

THESE DON'TS BEAR REPEATING:

a   *Don't* let your dynamic center collapse, no matter how tired you are. The energy you put under your voice will put energy into you. It will put your voice where you want it, when you want it.

b   *Don't* yield to the contagion of loud voices at social gatherings, discothèques, and sports arenas. Instead, use exaggerated breath support.

c   *Don't* release your frustrations and anger by shouting or screaming. You will only tear your throat apart. Get and hold attention by quiet emphasis and projection, as much as was required earlier to blow up your make-believe balloon.

d   *Don't* clear your throat under the illusion that you are clearing your vocal cords. Pant the phlegm off.

Keep your voice vital—and it will keep you vital!

REMEMBER:

- ◄ Don't let your voice make you sound older than you are.
- ◄ Don't let your voice make you sound tired . . . frustrated . . . discouraged. Make it sound at least as good as you look.
- ◄ Work with the projection pairs of verbs to improve your projection.
- ◄ Use the suggested preventives to protect your voice from fatigue, hoarseness, and laryngitis.

6. Banish That Blemish

Mind your speech a little
Lest you should mar your fortunes.
—WILLIAM SHAKESPEARE

STRIDENCY AND NASALITY

How many Americans talk through their noses? The census
does not ask that question; but if they were to organize a
third party, I suspect they could cast enough votes to
throw the next Presidential election into the House of
Representatives.

And if all the strident speakers in the country joined up
too, their candidate would probably win the election.

To correct both nasality and stridency, and to arrive
at the velvet smoothness of chest resonance, you must
work toward relieving your general physical tension.
Specifically, learn to relax your jaw and tongue and open
your throat and mouth so that the sound can exit that
way, instead of being shunted into the passageway that
makes it come out the nose.

RELIEVING TENSION

Tension is as much part of modern life as smog. Start
ticking off on your fingers the reasons you may be tense
right now—perhaps the dreadful time you have just had
trying to get a taxi; or a note coming due at the bank;

or the strain of your work; or your concern over war,
poverty, racism, and all the other ills that flesh is here
to these days.

I cannot remove the causes of your tension. But at least
I can help rid you of some of the effects.

THE RELAXERS

By following these suggestions, you can relax the entire
head and neck and feel better all over.

R:
1. *The plopper*
   a   Let your head dangle forward and hang there,
eyes closed, for six slow counts.
   b   Again counting slowly to six, raise your head
from its drooping position until your eyes, gradually opening, see the ceiling. You should feel the tension begin to
melt away.
   c   Repeat several times.

R:
2. *The rag doll roll*
   With your head again dangling, let your jaw hang
loose, as if it were about to fall off. Roll your head slowly
to one side; then back and up; then to the other side;
then forward again.

THE JAW

To know how far your jaw can relax, first put your
finger tips in front of your ears, at the spot where your
lower and upper jaw are hinged together. With your
mouth closed, the place is a slight bump. As you drop
your jaw, the bump will go away and be replaced by a
cavity.

Watch yourself in the mirror. Once properly relaxed,

your lower jaw will drop behind the upper one. Don't worry about that row of double chins; they will disappear when these maneuvers are over. (Stridency, shrillness, and nasality will soon vanish too.)

Place your index finger against your chin and manipulate your lower jaw until it stops fighting you and swings free. It should become eventually as loose as Charley McCarthy's. You will feel like a ventriloquist's dummy—and you will enjoy it. (Before, with jaws clenched and lips drawn, you were more like the ventriloquist.)

R:
3. *Slower downer*

   a Drop your jaw and let your tongue hang limply over your lower teeth and lip. Breathe more and more sleepily, as if you were beginning to feel the effects of an anesthetic.

   b Silently count a slow 1–2–3–4 on each inhalation, and another on each exhalation. By now your breathing should sound the way it would a split second before you begin to snore.

   c Substitute a groan for the count on each exhalation. Be sure you do not pause between the outgoing and incoming breath. The flow should be constant. Don't stop until you feel a yawn coming on.

R:
4. *The groaner*

   Tuck your tongue between your lower lip and your teeth, relaxed and thick. Now groan "Aaaaah," dragging out the sound and directing it at the point where your tongue and lip meet. You will have the sensation that the "Aaaaah" is actually outside your mouth—which is exactly where it should be.

TONGUE TALK

If I ask you to let your head sag on your neck, you will have no trouble doing it. But can you relax your tongue? Go over to the mirror and check: Can you let it go limp, completely without tension, resting sleepily in the nest of the floor of the mouth? Most people cannot. It will probably hump up, it will furrow, it will pull back, it will stretch sideways. Talk to it as if to an untrained puppy. Say, "Down, tongue, down! Relax! At ease!"

Now, with jaw and tongue completely relaxed, say "la, la, la, la, la, la," as if you were a drooling baby. Your tension will soon drool away.

THE THROAT

Yawning is a number one relaxer. Can you yawn at will? Here is a way to:

1. With eyes gently closed, bring your lips together lightly.

2. Drop your jaw loosely, lips still closed.

3. Let a great big lazy yawn take over, opening your mouth and the back of your throat w–i–d–e; feel the stretch, up and sideways, of the muscles, opening the throat.

If, as you yawn, you look at the back of your throat in a mirror, you will see the uvula pull up and shorten like a rising curtain. That is the way it opens to make way for sound.

In all speech (except when you are saying "m," "n," or "ng") your throat should be open. To feel the difference between a closed and an open throat, say, "ng–ah, ng–ah, ng–ah," several times. On the "ah" sound, the throat is completely open. On the "ng" sound, it is completely closed. Try to have the sensation of the open throat in speech.

To combine the relaxed jaw and the open throat in one maneuver, try this:

1. Put your elbow on a table, resting your chin on the back, not the palm, of your hand.

2. Lift your head so that your chin is about two inches above your hand.

3. With the same sensation as the yawn, say: "yah, yah, yah, yah, yah"; "yaw, yaw, yaw, yaw, yaw"; "yoh, yoh, yoh, yoh, yoh." Let your jaw relax so that it hits your hand as you pronounce each syllable. At the same time, put your other hand flat on your chest, right under your collarbone, and feel the vibrations there. There is no nasality now— no clenched jaw—no tight flat mouth.

THE MOUTH

Make a "V for Victory" frame of the index and center fingers of one hand, putting the tops of the fingers lightly at the corners of your mouth. The cleft or point of your chin should be directly above the bottom of the "V." If, as you speak, your mouth moves out to widen the top of the "V," you are undoubtedly a nasal talker.

Say "Baa baa, black sheep, have you any wool? Yes, sir, yes, sir, three bags full. One for the master, and one for the dame, and one for the little boy who lives down the lane." As you speak, watch yourself in the mirror.

As I said before, there should be about a half inch of dark between your teeth as you talk. To help you tight-lipped, clamped-jawed speakers unlock your mouths and get the sound outside of your heads, use these two maneuvers:

℞:

1. *Knuckle down*

Put the knuckle of your index or middle finger between your teeth and try to read, aloud, the Lord's Prayer,

the Gettysburg Address, or any other familiar passage. The
sound will be almost unintelligible. Then remove the
knuckle and repeat the same words, still opening your
mouth widely to let the sound pass through unimpeded.

    ℞:
2. *Megaphone*
    Use your lips as if they were a megaphone. "W"
makes a wonderful megaphone, blowing away nasality and
mumbling like a sea wind blowing away a fog.

Here are some sentences to practice on:
a Why do wily women win wealth and wed well?
b Wilma worked woefully while Wallace wilfully wan-
    dered west.
c Weary Willy washes and wipes wet windows while
    Walter whistles.
d Welcome wagons wound their way westward while
    warped wheels wobbled weakly.
e Washington was a wizard warrior; his wisdom and
    wishes worked wonders.
f Women worried when Warsaw's wild, wet winter
    weather worsened and workers wearied.
g One weeping willow wisp waves wanly in the wind.
h Woolite warrants washing worn, wilted white wool-
    ens well.

To remove the sound from your nose when you talk,
memorize one of these sentences and repeat it aloud until
you can zip through it the way in your schooldays you
zipped through "Peter Piper picked a peck of pickled pep-
pers."

MUMBLERS

The above alliterative sentences also help mumblers.
The "w's" bring your lips alive. Men's lips tend, with no
apparent reason, to be lazier than women's. Notice on your
television set how often men speak with a literal "stiff up-

per lip" (and how do you suppose that phrase ever came to mean not letting events get you down?). They often look as if they had just shaved off their mustaches, and their upper lips had not yet had time to become as flexible as before.

Ordinarily, lazy lips and lazy middle muscles go, if not hand in hand, at least side by side. The mumbler is likely to leave whole syllables out of his words. "Hereditary" may become "hered'ty"; "American," "Murcan"; and the like.

Your best cure for mumbling is to recite polysyllabic words slowly. With full breath support, making sure that you give each syllable its due, say the following words. Don't chop! Glide from one syllable into the next. Make full use of your vital center on the accented syllable. Give the accented syllables extra physical impetus:

administration	non-representational
dependability	quietude
jocularity	theoretical
monosyllabic	whimsicality
polysyllabic	zodiacal
somnambulator	cantankerous
valedictorian	fertilization
Yugoslavian	individualistic
beautiful	libertarian
exuberance	overwhelmingly
hereditary	regenerative
kleptomaniac	unappropriated

I sometimes think that mumblers are more common in the legal profession than in any other. One would think the essence of courtroom debate and pleading would be a clear and powerful voice. Yet again and again, lawyers enter my classes with lips that barely move when they talk. They mumble. Their breath support abandons them. Could it be because they don't want the opposing lawyer to catch their confidential asides?

PITCH

The owner of a leather company came to me for help because, as he complained quite legitimately, he sounded like a twelve-year-old boy. When he reached a prospective client on the telephone, he could not talk business until he had proved he was the head of the company and not the office boy. In three sessions he lowered his pitch to an attractive level and left pinched, nasal resonance behind.

(Once, he told me later, his new, lower voice cost him money. Before he joined the class, he and his wife had fallen in love with a crystal chandelier at an antique store, and he had called to ask its price. The woman who answered the telephone said, "What does a boy like you want with an expensive chandelier?" He explained his interest without giving his age, and the woman, much impressed by such appreciation on the part of one so young, suggested a price that she thought might be within his means.

(Later he called again in his new basso voice. Mysteriously the cost of the chandelier shot up. The price of sounding like an executive evidently was to be charged executive prices.)

A high-pitched voice is a serious handicap for a businessman not only because it irritates but because it lacks authority. In a woman it sounds like chalk squeaking on a blackboard.

An airline asked me to help one of its Spanish-speaking stewardesses, a candidate in a beauty contest. Beauty of form and figure was not the only criterion in the competition; the contestants were judged also according to their speech, and this poor girl whisper-talked and whined. She also inflected upward at the end of every sentence like a cat discussing its love affairs on a back fence. A few lessons brought her pitch down four tones, and gave her the velvet chest-tone that her lovely figure deserved. She was one of the runners-up in the contest not just because of her classic Castilian beauty, but because of her voice. My

tapes show that only five of the eighty-seven contestants
had voices to match their looks.

Think of how a cow moos; contrast the sound with the
bleat of a billy goat. The moo is low, the bleat is high. I
do not ask you to sound like a cow, but for contented listeners it is better to have the pitch of a cow than a goat.

How do we lower the voice? Low pitch and low resonance usually go hand in hand.

BE A LOW PITCHER

To find out how low your potential pitch may be, put
your hand flat on your chest right under the collarbone
and groan or say, "Aaaaah," as if for a doctor. Now, as if
you were going down cellar steps one at a time, go down
the steps of your available pitches till you hit bottom. Be
aware of the vibrations in your chest as your voice descends.

Next, with your hand still on your chest, say "*I* don't
think it is going to snow." Again, go down step by step,
lowering the pitch each time till you feel you cannot go any
lower. Try a few sentences at the lowest pitch you can
maintain naturally.

To help make this new low pitch part of your regular
vocal equipment:

℞:
1. *Be a floor talker*
Sitting in a chair, place your feet squarely on the floor,
twelve inches apart. Set a book between your heels. Bend
over from your waist toward the book, your head dangling,
your arms hanging loose. Your fingers should be like limp
tassels touching the floor. Relax completely. Now begin
reading, using your girdle of breath support. Your speech
will automatically resonate in your chest. Your pitch will
be lower. Listen carefully to this sound—it is the one you
want. Then straighten up, trying to retain the voice quality
you had in the dangling position. You are not supposed to
read for interpretation but purely for voice quality.

℞:
2. *Palmer penmanship*

In grammar school when they taught you how to write with flowing, rounded, unbroken lines, you were told to make endless connected circles like this:

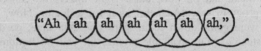

Standing chest up, stomach in, describe full rich vocal circles on

"Ah ah ah ah ah ah ah,"

with unbroken supported sound, while you make circles with your hand for your eye to see. As each sound hits the bottom of its circle, give it renewed energy by pulling in your vital center. You should remind yourself of a broken record when the needle gets stuck in the groove. The sound rolls over and over.

Try this on "ah" . . . "aw" . . . "oh."

Remember to give each circle of sound a new push with your vital center. Dig down, down, down as though you were dredging for a new low in voice range. Scoop up your voice from the bottom of the bay—haul the bucket up from the bottom of the well.

It is also a good idea to read aloud, with your hand on your chest to remind you to use chest resonance. Never let yourself inflect up at the end of a sentence. It tends to make your overall speech sound higher and gives you the tentative sound of uncertainty instead of the positive sound of authority. Even questions can be asked effectively inflecting down. Try some:

```
                    OVER  TO—
CAN  YOU  COME                  MORROW?

              DO  IT  TO—
WILL  YOU                DAY?

          GLAD
YES  I'LL  BE          TO.
```

Emphasizing down is much more effective than raising pitch.

```
I              I              You
   want it!       hope so!          must do it!
```

There is no sound of uncertainty or hysterics this way.

To attain a voice that charms, beguiles, persuades, convinces, commands—and, above all, *communicates warmly*—you must THINK LOW constantly.

(I do not mean morally; I mean physically.)

You have to keep your breath support LOW!

You have to keep your pitch LOW!

You have to keep your resonance LOW!

You have to keep emphasis and inflection DOWN!

Write on six self-adhering stickers, in big letters, and preferably in bright red ink, the words, "THINK LOW!" Place them on your telephone at the office and at home, on the mirror before which you shave or comb your hair, on your desk, in your diary. Remind yourself to "THINK LOW!"

And think low in all talking situations. If you spend much time on the telephone, turn your telephone calls into exercise sessions—hold a pencil about sixteen inches away from your lips at lap, waist, or table level, and talk down into it.

REMEMBER:

◄ Use some of the "relaxers" in this chapter every day to

relieve daily tensions. Use them to relax your head . . .
jaw . . . throat . . . neck.

◄ Don't clamp your teeth when you talk.
◄ Learn to feel the sensation of an open throat, as in yawn-
   ing.
◄ Don't contract the sides of your mouth when speaking.
◄ Make your lips lively, not lazy.
◄ Be a low pitcher.
◄ Be a smooth talker.
◄ Emphasize and inflect *down* wherever possible.

7. Speak in Living Color

He spoke in Hell's and Heaven's name,
Yet all he uttered seemed the same.
                              —ANON.

Think of a face with no smile, no frown, no flicker of emotion, with eyes that don't light up or crinkle with laughter. It's a pretty dull face, isn't it? Well, your voice too can be deadpan. If you take away variety of pitch, pacing, expression, and language, what remains is without luster or sparkle. You've robbed yourself of enthusiasm and warmth and humanity, no matter how much of each you may feel.

If you're afflicted with monotony, you're probably not using as many notes in your speaking voice as you should. Try singing "Do, re, mi, fa, sol, la, ti, do." Keep climbing for another four or five notes in the scale—"re, mi, fa, sol, la."

If you use as wide a range of pitch as that when you speak, your voice will have color and vitality. Now sing just "do, re, mi, fa, sol"—and stop. This is the limited range of a monotonous speaker. It has about as much variety as the drone of a bumble bee on a hot summer afternoon.

In London, television star Eve Arden absent-mindedly sat down on a piano keyboard. At the sound of the jangled notes, she wryly commented, "Gosh, two octaves! I'll have to reduce." Sixteen notes are perhaps too broad a spread for one's derrière, but for the voice they're wonderful!

As I pointed out in the last chapter, one way to achieve variety is to lower, not raise, the pitch of any word you wish to emphasize. Lower your pitch on the adjectives in the following lines:

> Tall men, short men, fat men, lean men, proud men, humble men, indifferent men, concerned men.

Now try emphasizing whole phrases, giving the key word within the phrase just a little more emphasis than the rest. Read this passage of Henry Ward Beecher's, guarding against ending each sentence on the same note:

> Thinking cannot be clear till it has had expression. We must write or speak, or act our thoughts, or they will remain in half torpid form. Our feelings must have expression, or they will be as clouds, which, till they descend in rain, will never bring up fruit or flower. So it is with all the inward feelings; expression gives them development. Thought is the blossom; language the opening bud; action the fruit behind it.

Pauses for effect are another coloring agent which, skilfully used, can give your speech added expression and feeling. You will find the places to pause self-evident in this Arabian proverb:

> He who knows, and knows he knows,
> He is wise—follow him.
> He who knows, and knows not he knows,
> He is asleep—wake him.
> He who knows not, and knows not he knows not,
> He is a fool—shun him.
> He who knows not, and knows he knows not,
> He is a child—teach him.

Say aloud, "Oh, I don't think he will ever do that." Repeat the sentence again and again, emphasizing a different word each time. You will find that this undistinguished nine-word sentence can have innumerable overtones of meaning. When you begin to vary your emphasis, you can play almost as many combinations in a sentence as in a hand of seven-card stud. (This is coloring through emphasis.)

Say two words, "Come here," in five ways—as if you were

1 calling for help when caught by an undertow while swimming;
2 luring your lover to your side;
3 bursting with news for a friend;
4 an army sergeant speaking to a private;
5 a parent summoning a misbehaving child.

(This is coloring through tone of voice.)

Say "hello" or "good morning" into the telephone (not necessarily with someone at the other end of the line) with these overtones:

1 I'm glad you called, whoever you are;
2 I hate the world;
3 I'm ready for a long gossip session;
4 I'm in a hurry; there is no time for a long chatty visit; say what you have on your mind and get it over with.

Can you say, "I love you," so that it feels like a warm embrace? Put all the love you can feel in "love." Then pitch it lower than the "I", like this: "I *love* you." Now try it on someone you love tonight. Color it according to the message you wish to convey:

"I love you" (I can't live without you);

"I love you" (you make everything seem like fun);

"I love you" (don't you understand, you fool); etc.

(I'm for using the word "love" more freely. Maybe the habit started when I played supper clubs. When an audience responded warmly, I just had to say, "I *love* this audience." I find I'm still saying it to lecture audiences and to my classes. And you know—I mean it!)

Newspapers can help you not only to check your voice for monotony, but also to correct that defect. Read an editorial out loud to your tape recorder if you have one. Does it sound as though you were reading a grocery list? Now

read the editorial again, bringing out the meanings of
words; then emphasize all the adjectives; here and there
try emphasizing a whole phrase, with the peak of the emphasis on the most important word. Vary the pacing—a
little quicker here, a little slower there. Find the appropriate places for pauses. Now listen to yourself on the recorder. Doesn't the editorial sound more interesting?

Read selections from great writings or speeches. Here is
one from John F. Kennedy's inaugural address:

> To those peoples in the huts and villages of half the
> globe struggling to break the bonds of mass misery,
> we pledge our best efforts to help them help themselves
> for whatever period is required—not because the
> Communists may be doing it, but because it is right.
> If a free society cannot help the many who are poor,
> it cannot save the few who are rich.

Without color, that passage might as well be from a sec-
ond-grade reader. Remember that adjectives, properly
chosen and emphasized, are a speaker's best friend. So un-
derline the words or phrases you think should be stressed,
and read the passage again. Notice how the stressed words
shed luster on those around them. You will find the whole
quotation passing through a sea-change. All at once it is
alive and compelling.

Listen to William Pitt the elder, addressing Parliament
in 1766 on taxation of the North American colonies:

> My lords, I am old and weak, and at present unable
> to say more; but my feelings of indignation were too
> strong to have said less. I could not have slept this
> night in my bed, nor reposed my head on my pillow,
> without giving this vent to my eternal abhorrence of
> such preposterous and enormous principles.

Imagine that you are William Pitt—an indignant man
of conviction. How would you have brought those great
lines to life?

WORDROBES

Even the most vivid voice with the most varied pacing cannot make up for a drab vocabulary. For a while, you may be able to imply by the tone of your voice a meaning that does not exist, and you may be able to make dull expressions sound bright, but all too soon it will become apparent your colorful sound should be working through more colorful words.

There is no better way to increase your variety of expression, your self-confidence, and your breath of knowledge than to add regularly to your working wordrobe. Look up new words as they come into your experience and then, if you think they are likely to prove useful, put them into practice. Use a word sparingly in general conversation until you are familiar with its nuances, and it comes naturally to your tongue. Then use it whenever it is appropriate. (But avoid words with which your listeners are not likely to be familiar. Your purpose is to communicate, not to show off.)

Reading is the best way to increase your vocabulary, partly because you are bound to run into new words and partly because they are likely to be surrounded by a whole clutch of familiar ones that give clues to the meanings of those you don't know.

If the words great, nice, awful were outlawed, would you have trouble getting along without them? Consider the following alternatives, noting, however, how the meanings differ:

Nice	*Great*	*Awful*
amiable	admirable	appalling
attractive	agreeable	alarming
captivating	commanding	base
dynamic	celebrated	commonplace
charming	distinguished	contemptible
handsome	delicious	calamitous
winsome	elegant	deadly

lovable	engaging	distressing
personable	impressive	dire
prepossessing	glorious	dreadful
stimulating	outstanding	foul
forceful	pleasing	fearful
irresistible	powerful	frightful
	superb	horrible
	unique	inferior
	extraordinary	inept
		inordinate
		low
		nefarious
		repulsive
		shocking
		unattractive
		unworthy
		wretched
		worthless

A well stocked wordrobe is a big part of colorful speech, but it is by no means the only criterion. The question is not just how many words you know, but in what unexpected designs and how freshly you employ them. You may have a voluminous vocabulary and still sound dull as ditch-water.

I may have used many clichés inadvertently in this book, but I said "dull as ditchwater" (some say "dish-water") to make a point.

"Dull as ditchwater" caught on originally because it was the most vivid and unmistakable description of dullness that had been coined. It deserved its place in the language.

But times change. Most of us today are not very familiar with ditchwater—and even dishwater is vanishing into the washing machine. Turns of phrase, like knives, lose their edge from years of cutting. If they cannot be resharpened, they eventually have to be replaced. Can you think of a present-day replacement for "ditchwater?"

The language is full of old, tired words that in a different setting would turn young again. The accepted euphemisms of one era become ridiculous in another. Your thrice-great aunt was only expressing spinsterish modesty when she referred to the "limb" instead of the leg of a bed, and asked for the part of the chicken that came over the fence last. Harry Golden, in *For 2¢ Plain,* cites as an example of our decline in modesty—or our increase in frankness, if you prefer—the following language changes:

1856.   She has canceled all social engagements.
1880.   She is in an interesting condition.
1895.   She is in a delicate condition.
1910.   She is knitting little booties.
1920.   She is in a family way.
1925.   She is expecting.
1956.   She is pregnant. (it took one hundred years
        to be able to say it straight out)

SHUN THE SESQUIPEDALIAN WORD

No speech habit is more repulsive than the use of large words, unfamiliar to speaker and listener alike, simply to create an impression.

George Orwell, in a volume of essays called *Shooting an Elephant,* fired dead on center at a present-day tendency, centered in writing but often painfully evident in speech, to use big, round words where little, sharp ones will do the job better. He took this model of plain powerful prose from Ecclesiastes:

> I returned and saw under the sun that the race is not to the swift, nor the battle to the strong, nor yet bread to the wise, nor yet riches to men of understanding, nor yet favor to men of skill; but time and chance happeneth to them all.

Orwell gobbledygooked this shining passage into:

> Objective consideration of contemporary phenomena compels the conclusion that success or failure in

competitive activities exhibits no tendency to be com-
mensurate with innate capacity, but that a considerable element of the unpredictable must invariably be
taken into account.

A great scholar can bring great words to heel, and a great
poet can make any word fly or burrow, burn or freeze. If
a Samuel Johnson chose to speak of the inspissation of
gloom and the anafractuosity of the mind, he had a right.
He knew his listener. He was speaking to men of his own
time, who knew their Greek and Latin roots as you may
know your friends' telephone numbers. Winston Churchill,
who loved to amuse himself with orotund language, could
call the coming of old age "the surly advance of decrepi-
tude"; but when the chips were down he spoke in Anglo-
Saxon: "We shall fight on the beaches, we shall fight on
the landing grounds, we shall fight in the fields and in the
streets, we shall fight in the hills; we shall never surrender."
The only foreign-bred word in the lot was "surrender"—
the one concept that Churchill found unthinkable.

Oscar Hammerstein went straight to the hearts of all
women with the words of the song I used to sing in *The
King and I*:

> He may not always say
> What you would have him say
> But now and then he'll say
> Something wonderful.

(In case you are interested, it is on Decca Record No.
DL 9008.)

Ivor Brown, in his delightful *Mind Your Language*, lists
the following examples of long words that sound stilted
today and have shorter, usually preferable, alternatives:

commence or initiate	begin
terminate or finalize	end
in the present circumstances	as things are
with reference to	as to, or about

domicile	home
optimum	best
in the eventuality of	if
endeavor	try
visage	face
edifice	building
infringement	breach
regulations	rules

Many of the words in the left-hand column are words which are comfortable to the eye but awkward to most ears.

Every word leads a triple life. It is read; it is written; it is spoken. The chances are that you read with ready comprehension at least three times as many words as you can dredge from your mind in spontaneous talk. Your writing vocabulary is somewhere in between.

Notice how lively the language becomes if given a chance. Loosen the reins, tap with your heels, and it is off at a gallop. "Toward More Picturesque Speech," a delightful department in the *Reader's Digest,* regularly blows such iridescent bubbles as these:

◄ Texans discussing their oil-gotten gains.
◄ The sort of book that once you put it down you can't pick it up again.
◄ We motored through miles and miles of nothing but miles and miles.
◄ The idea caught on like measles in a kindergarten.
◄ The pebbly brook chattering with cold.
◄ Gold digger—a woman after all.

My mother regularly tosses off phrases like these:

◄ (of an attractive dinner guest) He arouses all my extra-sexual perception.
◄ (reporting on a visit to the dentist) He said it was a matter of the tooth, the whole tooth, and nothing but the tooth.
◄ (deciding she would go on a diet) I've got to break through the pound barrier.

When I was playing in *Rosalinda* on Broadway, in one scene I stripped down to long old-fashioned underwear, removing six petticoats of different colors. I never put the petticoats on in the same order; the members of the orchestra would have a kind of ship's pool betting on what the last color to come off would be. I had two fun games going at once—one with the audience and the other with the betting musicians in the pit.

You can vary coloring in words, too. Start creating your own unexpected—but not forced—expressions. They do not have to be elaborate. "Imp" is more vivid than "mischievous boy," "small tempest" than "fuss," "testy" than "easily irritated." If you cannot create vivid phrases yourself (and don't be ashamed if you cannot—not many people can), give your speech a little added flavor by the tasteful use now and then of appropriate quotations, anecdotes, aphorisms. You will find them in many paperback book collections and in newspapers and magazines. Start a collection of your own and file them on cards.

Be clear when you speak. Be concrete. Be colorful.

REMEMBER:

◄ Don't be stingy—use *all* the notes in your speaking register.

◄ Emphasize adjectives *down* for a dash of quick color.

◄ Enrich color by working on meaning . . . pacing . . . pauses for effect.

◄ Turn to the Appendix, and read selections from "Reading for Color and Effectiveness" into your tape recorder. Listen critically, and correct your mistakes.

◄ Add regularly to your wordrobe. Look up unfamiliar words and make them part of your vocabulary.

8. Perfect Pacing

Speech finely framed delighteth the ear.
—2 MACCABEES 15:39

SPEED AND CHOP TALK

The advertising director of a famous newspaper was on the telephone. "Would you help me save the job of a wonderful woman?" he asked. "She is in her sixties, and she has been my secretary for fifteen years. I am devoted to her. But she talks faster than I can listen. A few years ago I didn't mind so much, but as the pressure of my job builds, her voice gets on my nerves more and more. I don't want to fire her, but if she doesn't slack off on that riveting-machine delivery I'll have to let her go to keep my sanity."

When his secretary arrived for an interview, I sympathized with his problem. But I also sympathized with hers. Busy. Busy. Deadlines. Crises. She fitted her speech to the tempo of her day. She went so fast that often she missed a syllable completely.

Before even starting her on slow-down techniques, I prescribed stickers, to be applied to her telephone and to any place else where she would notice them and others would not. They said:

SLOW

Since her speech, like that of most speed talkers, was as choppy as it was fast, I particularly emphasized the necessity for joining her words together in phrases, gliding like this:

The Lord is my shepherd; I shall not want.

He maketh me to lie down in green pastures;

He leadeth me beside the still waters.

He restoreth my soul.

No stops between words within a phrase.

For three weeks she watched her pacing. Gradually blessed peace descended on her office. One day the advertising director telephoned again. "She used to rattle like hail hitting a tin roof; now," he exulted, "she ripples like a brook!" (Well, he *was* in advertising!)

Next day it was the secretary's turn to call, all aglow: "Miss Sarnoff," she said, "I'm in seventh heaven. Mr. Blank says I don't remind him of a machine gun anymore!"

Her speech had subsided from a headlong 200 words a minute to a smooth 135. She had learned to speak as a river runs toward the sea—not in a series of discontinuous droplets, but in a smooth flow of phrases, each word clasping its neighbor, a natural part of the whole.

LEGATO VS. STACCATO

Two important words in music are *legato* and *staccato*. Legato, says Webster's Second International Dictionary, is "smooth and connected with no breaks between successive tones." Staccato is "disconnected; cut short or apart in performing."

Speech cannot be all one or the other. The more staccato your speech, though, the less pleasant it will sound. The voice tone of the legato speaker is a thread on which the syllables are strung like beads, with no knots separating them. The staccato speaker chops his phrases into words and his words into separated syllables. A person who still reads word by word is likely to speak jerkily.

Do you talk in jolts, like an ancient car traveling a bumpy road? "Our kitchen—certainly needs—redoing." That is staccato. It is the short, dry sound a violinist makes when, instead of bowing his strings, he plucks at them. Learn to draw a bow across the violin strings of your words.

If you are a staccato talker, you shortchange your vowels and exaggerate your consonants. Your words emerge not in the flow of violin music, but in the broken phrases of a horn when the player hits the stops: "P – p – p – p."

MAKE THE MOST OF THOSE VOWELS

Read the following lines aloud. S – t – r – e – t – c – h each vowel like a rubber band, for no less than two beats.

> I could have danced all night,
> I could have danced all night
> And still have asked for more.
> I could have spread my wings
> And done a thousand things
> I've never done before.

Make it sound like this looks: "IIIIII cooooould haaaave daaaaanced aaaaall niiight." Intone the vowels with love, as if the words were a Gregorian chant. For a while, let m – o – l – a – s – s – e – s be your guiding word.

Remember: *Don't* sound like the Morse Code. *Don't* emphasize your consonants; let them float on top of the tone. Rearrange the relationship between your vowels and your consonants, so that you dwell longer on the vowels and as briefly as possible on the consonants.

While you are dr–aw–ing out the vowels, make large, slow-motion, Palmer-penmanship circles with your hand.

Don't stop. Let the syllables flow into one another. Connect the words.

Practice on these familiar lines:

> Rain – rain – go – away –
> Come – again – another – day.

> Row – row – row – your – boat
> Gently – down – the – stream;
> Merrily – merrily – merrily – merrily,
> Life – is – but – a – dream.

PACING

The opposite number to the chop talker is the man or woman whose speech is perpetually stuck in low gear.

A salesman came to me because he often found himself unable to compress his sales talk into the time given him. He would drive a hundred miles to meet a prospective customer, only to find that he had been allotted just fifteen minutes in which to present his case. Part of his trouble was organization; he had to learn to arrange what he had to say so that, if necessary, he could abbreviate it without weakening it. More urgently, though, he had to learn how to alter the rate and pacing of his speech as the situation required, without losing clarity and conviction. Before he began to practice pacing, it took him fifteen minutes to cover the ground that an average talker would have covered easily in ten. Today, if he has to, he can make in ten minutes, and effectively, the points that would take most men twenty. He can speed up or slow down at will.

Pacing, you see, works both ways. The following hints can slow down your speech if it is too fast, or speed it up if it is too slow:

1. Count from one to ten, first in five seconds, then in ten, then in twenty.
2. Make a daily practice of reading newspaper editorials

aloud, first putting a penciled bracket under each phrase you wish to connect. As you read, move your pencil smoothly along the lines, leading your voice. If you find that your normal rate is too slow, go faster; tighten the phrases. If your tendency is to speak too fast, loosen them.

3.   Read into your tape recorder. Play it back and check for speed. For flow. For choppiness.

4.   Record good newscasters. Try to imitate their pacing; feel the flow of their speech.

As I write, I am in the midst of a series of classes for southern executives whose firm flies them to New York for a session with me each Monday. They had found that though the pacing of their talk was fine for the south, it seemed turtle-like in the north. Most northerners count their business minutes as jewels, and want business conversations to move crisply forward.

I am proud to report that these Virginians can now speed or slow their rate of delivery as the situation requires. They, I think, are as pleased with their progress as I am. (They may be even more pleased that I sternly resisted the temptation to tamper with their southern speech patterns.)

Once you have your speech under control, it is yours to do with as you wish.

You can temper it to meet the needs of your listener, as the wind in the Bible was tempered to the shorn lamb. You can adjust your pacing according to the time of day . . . the nature of your audience . . . its mood. The speed of speech varies in business and in social life, from Monday morning to Friday afternoon, from lunch to dinner, from face-to-face to telephone conversation.

There is no need for your speech to outspeed a bullet; nor should it wallow along as though it were a hippopotamus. Be not too fast and not too slow, but greyhound-smooth.

REMEMBER:

◄   Speak at the rate that is best for you and the situation of the moment. Don't be as fast as a machine gun, or as slow as molasses on a cold day.

◄ Note the pacing of the better newscasters on television
   and radio; then check yourself against them on your
   tape recorder.

◄ Speak in phrases; don't chop talk.

◄ Honor your vowels.

9. Don't Upstage Yourself!

Er was wicked in the sight of the Lord; and the Lord
slew him.   —GENESIS 38:7

PADDING

The Lord was right. To err is human, but to "er" should
be considered a capital crime. My only complaint about the
slaying of Er is that it should have been done before he had
a chance to start a family; his descendants today threaten to
take over the world.

And "er," or "ur" if you prefer, is only one of numerous
padders that uglify the speech of far too many of us. My
present-day version of the Holmes warning I mentioned
earlier ("Don't strew your pathway with those dreadful
'urs'") is:

To save your list'ner misery and woes
Don't strew your way with those—you know—*you know's.*

"Er" and "you know" are meaningless pause fillers—
padders—sounds that fill in a pause. Other padders with
which we are all familiar—either standing alone or tacked
onto other words—are "so," "uh," "and uh," "and," "now,"
"darling," "dear," "they say," "you know what I mean,"
"do you understand?", "etcetera, etcetera, etcetera," and
such wordless fill-ins as gasps, lip-smacking, throat-clearing,
and giggling.

Throat-clearing not only irritates the throat of the speaker—it irritates the ear of the listener as well. It may make
him want to clear *his* throat.

One of my students, a labor lawyer, complained that whenever he spoke he saw pain in the eyes of his listeners. "I know," he said, "that I write a darned good speech. What is wrong with my delivery?" What was wrong was simply that he continually cleared his throat. Once aware of this speech tic, he put a quick and complete stop to it. (In all the vocal problems I have described, please do not underestimate the power of self-discipline. With self-discipline, most speech blemishes are curable.)

Then there is giggling. Giggling is forgivable for those under fourteen. For anyone older, it should be a penal offense.

A plump, abbreviated, middle-aged woman came to me with the highest, most persistent giggle that ever scraped a human's ear drums. I moved the giggle down her vocal register until it became a not unpleasant chuckle and finally vanished altogether.

To attain this result, I simply used the devices I have already described. One was a scattering of stickers, with the word "giggle" crossed out. Another was exercises to keep her breath flowing throughout each phrase, so that she did not stop to giggle.

I used a psychological argument, too. A giggle is associated with adolescence. "If you giggle," I asked her, "shouldn't you wear a teen-age miniskirt, too?" The first step toward eliminating any speech tic is to become aware of it. Indeed, awareness alone is often sufficient to cancel it out.

Stickers are the ideal reminders. If you find yourself saying "Uh" between words, write "Uh" on your stickers, and then cross it out by drawing a line through it. Make at least six of these stickers. Keep them where you cannot help seeing them—on your desk, by the kitchen range, alongside your telephone. Use them faithfully, and within a few days your padding should be a sorrow of the past.

VISUAL DISTRACTORS

The owner of a prosperous real estate company confided to me his worries about Bill X, one of his most promising young executives. He was bright, energetic, and he was invaluable to the company—indeed, he had just brought off a two-million-dollar deal. He was personable; but somehow, complained my friend, he was irritating; he did not enhance the company image.

What was the trouble? His dress? His speech? His voice? The real estate man could not put his finger on it. He did, however, send Bill to see me. He was all that I had been told—bright, competent. And his problem almost literally hit me in the eye. It was his right hand.

That hand was in constant motion. It cut in and out, sawed the air, darted like a striking snake. It flashed past my eye like a flying saucer; rotated before my face like the vanes of a windmill.

In East Indian dances, gestures substitute for words. Hands talk a language of their own, telling the most intricate stories by adjustment of position and movement. Similarly, deaf mutes exchange remarkably subtle ideas entirely through hand signs and bodily gestures.

Now, there is nothing wrong with gestures, properly used. A gesture is fine for splendid emphasis—but only if it emphasizes, not if it distracts. There is no need to raise a finger every time you say "one," and a second finger every time you say "two." The words speak for themselves.

When your listener pays more attention to what your hand is doing than to what you are saying, you are being upstaged. Your hand should be put in its place.

My cure for Bill may have been unorthodox, but it worked. When his turn came to talk before the class, for instant television playback, I tied a broad red bow to his right wrist. "Whenever that hand comes up," I told him, "you are going to see that bow, and so will we. We won't be concentrating on your message; we'll be watching the bow."

The trick was successful. His hand quieted down. When the lessons were over, he took the bow to his office and put it under a glass bell as a reminder. From then on, his hand was under control.

You *can* correct, or at least modify, untoward gestures. Tom Wicker, in the New York *Times*, described the 1968 campaign gestures of Richard Nixon: "breast strokes, veronicas, karate chops, jabs, uppercuts, and one-hand push shots"—and acknowledged that once Nixon had become President, these distractors had diminished or vanished.

Hand gestures are the most common of the physical distractors that interfere with communication, but there are many more. Some people incessantly nod or shake their heads. Others lick or bite their lips, fidget with pencils or jewelry, brush nonexistent lint off their clothes, weave from side to side, sway back and forth on their heels like rocking horses, pace the floor like lions, swing crossed legs like pendulums, shrug their shoulders, curl their forelocks with their fingers, drum on the table, examine or pick at their nails.

Many of these physical distractors stem from nervousness—a common speech problem, and one which will be considered at length later in this book.

No less distracting are a gap between a woman's stocking and her skirt when she sits, or a zipper that stops halfway along the track.

Clarence Darrow, the famous trial lawyer, sometimes used a physical distractor when his adversary was summing up to the jury. Darrow, smoking a cigar at his council table, would let the ash gradually lengthen until every eye was on it, waiting for it to fall; his opponent might as well not have bothered to speak.

(One physical distractor that may have something to be said for it is the askew tie. An English friend of mine reports that he deliberately sets his tie a bit off center so that women will want to come close and straighten it.)

Unless a distractor is a true tic, it can be painlessly removed. If you are a head-wobbler, for instance, balance a book on your head while talking on the telephone. (I assume that you are alone. Otherwise you might be thought a bit odd.) If the conversation falls off before the book does, you are whipping your problem.

I repeat: stickers in appropriate locations are invaluable reminders and discipliners. They are like speech nursemaids. The editor of a highly regarded woman's magazine asked me to help her become more effective in meetings. She was utterly unaware that her nose twitched like a rabbit's when she spoke. I had her write out a dozen stickers bearing the pregnant directive:

Within a week she had stopped being a rabbit, and rejoined the human race.

EYE CONTACT

The head of a banking organization came to me with a personnel problem. It is bad enough, he said, that the public think of bankers as aloof and cold. But—even worse—many young men training for high banking positions seem to think of themselves the same way; they freeze just when they should thaw. Since modern banking is a matter in no small part of public relations, executives should appear warm, not cold. Could I do something, he asked, to give his young executives a warmer image?

Part of the chilliness that emanates from too many executives comes simply from nervousness and lack of self-confidence. Part, perhaps, is a matter of tenacity and single-mindedness which leave no room for the social graces. But most chilly executives simply do not realize the need for communicating warmly. It literally does not occur to them

that they are shutting out their peers and juniors by showing no sign of interest and approval—sometimes even failing to smile "hello."

Older men, who have come to take their board chair-
manships for granted, often mellow. They discard the mask
of aloofness that accompanied them on their climb. They
turn again into human beings who enjoy a joke. Their smile
is ready and warm; their interest in others spontaneous and
sincere.

One of the quickest ways to eliminate the appearance of
aloofness is to practice direct, pleasant eye contact. If you
are talking with a subordinate, or, for that matter, with a
superior officer, do not let your gaze flutter around the
room or out the window. Be interested—and let your eyes
show it. This does not mean to impale people with your
look—on the contrary. It does mean to look directly into
their eyes—not at them, into them.

In any business conversation—as in any public talk—
look into others' eyes a good ninety per cent of the time
remembering that your eyes communicate no less than your
voice does. If you are talking to more than one person, your
gaze should pick up each in turn, and rest on him for five
or six beats. It should convey interest and approval, not
blankness or hostility.

I had one student whose principal distractor was contin-
uous blinking. He was like a defective neon light. His flut-
tering eyelids made him appear unsure of himself. Once he
was aware of his habit, it was only a matter of hours before
he slowed his blinking rate to normal.

Another student, quite to the contrary, seemed detached
from anyone to whom he was speaking because he scarcely
blinked at all. He stared out of the corner of his eye, like
the villain in an old-fashioned murder mystery. When I
taught him to blink more often, the severe look disappeared.

If you find yourself avoiding the gaze of the person you
are talking to . . . if you stare like an owl or blink like a
sleepy child . . . write down a reminder and work on your
"problem."

A CLOVE OF GARLIC, A JUG OF WINE AND THOU

Good grooming includes personal cleanliness. Body odors may have stimulated other generations, but they distress ours. Avoid, too, musky perfumes that suffocate those near at hand. Be chary of alcohol and onions at lunch. As for garlic, don't take that even the night before.

An amusing incident in my life behind the footlights— though it did not seem so to me at the time—had to do with garlic. My first Broadway show, *Rosalinda,* ran a long time. During the fourteenth or fifteenth month, the tenor, with whom I shared passionate love scenes, developed the garlic habit. You can imagine how difficult it was to make love in the midst of chemical warfare.

We discussed the problem at length, and he finally promised never to eat garlic again before a performance. For the next few weeks, harmony reigned. Then one evening, just before the show, the doorman brought me an envelope containing a clove of garlic and a note saying, "Defend yourself—I've slipped."

To appreciate my retaliation, you must know that in the second scene of the play, the tenor entered Rosalinda's parlor, donned her husband's velvet robe and slippers, settled back on the sofa, and was served his supper by a pert maid, Adele. The supper, brought in on a tray, included a delectable wiener schnitzel under a large silver cover. The tenor would lift the cover to savor rapturously the aroma of his favorite dish.

So-o-o—before the show I slipped into the prop room where the schnitzel was kept. I mashed the clove of garlic into it and set the platter on a hot radiator to ripen.

Curtain time: enter tenor. He gaily removes his jacket, dons the robe and slippers, settles back on the sofa and welcomes the silver tray. He lifts the cover and takes a deep breath. Complete asphyxiation!

But my scheme boomeranged. I had forgotten that four

lines later, the tenor exited. I was left to play the balance
of the scene by myself in a noxious gas chamber.

REMEMBER:

◄ Stickers can help you get rid of padding—those "er"s
   and "ah"s . . . those giggles . . . those "you know"s.

◄ Your eyes are almost as much a part of your speech as
   your voice is. *Look* at the people you are talking to;
   it will help them to listen better!

◄ Be considerate not just of your listeners' ears and eyes,
   but of their noses, too. No garlic, *please!*

10. "Everybody Says Words Different"

> "Everybody says words different," said Ivy. "Arkansas folks says 'em different, and Oklahomy folks says 'em different. And we seen a lady from Massachusetts, an' she said 'em differentest of all. Couldn't hardly make out what she was sayin'."
> —JOHN STEINBECK, *The Grapes of Wrath*

REGIONAL ACCENTS

Shortly after giving a lecture in Richmond, I received a long-distance call from a man who reported that his wife had recorded the whole talk on tape and brought it home for him to hear. He wanted to send her to New York to take lessons, so that I could match her accent to his. He had lived in Richmond all his life; she came from a town sixty miles away where the pronunciation was quite different. His work brought him into contact with businessmen from many countries, and he found that though they had no trouble understanding him, they could barely understand his wife at all. He sent me a tape with a sample of his own speech. Soon afterward his wife came to New York, where she took three lessons weekly for four weeks. The result was "his and her" accents—accents that matched!

There are nearly as many different accents in America as there are people. Lewis and Marguerite Herman report that in Richmond alone they heard the word "aunt" pronounced eight different ways, while in another limited area "yes" was pronounced thirty-seven different ways.

There are three principal streams of speech in the United States: the eastern; the southern; and the midwestern, which seems to be slowly gaining the day. Notable subcurrents flow through:

New England
New York City, Jersey City, Hoboken, etc.

Pennsylvania (two branches: the Philadelphia and the Pennsylvania Dutch)

Louisiana

The rest of the Southern and Gulf Coast, in three broad parts: East Texas; DelMarVa (sections of Delaware, Maryland, and Virginia); and Tidewater (Southeastern Virginia, eastern North Carolina, and most of the coast of South Carolina)

The Middle and Far West, including upstate New York. A regional accent is perfectly all right wherever it is understood and accepted. But when accents stand in the way of instant comprehension they need replacing.

Since my home and business are in New York, New York accents predominate among the speech detractors I am asked to cure. As Richard Shepard pointed out in the New York *Times:*

A fine German accent may bolster a psychiatrist's fee. A crisp British accent simply cries for a lecture tour. Regional variations across the city line command affectionate toleration. To speak as they do in Dixie—as long as it's intelligible—is a sentimental plus. The New England twang conjures up visions of democracy in the raw, small townsmen going to meetings and debating about raising money by lottery. The pioneer spirit infests the Western drawl, even when it emanates from a mouth that never shouted at a cow. Modified Midwestern is to us what Florentine is to Italian, the standard, the stated norm that few from elsewhere can more than approximate.

But [out-of-New Yorkers] abominate the New York accent. New Yorkers abominate it, too. In school, patient teachers, with frustrating results, try to extirpate local aberrations, such as oi for er, er for oi, the dese, dems and doses, the whatch for what are you and the lamentable, mystifying disappearance of the r that makes Noo Yawkers rush to fi-uhs when the alahm bell rings.

Add to this ethnic variants with rising intonations and brutally mis-emphasized consonants, and the city emerges as a linguistic disaster area, a desperate zone of pear-shaped poverty, in which even sizable Federal aid will show no pronounced results . . .

Now, is the New York accent really all that bad? The answer, doubtless, is a resounding yeah. But it need not be so; that is a culturally bred reaction and nothing that a little positive thinking can't cure . . . It is the dialect that unifies the fastest town in the world. It wastes no time on colorful metaphors and drawled verities. It runs toward a deed, a deal or a dollar, anything that has a goal . . . It is the hurry-up, short-order accent of America.

This doesn't make it the best . . . But must our accent be rooted out? Under New York's landmark laws, certain ancient buildings may be built anew inside but not a brick on the outside may be touched. Is there no way to harness the accent and its vigor, to reach a happy medium that will allow for some internal refurbishing while preserving the rugged exterior? Something between Mayor Lindsay and Zero Mostel?

If you have a regional accent, don't be ashamed to keep the best of it. Wipe out only the part that is genuinely disagreeable to most people with whom you are in contact or that is difficult for them to understand.

Television and radio are responsible for fusing dialects, so that many communities are losing speech characteristics which were once theirs alone. Speech sounds of the midwest have come to predominate on most American tongues. Midwestern speech is often called "standard" or "average" American because it is spoken by more Americans than any other dialect. It has had such an influence on the speech of the rest of the country that it has fused the broad, dark "ah" sound (once found in cultured speech in words like dance, bath, half) with the lighter "ă" vowel usually found in words like "cat," "fact," and "match." It has also put the consonant "r" back into words where British, New England, and southern influence had caused the "r" to be omitted (as in "aht" for "art").

The same person may pronounce the same word in different ways, according to circumstances. In business and other somewhat formal situations, speech is apt to be more careful and precise than it is in casual conversation. It often loses polish in an informal social situation, loses still more in a family situation, and becomes most lax (often with complete reversion to early speech habits) under the influence of alcohol, fatigue, or special stress.

MISPRONUNCIATION

What you have to say is presumably more important than the way you say it. Still, human nature being what it is, people's impressions of you are often based on the way you speak. Frequently heard words become code words in listeners' minds. The way you handle them reflects your education, culture, taste, and personality.

Commodore Cornelius Vanderbilt, a self-made man with little formal schooling, complained that he was embarrassed when he had to deal with "all them British Lords," because, he said, "I know I am smarter than they are—but they *sound* smarter."

Sometimes a mispronunciation may become fashionable. When George I arrived from Hanover to reign over England, he was unable to pronounce "either" in the English fashion; he said "eye-der." Obsequious courtiers picked up the sound, gradually restoring the "th" sound, and today "eye-ther" is acceptable wherever English is spoken.

If you have a reasonably sensitive ear, you will hear mispronunciations all over the place, very nearly as many in the hallowed halls of academe as in Luigi's trattoria. I have a friend who regularly says "mumbuling" for "mumbling," "off-ten" for "often," and so on; yet he considers himself a meticulous speaker.

If you regularly make the kind of sounds in the right-hand list below, expect a raised eyebrow from a discerning listener.

The words	The sounds
Did you	Didja
Goodbye	Guhby
Ought to	Otta
That's what I	Swateye
Going to	Gonna
Saturday	Saddy
Want to	Wanna
Let me	Lemme
Government	Govmint
Because	Becuz (or becawss)
Strength	Strenth
Length	Lenth
Width	With
Fifth	Fith
Often	Off-ten
Library	Libery
Height	Heighth
New	Noo
Athletic	Athaletic
Avenue	Avenoo
Extraordinary	Extra-ordinary
Mischievous	Mischeevious
Ask	Ax

Particularly in New England and New York, watch out for the unwelcome "r":

The word	The sound
Idea	Idear
Sofa	Sofer
Plaza	Plazer
Banana	Bananer
Draw	Drawer
Law	Lawr
Saw	Sawr
Indiana	Indianer
Florida	Florider
Soda	Soder

If you know someone who is the victim of an unwelcome "r", you can suggest a very simple way of curing it. Tell him to push his tongue tip down into the lower gum ridge at the end of words like "idea" or "soda," so that it cannot go up to form the "r" sound.

Acceptable pronunciation alters (which does not always mean it improves). More and more the ugly "bokay" shoulders aside the soft "bouquet"; "kewpon" has all but replaced "coupon." More people now say "noo" than "new," and "Toosday" than "Tuesday."

The word "beautiful" is often so distorted nowadays that there is no longer anything beautiful about it. Some people say "bee-you-dee-ful." I do hope you simply say "b'yootiful," so that its sound lives up to its meaning.

CONFUSED CONSONANTS

T's and D's. Avoid an explosive "t" or "d." Leave that sound to Mae West.

The secret of an attractive sounding "t" or "d" is a delicately pointed tongue tip—a feather, not a bludgeon—that lightly touches the upper gum ridge and instantly retreats, cutting the consonants short. To develop this delicate "t," say "Tuh, tuh, tuh, tuh, tuh," as if you were imitating a woodpecker, or a *dripping* (not a splashing) faucet.

In pronouncing "d", too, cut off the sound as soon as the tongue tip touches the gum ridge. No after-splash!

Don't substitute "d" for "t," making

"thirty"	come out	"thirdy"
"party"	come out	"pardy"
"Saturday"	come out	"Sadday"

Avoid substituting "d" for "t" when the "t" is doubled:

"utter"	not	"udder"

"letter"	not	"ledder"
"batter"	not	"badder"

Only pronounce one "t" when "t" ends one word and begins the next as in:

> want to
> at times
> hit twice

Otherwise you will sound overprecise.

Do not let "d" replace the hard "th" sound, so that "the other brother" becomes "de udder brudder." Practice saying the following very fast:

> the
> these
> them
> those
> there
> that

For the sound "th," the tongue tip pushes against the cutting edge of the upper teeth.

R's. When your tongue forms an "r", the sides lift to make contact with your upper teeth, the tip pointing upward but not touching. To insure a good "r", practice growling: Grrrr. Grrrr. Grrrr. Then drop the "g" but keep the hint of a vowel sound before the "r":

> Errrrr-rabbit
> Errrrr-race.

Drop the "er" when you are sure you have counteracted any tendency to turn "r" into "w".

Some foreign-born people suffer from the reverse defect, a guttural or rolled "r." If this is your problem, make your tongue relax. Do not let it vibrate. Run through the "r" page in the Appendix, saying before each word (first aloud, and later silently), "No tongue tension." Thus:

No tongue tension — *rose;*
No tongue tension — *run;*
No tongue tension — *riddle;*
etc.

L's. "L" is formed much as "t" is, with a delicate tongue tip briefly touching the gum ridge. Look at the mirror and say "ell" again and again. Then say "la, la, la, la," keeping your tongue pointed and narrow and feeling light.

Lolling L's. The lolling "l," like the lisp, is baby talk that was never outgrown. The tongue tip widens, as though to make a "w." Both blemishes are particularly injurious to a man, since they deny him his masculine authority and, in business, sometimes his credibility.

At his wife's insistence, a broker came to see me about his lolling "l's."

"How wong wiww it take me to wose them?" he asked.

I assured him that it would not take wong; nor did it. He was saying "w" for "l" because his tongue tip remained wide and lazy and failed to touch his upper gum ridge. Once he learned to point his tongue instead of widening it, the lolling "l" disappeared.

Lisping. A middle-aged woman of Hungarian parentage asked me to soften her harsh voice. I asked, "Do you mind if I correct your lisp, too?" She burst into tears. She had long since abandoned hope that her lisp might be cured.

In her childhood, she told me, her mother had traveled from one end of Brooklyn to the other every Thursday to buy ducks' tongues from the only butcher in the borough who sold them. Hungarian peasants believed that cooked ducks' tongues would cure a lisp. The child ate the tongues faithfully, but the lisp persisted.

It was gone forever by the time she left for home that evening.

The tongue forms an "s" by retreating, furrowing lengthwise and curling up a little on the sides, leaving just enough room for the air to get through. If the tongue tip touches the upper or lower teeth, the "s" turns into a baby "th." In pronouncing "s," the tongue tip should not touch *anywhere*.

I instructed the lisper to drop her head back loosely, so that she was looking at the ceiling, and let her tongue fall back in her throat. In that position, with her teeth loosely together, she practiced hissing. Then, with her head again in normal position but her tongue still retracted, she began reading aloud a list of words beginning with "s". Before each of the words she repeated aloud (and then to herself), "Retract the tongue." So:

> Retract the tongue — *sssaint;*
> Retract the tongue — *sssinger;*
> Retract the tongue — *sssslowly.*

That was all there was to it. In an hour her lisp was gone.

Dentures, particularly new ones, frequently cause lisping. This is because, as you have noticed if you ever have had a tooth drilled or pulled, the tongue is as curious as a monkey. It cannot resist investigating any new situation in the mouth. It is particularly fond of dentures and keeps nestling against them.

The cure is the same as for a non-denture lisp. Simply get into the habit of retracting the tongue when saying "s." *The sibilant SSSSSSS.* If your "s's" whistle, you need to put interference in the way of the breath stream. Instead of retracting your tongue as you would to prevent a lisp, let the tongue tip touch the lower teeth and blow the "s" lightly over it and the lower lip.

DEFECTIVE VOWELS AND DIPHTHONGS

To return tarnished vowels and diphthongs to mint condition, first familiarize yourself with the chart of sounds in the Appendix. It is as clear and simple as I could make it. The sounds are presented not in forbidding phonetic symbols, but in letters that you should easily follow.

Bear in mind as you are cleaning up your tarnished sounds that the explanation of each pronunciation will help you recognize proper tongue and lip positions, and help your ear correct by identifying the sound. Otherwise your mispronunciations will continue no matter how relentlessly you practice.

Here are summaries of some tongue positions:

"ah" as in "father." Your tongue must be completely relaxed and flat. Your jaw drops lower than for any other speech sound.

"a" as in "apple." Lower only the front of your tongue, and drop your jaw again. Do not let the sound detour upward through your nose, twanging as it goes. Avoid letting one syllable turn into two ("may-un" for "man"), or a soft "a" into a hard "a" ("Hairy" for "Harry").

"aw" as in "talk." Raise the back of your tongue slightly, while its sides touch your upper back teeth. Do not overpurse the lips!

"uhr" as in "bird." This sound should not become "buh-eed" or "boy-eed." Here "uh" should go into "r" not "ee."

Diphthongs (A diphthong is a combination of two vowels, one gliding into the other, with the stress on the first)

"oy" as in "voice." "aw" plus "ih" or "ee." It should not become "uh-ee." Not "vuhees" but "vawees" or "vawihs." Up with the back of the tongue for "aw" . . . then up with the middle for "ih" or "ee."

The "eye" sound. "ah-ih" or "ah-ee." The tongue stays flat on "ah," but rises as "ah" goes into the "ih." Do not say "awee."

"ow" as in "how." "ah-oo." The tongue again stays flat on the "ah," and the lips shape the "oo" by pouting. Do not say "ayoo" like Eliza Doolittle and end up twanging.

REMEMBER:

◄ There is no one correct speech. But do eliminate regionalisms, mispronunciations, and tarnished sounds that distract from what you are saying.

◄ Not all accents are unattractive—and most of those that are, are easily corrected.

◄ When you use a word, make sure you know its meaning —and are pronouncing it correctly.

◄ First, identify your confused consonants, your lisps, defective vowels, or diphthongs. Then turn to the section in the Appendix dealing with those troublemakers —and go to work on them.

PART II

CONVERSATION

11. Conversation Is a Two-way Street

Conversation has fallen upon evil days . . . It is drowned out in singing commercials. It is hushed and shushed in dimly lighted parlors by television viewers who used to read, argue, and even play bridge, an old-fashioned card game requiring speech.   —WHITNEY GRISWOLD

IS CONVERSATION A LOST ART?

Some years ago a friend of mine started to collect glass paperweights for a few dollars apiece. Today some of the same paperweights sell for thousands of dollars. Why? Because the making of paperweights flourished for only twenty years, around the middle of the last century, and then died out as an art form.

I hope that good conversation will never become a lost art; it is already precious enough without that. But there are times when it too seems in danger of extinction.

Probably the heightened speed and tension of modern life have contributed to this decline in conversing. The TV age may have something to do with it, too. Instead of interchanging talk, small or large, many of us sit for hours in front of a one-eyed box, absorbing entertainment or news without even having to open our mouths. How can one become verbally involved—unless he talks back to the commercials? If television instead of conversation is the floor show for you at dinner, or on other occasions where you might be talking with family or friends, you are cutting yourself off from one of life's enriching experiences.

Television need not be a boob tube. A balanced diet of television can be a stimulus, not a deterrent, to conversation. Along with the trash that clutters the airwaves are enough excellent documentary, feature, and discussion programs to give us all useful information for thought—and talk.

Men have celebrated the virtues of conversation since the beginning of recorded time. A Chinese proverb declares, "A single conversation across the table with a wise man is worth a month's study of books." The French essayist Michel de Montaigne wrote, "It is good to rub and polish our brain against that of others." And the English philosopher John Locke said, "I attribute the little I know to my not having been ashamed to ask for information and to my rule of conversing with all descriptions of men on those topics that form their own peculiar professions and pursuits."

Good conversation can leave you more exhilarated than alcohol; more refreshed than the theater or a concert. It can bring you entertainment and pleasure; it can help you get ahead, solve problems, spark the imagination of others. It can increase your knowledge and education. It can erase misunderstandings, and bring you closer to those you love. If the art of conversation is dying in *your* life—revive it now!

YOU *CAN* BE A GOOD CONVERSATIONALIST

I have heard politicians, businessmen, famous writers, and even actors confess that they were at a loss for words and felt like wallflowers when the subject of a conversation veered away from their own specialty. Less famous people say routinely, "I'm just no good at talking." They give alibis like these:

◄ I don't know what to say.
◄ People aren't interested.
◄ People don't listen to me.
◄ I just like to listen.
◄ I'm too shy.
◄ I bore people.

In most cases none of these excuses is valid:

◄ Probably you *do* have something to say, but are simply diffident about saying it. If you really have nothing interesting to talk about, *find* something. Read the daily paper—and not just the sports or social columns. Read newsmagazines. Follow world events. Read, until reading becomes a delightful and irresistible habit. Follow books, music, art, baseball, space flights. There are thousands of things to read—and talk about!

◄ People can be interested in anything—*if you make it interesting.* I have heard a man describe nuclear fission so clearly and absorbingly that twelve ignoramuses (including me) sat spellbound for half an hour.

◄ You're *not* too shy. "Shy" is just "I" with a "sh" before it. Shyness is really I-ness. The shy person is so busy thinking about himself that he says "sh" to any other subject. Think *out,* not *in*—and the words will follow.

◄ Yes, people *will* listen to you—but not if you start apologetically, drearily—not if you mumble. Change your approach. Speak up. Start with a provocative opening. Or if you don't feel ready for that, start with a simple question like, "How did you happen to come to San Francisco to live?"

Even if you are not ready to plunge into conversation feet first, you can at least make reinforcing comments: "Yes, you have a good point there" . . . "I've never heard it put so clearly." Soon you will find that these "filler" sentences are growing into a meaningful part of the dialogue.

Listen to a good conversationalist, and you will find that he is enthusiastic; that he speaks to the point; that he interests his listener; that he is sincere, and that his remarks are well balanced.

Look at him, and you will find that he is animated. Again and again his face lights up in a natural smile.

SMILE TALK IS THE BEGINNING

I am a great believer in what I call "smile talk"—not just in full-scale conversations, but whenever two people exchange words.

Why *not* smile a good morning at the old lady next to you in the elevator? Why *not* be the first to speak if you are seated in a restaurant opposite someone who appears respectable and lonely? Why *not* learn whether your seatmate on the plane is in the mood for a chat?

I am not proposing that you disregard courtesy or common sense. Does someone appear to be the sort you would enjoy talking with? Approach him tentatively. If you are rebuffed, don't feel offended; anyone has a right to solitude if that is what he prefers. But try.

In smile talk, as in any conversation, a compliment often helps. If you are talking to someone whose appearance has something about it you admire, say so. Abraham Lincoln pointed out—and he was not the first to discover this aspect of human nature—that "everybody loves a compliment."

It is essential, though, that the compliment be credible. If it is patently insincere, it might as well be an insult. Archbishop Fulton Sheen once remarked that a compliment is baloney sliced so thin that it is delectable. Flattery is baloney sliced so thick that it is indigestible.

If the shoe is on the other foot—if a stranger or casual acquaintance wants to strike up a conversation with *you* —there is no reason to accept the gambit if you would rather not. If you would prefer to be alone with your thoughts, say frankly, but politely, that you are tired, or would like to read, or work, or sleep. Only once in the thousands of miles that I have had to fly for lecture engagements have I found a neighbor so importunate that I had to change my seat. Even then I did not need to hurt his feelings; the stewardess, noting my dilemma, simply paused beside me to say that if I wished, I could spread out my working papers on two seats in an empty section of the plane.

Have you ever noticed how friendly people become in an emergency or disaster such as the great New York blackout of 1965? What a shame that it takes a blackout, a garbage strike, a flood, or a blizzard to end the restraint between people who may have lived next door to each other for twenty years without even exchanging a smile!

Yes—as Saint Paul told the Ephesians—"Be not forgetful to entertain strangers; for thereby some have entertained angels unawares."

REMEMBER:

◄ *You can* be a good conversationalist.
◄ People will listen—if you have something worthwhile to say.
◄ Read magazines that discuss important events. Read newspapers. Read books. *Read!*
◄ Listen to radio conversation stations. Turn to television for documentaries . . . panel shows . . . coverage of important news events.
◄ SMILE!

12. The Ten Simple Secrets of Conversation

> True happiness arises from . . . the friendship and conversation of a few select companions.
>
> —JOSEPH ADDISON

THE FIRST HINT: STIMULATE OTHERS

You have a responsibility to talk with others in such a way that you not only interest them but stimulate them to participate in turn. Are you calking their self-confidence, or scuttling it? Are you offering them an opening to make a point of their own, or locking them out? Above all, are you showing interest in them—or only in yourself?

Conversation, like a game of catch, cannot be just one-sided. If someone drops the ball, there is an embarrassed silence until it is picked up and tossed again.

My younger students frequently complain to me that they cannot keep conversation alive on a date. Actually, the technique involved is very simple: ask questions that require answers which in their turn will carry the conversation forward. If you only ask, "Nice weather, isn't it?" the other person may bring the whole exchange to an end by replying, "Oh yes, it is." (Mark Twain, by the way, was told one day, for the dozenth time, "Nice day, isn't it, Mr. Clemens?" He replied, "Yes, I've heard it very highly spoken of.")

"Nice weather, isn't it?" can be a dead-end question, but it does not have to elicit a dead-end answer. After all, there must be some interest in weather, or the eleven o'clock TV news would not give a full five minutes to it, with diagrams.

If you find it difficult to draw out your conversational partner, start your sentences with handles like these:

> *"Why* would a . . . ?"
> *"What* do you think will . . . ?"
> "In your opinion what . . . ?"
> *"How* did you happen to . . . ?"
> "How do you explain . . . ?"
> "Could you give me a 'for instance?' "

"How, what, why"—three good friends.

A dead-end answer, of course, is as unproductive as a dead-end question. Keep that conversational ball in the air.

But if you think that the query about the weather reflected nothing more than the speaker's desperate desire to say something to break the silence, perhaps you can launch into your experiences in the blizzard of '88.

If your opposite number responds stingily at first, he may be shy, he may be indifferent, he may be stupid—or you may not yet have hit upon the area that engages his interest. It helps, at a party, if you can learn from your host or hostess something about the person who has been thrown together with you; but even with that knowledge, you cannot be sure of breaking the ice, and triggering his tongue.

You may have to sit at dinner by a llama-like, aloof lawyer who could not be induced even by the tortures of Torquemada to so much as turn and look at you. Keep trying, though. If a reference to the problems of Mexican wetbacks brings no response, maybe a word about scuba diving will do the trick. Or you might mention the breeding habits of whales.

As a last resort, you can always knock a glass of water into his lap. If even that fails to produce a spirited exchange, at least it will have relieved your feelings.

Take an Interest in People and Ideas

Sir Noël Coward once remarked, "My importance to the world is relatively small. On the other hand, my importance to myself is tremendous. I am all I have to work with, to play with, to suffer, and to enjoy."

True enough, mankind is—and indeed has to be—self-centered. Once that basic fact of life ceases to shock you, you can adjust your discourse with others accordingly. To be blunt, it is to your advantage to discuss subjects that interest others, even if their prédilections do not happen to be your own. You can afford to throw a sop to their self-esteem, even if your own self-esteem has to wait its turn for a little.

Cynical? Not at all. If you go a little out of your way to treat your family and friends as if they were important to you, you may well find that they do mean more to you —and you will mean more to them. Everybody wants approval and thrives on it. You may stumble on the fortunate fact that there really is something wonderful about every imperfect, mixed-up, uncertain human being who ever took his place in the queue shuffling continually from womb to tomb.

Psychiatrists say the mental patient who starts taking an interest in people and things outside the prison of his own ego is on the way to recovery. To the extent that self-absorption is a reflection of insanity, none of us is completely sane. But the more we reach out to others, not to get but to give, the saner we become. And a selfish reward ensues: the more thoughtful you are of others, the more thoughtful they will be of you. The more you respect them, the more you will win their respect.

If you are really interested in someone, your interest will shine through what you say. You will share his problems as well as his pleasures. You will look for ways to help when help is needed. You will be less taken up with what you can teach him than with what he can teach you.

So don't hesitate to toss out the conversational ball, and keep tossing it out until someone catches it and tosses it back again. The more skillfully you throw, the more exciting the game becomes.

THE SECOND HINT: EDIT

"Don't let the weeds choke the plant you want to keep alive," I tell my classes. There is no more hurtful speech habit than not knowing when to stop, or what to leave out. The non-edited talker, the repeater, the rambler, the overdetailer, soon finds he is talking only to himself; his audience dematerializes, like the Cheshire cat in *Alice in Wonderland*.

General Alexander Smythe, whose speeches in Congress were better known for their length than their cogency, said to his rival Henry Clay: "You, sir, speak for the present generation; but I speak for posterity."

To which Mr. Clay replied, "Yes; and you seem resolved to speak until the arrival of your audience."

Rambling is a hard habit to overcome. Most of us feel a certain sympathy with Sancho Panza when, replying to Don Quixote's complaint that Sancho's tale is too full of repetitions and diversions, he defends himself thus: "The way I'm telling it is the way all stories are told in my country. It isn't fair for your worship to ask me to get new habits."

Yet if there is any single injunction on conversation that should be blazoned in red, whether you are chatting with a friend or addressing an audience of thousands, it is this: *Come to the point and stay with it.*

Executives in my classes report almost without exception that the habit most annoying to them in business conversation is non-edited talking. Millions of man hours go down the drain of this habit—the drain of rambling, forgetting the point, never coming to the point, saying the same thing again and again.

One of my students was a consulting engineer who advised manufacturers on cutting production costs. He found, for instance, that often they used five or more drops of glue where two would have done the job at least as efficiently. Not only did wasted glue add to plant costs, but workers had to take time to wipe the overspill away.

In conversation, too, there is often a wasteful overspill, with a dozen words used where one would do the job. Women especially, when their children are grown and their time stretches empty ahead, are likely to dwell interminably on unimportant details: only their hairdressers or manicurists really have to listen—that may be part of what they're paid for.

> "John," says Mrs. Smith, "I know it was last Tuesday at eleven o'clock because just before you called, Mrs. Jones came across to borrow some flour. I remember it especially because she was wearing a brand new dress, bright pink with gold buttons . . ."

I hope that Mrs. Smith does not remind you of yourself. When your principal purpose in conversation is to make a point, make it—and not too much more.

Rambling may be an indication of a vague way of thinking. It may be a means of clinging to the center of the stage. More likely, though, it is simply a bad habit, of which you can rid yourself much more easily than a cigarette addict can rid himself of the habit of smoking.

If you are aware of a tendency to talk endlessly, try to imagine that you are talking on the long-distance telephone at day rates.

THE THIRD HINT: AVOID "I" DISEASE

"I" is the smallest letter in the alphabet. Don't make it the largest word in your vocabulary. Say with Socrates, not "I think," but "What do *you* think?"

A speaker at a garden club meeting used twenty-six "I's" in the first three minutes of his talk. If he departed from "I," it was only to substitute "my": "My garden . . . my hedge . . . my bush." An acquaintance went up to him afterward and said, "I'm awfully sorry you have lost your wife." "Lost my wife?" said the speaker. "Not at all; she's fine." "Well, didn't *she* have something to do with the garden too?"

Henry Ford II described a bore as "someone who opens his mouth and puts his feats in it." A bore is also a man who puts the "I" in "monopolize": "monopol–I–I–I–ze."

Soliloquies are fine in Shakespeare, where an actor is on stage alone, but they are out of place in a social group. The monopolist cares for no joke, no story, no point of view save his own. "Yes, my boy (or 'my dear')," he says when someone tries to break in, "but . . ." and he rushes on. Conversational monopoly is ego run wild. It is impervious to sighs, glazed eyes, faint yawns, disclaimers, and timid introductions of other subjects. And, sadly, the monopolist's infatuation with his own words is usually a lifetime love affair.

There is one important exception. Some people are so expert, entertaining, or charismatic that everyone *wants* them to keep on talking. It would be a sin not to let them hold the floor. There is a story of how Senator Eugene McCarthy entered a room of political admirers during the 1968 Presidential campaign, presumably to talk politics. He saw an agate marble lying on a table. Forgetting the election, he plunged into a fascinating half-hour monologue on marbles: how the game started; how it is played in various countries; why marbles are made less often nowadays of marble than of bakelite, porcelain, or glass; what the preferred shooting techniques are. For that half hour, his absorbed listeners forgot Vietnam for marbles.

Like the automobile driver, the conversationalist has to keep an eye out for traffic lights. For him these are his listeners' signals of enjoyment, attentiveness, and general receptivity on the one hand, or boredom, irritation, and frustration on the other. If he doesn't see the red light and fails to stop talking, he may find himself the cause of a conversational traffic tie-up.

There may be times when the mouths of the listeners are truly open in sheer ecstasy rather than a desire to break in. Even so, remember the traffic lights. There is nothing to lose by giving others the right of way; if your listeners are truly enchanted by your wit and wisdom, they will keep flashing the "go" signal.

Jokers are no exception to this rule. Many people feel a curious compulsion to tell jokes, even when they don't tell them well. The nonstop joke teller can be a real conversation killer.

I remember a long-awaited reunion with a friend who for five years had been living two thousand miles away. She arrived back in town with a brand new husband. He dominated our conversation from the start, telling one joke after another—not too well; and she urged him on. When they left, I knew little more of what had happened to her in the five years of our separation than I had when they arrived.

In vaudeville days, if an act dragged on too long, the manager, standing in the wings, extended a hook on the end of a ten-foot pole, caught the offender by the neck, and dragged him from view.

There should be a hook to rescue us from the man or woman who suffers—and makes us suffer—from "I" disease and monopolizing.

THE FOURTH HINT: DON'T INTERRUPT

One such hook is to interrupt. Interrupting, however, should be only a last resort; it is usually a cure worse than the disease. "There cannot be a greater rudeness," said John Locke, "than to interrupt another in the current of his discourse."

Suppose someone is arriving at the climax of his anecdote. The listeners are following his words as eagerly as a bridesmaid follows the flight of the bridal bouquet. Then all at once you break in: "Say, did that happen the week you were in from Easthampton?"

The person talking is certainly not going to love you, and chances are nobody else will either.

So:

◄ Don't interrupt by irrelevant questions;
◄ Don't interrupt by irrelevant remarks;
◄ Don't interrupt by finishing others' sentences;
◄ Don't interrupt to help tell a story;
◄ Don't interrupt to argue unimportant details (this often happens between husbands and wives). In two words,

Don't interrupt.

Except—

When the act has clearly been going on too long . . . when the speaker is not getting attention or is putting people to sleep . . . when he is moving into conversational areas that may be seriously offensive . . . when in effect he has become a public nuisance . . .

Then, it is kind and charitable to *get the hook!*

THE FIFTH HINT: AVOID BORING TOPICS

Few people are enthralled when you talk about your

> Dogs;
> Children;
> Recipes and food;
> Health complaints;
> Golf shots or other sports triumphs;
> Domestic complaints.

Keep your health complaints for your doctor . . . send your recipes through the mail . . . play your golf on the course, not in the living room . . . keep your domestic difficulties a family affair.

Dogs and children can steal scenes from the greatest actor, but they don't do so well as subjects of drawing room conversation. I remember sitting next to a brilliant lawyer who could have entertained and informed our entire dinner party about crucial happenings in the New York

City Administration. Instead, he spent a good half hour telling how he had looked for a lost spaniel. By the time he finished, I felt that I knew every crack in the pavement over which he had walked. All his listeners had begun to take on the appearance of the lost spaniel, sad-eyed, wilted, droopy-eared.

Winston Churchill felt children were not fruitful subjects for conversation. On one occasion an ambassador said to him, "You know, Sir Winston, I've never told you about my grandchildren." Churchill clapped him on the shoulder, and exclaimed, "I realize it, my dear fellow, and I can't tell you how grateful I am!"

THE SIXTH HINT: DON'T OFFEND

It is fashionable today to equate good manners with hypocrisy. If the equation is correct, there is much more to be said for hypocrisy than I had realized.

The best manners don't come from hypocrisy at all—they come from empathy. Empathy, a key word to the actor, means feeling as though you *are* the other person—putting yourself in his place. Sensitivity is what good manners are all about. They are simply expressions of the decent respect that one human being owes another and is owed in return.

Try to be sensitive to the climate around you. You cannot always assess it correctly, to be sure; but *try*. Once, at a small gathering, the conversation turned to a city where I had just finished an engagement, and I mentioned complaints I had heard there about the incompetence and corruption of its administration. Later I learned, to my horror, that one of the men in the party was executive assistant to the city's mayor.

Another time, I was introduced to Mr. X, a reporter for a major newspaper, a distinguished-looking man, dressed in morning jacket and striped trousers, with a red rose in his buttonhole. Certain I had seen his name by-lining leading reports, I told him how much I enjoyed everything he wrote. "You know," he said, "you are the first person ever to tell me that. I write the obituaries."

Whether a conversational subject is risky or safe depends on the people around you and the mood of the moment. Subjects such as politics, race, or religion may be rewarding in some groups and lethal in others. Just before election, tempers may run high. In these days of the generation gap, reactions to the activities of certain young people are likely to be extreme, one way or the other. Jean Cocteau said, "Tact consists in knowing how far to go." Be tactful. Unless you have friends who enjoy brawling (some do, you know), avoid bringing up topics that will put them at each others' throats.

Do not invade others' privacy. Maybe the FBI has to do that, but you don't. Stay away from the personal, petty, probing question. I am taken aback at the number of people who do not hesitate to ask a woman how much her husband earns, or how old she is. A little old lady of my acquaintance had the perfect put-down for the latter query. "Can you keep a secret?" she asked in her turn. "Of course," said the other. "Well," said the little old lady, "so can I!"

If you have just taken off twenty pounds, or stopped smoking, it may be a kindness to tell a fat man or a cigarette addict how you did it. But don't insist on reciting all the details if it is obvious that you are simply embarrassing the other person.

And don't, please, employ, however harmlessly you mean them, expressions which might hurt feelings. I don't know whether people are more sensitive to implied racial or ethnic slurs today than they used to be, but they certainly react more vigorously. In a recent campaign for high office, one of the candidates put an all but indelible blot on his image by referring to racial minorities in terms which showed perhaps not bias but, almost worse, insensitivity.

Don't use locker-room language except in the locker room. (There is no real necessity, for that matter, to use it even there.) Filthy speech, like topless waitresses, seems to be on the increase, but that does not make it more aesthetically acceptable. Language that once would have ap-

palled a longshoreman now falls trippingly off the tongues
of men in Brooks Brothers suits and matrons in Pucci
dresses—not to mention actors in certain much publicized
plays.

Good taste, which Schiller called "the finer impulse of
our nature," seems to be in trouble at the moment; some
say it is following Steller's Siberian sea cow into extinction. But I have more faith in my fellow man than that.
People are still people, with human hearts. Most conversational gaffes spring simply from thoughtlessness or ignorance. Consideration for others is still a custom honored
more in the observance than the breach. Indeed, it has to
be; for it is the touchstone of civilized intercourse.

THE SEVENTH HINT: DON'T GOSSIP

"Thou shalt not bear false witness against thy neighbor,"
says the Bible. A good many of us, though, are willing
to spread dubious rumors—and a rumor is about as hard
to unspread as butter.

To gossip, says Webster's Second International, is to
"run about and tattle; to tell idle, esp. personal tales." In
other words, to talk about someone behind his back.

My quarrel here is only with gossip that hurts. Some
gossip is fun for all concerned. And it is perfectly possible
to say something *nice* about your neighbor behind his back;
I have heard it happen. But sometimes a pat on the back
is just to know where to put in the knife. There is no excuse for damaging others, either intentionally—which is
plain mean; or inadvertently—which is one of those
failures of sensitivity we were discussing a page or two
back. To pass on hurtful facts or allegations out of envy
or malice, or in order to boost your ego by appearing
privy to things others don't know, is beneath contempt.

In the question and answer period after a talk to a group
of women, I sometimes ask whether they consider gossip
to be largely a female activity, as men assert, or whether
men indulge in it too. The almost invariable reply is that

men gossip at least as much as their wives. But women are remarkably charitable to their opposite numbers on one vital count: they agree that men are usually less *malicious* in their gossip.

Ninety per cent of conversation is chit-chat, revolving around people and personalities. Most of us would find conversation as dull without personalities as a soft-boiled egg without salt, or as watered wine. People's greatest interest, outside of themselves, is other people—and why should it not be?

So I do not expect you to avoid all mention of anyone who is not in the room. Go ahead—gossip a little. But when you find yourself about to say something slightly nasty, I suggest that you instead recite quickly under your breath this Hindu version of the Golden Rule:

"This is the sum of duty: do not to others which, if done to thee, would cause thee pain."

You will work out your applications for this rule according to circumstances. If you mention to Anne that Sally is putting on weight, you aren't being unfair to Sally. The fact is that she should go on a diet. But if you reveal something real or fancied about Sally that has the effect of a deliberate slap in the face, then you would be much more honest to slap her in the face and have done with it.

If you wash others' dirty linen in public, *you* may be the one who comes out tattletale gray.

THE EIGHTH HINT: DISCUSS, DON'T ARGUE

"Good nature," said essayist Joseph Addison, "is more agreeable in conversation than wit."

Discussion, as long as it is good-natured, is what conversation is all about. Angry argument, on the other hand, with each side hotly attacking the other and as hotly defending itself, is the enemy of good talk.

One difference between a conviction and a prejudice is that a conviction can be explained without getting angry. The Chinese have a saying that the man who shouts first has lost the argument. This does not mean that the man who becomes angry is necessarily wrong in his opinion; but he certainly does not know how to handle himself in expressing it. A good rule for discussion is to use hard facts and a soft voice. Try not to irk or to silence but to persuade.

As long as tempers remain cool, and reason and good humor reign; as long as you are willing to listen to me, and I am willing to hear you out; as long as we direct ourselves to the issues rather than to passion or prejudice—then discussion has not degenerated into quarreling. But when voices grow shrill; when "I think that's a pretty stupid remark!" becomes a cutting retort; when we see bystanders becoming uncomfortable and fidgety—then we should not be surprised if our friends take refuge behind a potted palm. There is small gain in winning an argument and losing a friend.

Quarreling splits people apart; discussion binds them together. Quarreling is barbarous; discussion is civilized. Arguments, and even quarrels, are sometimes inescapable and friendships and marriages have been known to survive them; but the scars remain. An outburst of temper in a family may clear the air, just as a thunderstorm may lift the heaviness from an August day; but even then both the quarrel and the reconciliation should take place in private.

A friend of ours belongs to a luncheon club where conversation ranges widely, and disagreements about facts and interpretation are everyday occurrences. Was Garrett Hobart Vice President under William McKinley or under Grover Cleveland? Where was the first cave art discovered?

Ordinarily some member can provide an acceptable answer to such a question, and the subject changes. Once in a while, though, the issue cannot be resolved at the luncheon table. In that event, a wager is made, with the conditions and the amount wagered going on record in the club's betting book. Then the facts are formally checked; the loser pays; and the outcome is memorialized in the book.

The exchange preceding such a bet may be vigorous. It is not, however, a quarrel, or even heated argument. It is discussion—first because it is in good clean fun, and second because both sides are trying not to make a debater's point but to get at the truth. They are bound by the laws of evidence, and the loser accepts the outcome as cheerfully as the winner.

THE NINTH HINT: INCLUDE OTHERS IN

To exclude others from conversation is as unthinkable as it would be for a hostess to omit serving one of her guests at dinner.

Without stopping to think about it, many of us are inclined to ignore the quiet man in the corner and devote ourselves instead to some approving listener or some absorbing raconteur. We too often concentrate on making a good impression on the lions of the party. But how would you like to be the one left out? Besides, what if the person you failed to include turns out to be the prize of the lot?

So don't leave *anyone* out. Reach out to them all. Let your eyes communicate cordially with each in turn. Be aware of everyone's reaction to what you are saying.

A lawyer of my acquaintance invariably directs his talk at just one person in any group. He talks delightfully, but only for that one. The rest of them, to all intents and purposes, are blackballed. They are all "odd men out."

Most social groups are likely to have at least one odd man out—a person who looks and acts like an outsider, and is likely therefore to be treated as an outsider.

Don't treat him that way, however uninteresting he may appear. You must have felt like an outsider at some time in your life. Put yourself in the shoes of the man who is feeling left out now. Make a point of setting him at his ease. Include him in!

THE TENTH HINT: LISTENING

"Know how to listen," said Plutarch, "and you can learn even from those who speak badly." •

Fifty per cent of good talk is listening—with not just your ears, but all your senses; and with your heart as well as your mind.

Listening is often as important as speaking. It is easy, when the talk is less than dynamic, to find yourself thinking of something else; to miss key words or phrases; to misinterpret what you hear; to decide in advance what point is being made, and fail to notice that it turns out to be a different point altogether.

Not only individuals but entire communities may fall into poor listening habits. I could name one city which contains some of the most unresponsive theater audiences in the United States. Noël Coward, who closed a show there just before I was to open in another, gave me this warning of what to expect:

"We played a preview for the veterans from the Soldiers' Hospital. That night we played for the wounded. The next night we opened, and played for the dead."

Do you listen with dull eyes and drooping ears? Is apathy, even boredom, written large on your face? Do you wait poised for the speaker to pause for breath, so that you can take over? Is your whole attitude negative, aimed at deflating, demoralizing, defying, and destroying the person talking, because you want to be talking yourself?

Then no matter how effectively you express yourself when your turn comes, you are a poor conversationalist.

In one of my classes, students took turns giving talks, which were then analyzed by the other students. I noticed that the speakers always avoided looking at one young man in the front row, and I wondered why. When I took the floor for my concluding analysis, I kept an eye on him. His face was cold and withdrawn, and his gaze was fixed on the ceiling.

Afterwards I took him aside, and said, "You are such an attractive man, and a sign of approval from you would raise any speaker's spirits. Why do you shut them out?"

He was shocked. *"But I don't!"* he protested. "I am listening all the time. I don't look at them because it might distract me from what they are saying. I constantly ask myself, 'Is this statement true? Is that one exaggerated? Does that theory hold up?' I *really* listen!"

Perhaps, I told him; but not empathetically. If you don't look at the speaker at all, as far as he is concerned you might as well clap your hands over your ears, or wear earmuffs. Would you like him to do that when you are speaking?

Two kinds of listening deserve special mention. One brings important information to the listener. And the other brings special inspiration to the speaker.

1. Listening that informs

Some show people have an extraordinary capacity for adjusting through listening.

Gertrude Lawrence was a fine example. She listened to the audience every moment she was on stage. She appraised her performance by the quality of their attention, of the silence. The rustle of a program, coughs, clearing of throats—all these are warning signals to a sensitive actor. Listening enabled her to play the crowd as an angler plays a trout, letting it run a little, reeling in, letting it run again, netting it at just the right moment.

Oscar Hammerstein was another. After a matinee during the tryout of *The King and I* in New Haven, I left the theater by way of the orchestra section. At the back of the house stood Oscar, who had adapted the musical from the book *Anna and the King of Siam.* Oscar, a big bear of a man, was leaning on the back rail, looking thoughtful and glum. When I asked him what the trouble was he said that he had spent the matinee *listening to the audience listen*—and he knew they were not satisfied. What they missed, he was convinced, was romance. He had kept his adaptation faithful to the book, which, being about a widowed English schoolteacher in an oriental court, really had no love interest at all. But audiences came to the theater in those days for a vicarious love life. Without it, they were disappointed. They fidgeted.

That evening Oscar and Richard Rodgers, the composer of *The King and I,* locked themselves in their suite in the Taft Hotel to insert the touch Oscar felt was needed. They added a scene in which the king, extending his hand to Anna, asks her to show him the steps of the polka. Then, as the two sing "Shall We Dance," he sweeps her into the dance, his arm lightly about her waist. Far from a full-fledged love scene; yet it filled the hunger for romance that Oscar, *listening,* had sensed in the audience.

Close listening for correct information is essential to good conversation, social or business. Did you ever play the game in which one person whispers a message to a second, who whispers it to a third, and so on around the room? The message almost never comes out at the end with more than a distant family resemblance to the way it started. Accurate listening is rare; it is not as easy as it seems.

After receiving an honorary degree in the United States, Marshall McLuhan boarded the plane for his home in Canada and ran into a friend. "What were you down here for?" asked the friend. "Getting my LL.D.," said Mr. McLuhan. Someone overheard him incorrectly, and when he landed at Montreal the customs inspector gave his luggage a piece-by-piece examination. "Come on," the inspector said at last, "where did you hide the LSD?"

One moral to that story is that when you listen, you should listen with a hearing ear. "The hearing ear and the seeing eye," says Proverbs, "the Lord hath made even both of them." And they are both badly needed.

2.   Listening that inspires

Appreciative listening, in addition to informing the listener, uplifts and even inspires the speaker:

In Agnes DeMille's *Autobiography* she tells how Charlie Chaplin came to one of her childhood birthday parties.

"My God," she writes, "what an audience he was; he sat giving us, the children, his undivided attention as we performed. Much has been written about his gifts as a talker, his virtuosity of improvisation—but has anyone ever paid him his due as a courteous, enkindling listener?"

When Toscanini conducted for singers, the expression on his face was one of rapture. He listened with such ecstasy that they could not help outsinging themselves.

Perhaps the most appreciative seeming listener I have ever observed is the Duchess of Windsor. One season when I was singing in a Palm Beach supper club, the Windsors reserved a table near the floor several nights in a row. Clearly, her ability to listen was not the least of the charms by which she had magicked the King of England. She would sit across from her husband, elbows on the table and hand under her chin, her eyes as well as her ears seeming to drink in every word he uttered. She appeared to be saying, "Tell me more—I'm listening—it's fascinating."

Take a tip from the Duchess. When you are dining with someone, don't play with the silverware or let your gaze wander about the room. *Listen.* I am not talking about uncritical listening, but friendly attention. Say to yourself, "I'm a sponge; I am going to soak up every word." The greatest compliment you can pay anyone is really to listen to what he has to say. And the way to show you have really been listening is to answer responsively. For though listening is half of good conversation, talking is still the other half.

The art of conversation is part of the greater art of leading your life with grace, with charm, and with love.

All this, and more, is summed up in the Book of Maccabees:

> "Do more than exist—live.
> Do more than look—observe.
> Do more than read—absorb.
> Do more than hear—listen.
> Do more than listen—understand.
> Do more than think—ponder.

Do more than plan—act.
Do more than talk—say something!"

REMEMBER:

◄ Don't just talk—stimulate others to talk too!
◄ Take an interest in others' ideas. Ask stimulating questions.
◄ Edit when you talk. Don't repeat—come to the point and stay with the point. Don't ramble—don't over-detail.
◄ Avoid "I" disease ("I"—"me"—"my"—"mine"). Don't monopol-I-I-I-ze.
◄ Don't interrupt with irrelevant questions and remarks. Don't finish others' sentences or stories.
◄ Don't bore. Your health . . . food . . . children . . . dogs . . . should be kept a family affair.
◄ Don't offend. Be sensitive to the feelings of others. Don't invade their privacy or step on their toes.
◄ Don't gossip. Don't damage absent people by what you say.
◄ Discuss—don't argue. Keep your boiling point high.
◄ Include others in. Don't ignore the quiet ones.
◄ *Listen*—with eyes, ears, heart, and mind.

13. Conversation Begins at Home

With three conversing, I forget all time,
All seasons, and their change; all please alike.
—JOHN MILTON

At the altar a bride used to promise to love, honor, and obey.

The "obey" has vanished from the wedding ceremony now. I suggest that groom as well as bride might profitably put in its place a simple pledge *to keep the dialogue going.*

Love may grow thin, honor may cease to be deserved, but as long as you can keep the dialogue going your marriage is in business.

Have you ever seen a couple sitting in a restaurant, more indifferent to each other than if they were strangers? There is no conversation until the menu arrives, and then it goes something like this:

"What do you want first, Ruth?"

"What are *you* going to have, John?"

"I'm not sure yet. Make up your mind, dear. What will it be?"

"Should I order the eggplant or the antipasto?"

"Whatever you want, dear. What do you feel like?"

"Maybe the shrimp. Should I have the shrimp, John? Or the eggplant?"

"Whatever you want, Ruth."

"Oh, I had shrimp for lunch. What are *you* going to have, John?"

So it goes, for each course. And that is the extent of the dialogue.

You have seen couples like Ruth and John, sitting
drearily, perhaps not frowning but certainly not smiling,
seemingly scarcely aware of each other's presence. What
are they thinking about, do you suppose? (Sometimes one
of them talks on and on, as if to himself, while the other is
obviously not listening at all.) The pain of their loneliness
can be felt the width of the room.

I use Ruth and John only as a reminder of the importance
of communication in marriage. In passing, though, let me
offer two quick rules about restaurant meals with your
wife or husband:

1. Make up your mind with dispatch about what you are
going to eat, and order it without all the discussion it takes
to get a bill through Congress.

2. Don't just sit there! Say something. Bring a few little
things to talk about when you go out for dinner. Otherwise,
you sadden not only yourselves but all those in the restaurant who look on you. Inject a few raisins of conversation,
as O. Henry wrote, into the tasteless dough of existence.

Dullness when dining out in all likelihood reflects dullness at home. We all have heard complaints like these from
husbands and wives:

SHE: He comes home, mixes himself a drink, and sits
down with his paper. If I ask him a question, he grunts a
one-word reply. If I try to make conversation, his mind is
far away, maybe still mulling over some problem at the
office. I've been with the children all day, talking their
language, and I am dying for a little mental refreshment.
But he shuts me out.

HE: Before I have even closed the door behind me she
begins her inventory of things that went wrong: the dish-
washer leaked, the cleaning woman didn't show up, little
Pete called her a bad name. So I stop on the way home for
a drink, to fortify myself for the twilight hour of complaints.

HE: (again) The minute I put down my briefcase, she
says, "What happened at the office today, dear?" Well
what happened at the office I would rather forget. The last
thing in the world I want to do is replay the events of the
day. Why can't she stop asking that question? Rather than
answer it, I turn on the television set.

People being people, it is not surprising that husbands occasionally seem a little less than perfect to wives, and vice versa. Nor is it surprising that complaints tend to fall into patterns.

Husbands say:

> She talks too much . . .
> She talks too loudly . . .
> She never finishes her sentences . . .
> She finishes all my sentences . . .
> She never gives a direct answer . . .
> She is always interrupting . . .
> She is always correcting me . . .
> She nags . . .
> She whines . . .
> She . . .

Wives have many of the same complaints, but their most common charge is that their husbands shut them out . . . don't try to talk . . . seem to be thinking of something else.

One wife asked me, "Why should women learn to talk more if their husbands want them to talk less?" I replied that if they learned to talk *better* their husbands would want them to talk *more*. "Love," said Antoine de St.-Exupéry, "does not consist in gazing at each other but in looking together in the same direction."

It may not be true in marriage that familiarity breeds contempt, but sometimes it at least breeds lack of appreciation. The husband of a woman I know has criticized her for years for timidity and indecisiveness in her speech. "You don't sound like the wife of a chairman of the board," he would tell her. The other day, as they sat down to talk over a party they had just attended, she started the tape recorder without his realizing it. Afterwards, she played it back. Listening to her objectively for the first time gave him a totally new appreciation of her conversational effectiveness and charm. The tape recorder, she tells me, served as a silent marriage counselor. (P.S. He was less pleased with his own half of the conversation.)

"The majority of men," says Kierkegaard, "are subjective

toward themselves and objective toward all others, terribly objective sometimes. But the real task is to be objective toward oneself and subjective toward all others."

DON'T CUSS—CONVERSE!

A recent book made headlines by advising married couples to spend more time fighting. "A fight a day," say George R. Bach and Peter Wyden in *The Intimate Enemy*, "keeps the doctor away." (Marvin Kittman, the humorist, retorted that one doctor, at least, will be kept away: the obstetrician.)

It is true that a quarrel in some circumstances may be the only way to burst an emotional boil, but too often a quarrel is simply a way to avoid facing unpleasant facts and making disagreeable decisions. The alternative to quarreling certainly need not be, as the authors assert, "a lifetime of fake accommodation, monotony, self-deception, and contempt." It should be, and can be, a constructive appraisal when something is going wrong, and a first step toward making it go right.

The authors of *The Intimate Enemy* lay down Marquis of Queensberry rules for carrying on the unpleasantness they advocate; but the trouble is that once a discussion becomes a fight, all rules are off. No psychiatrist is around to sit in as marital referee. Domestic quarrels, like wars, may escalate until the bomb is dropped. They enlarge like this:

1. A difference
2. A FUSS
3. A squabble
4. A *wrangle*
5. A QUARREL
6. A *FIGHT*

"Many domestic experiences," said George Bernard Shaw, "leave blacker and more permanent wounds on the soul than thrusting the bayonet through an enemy in a trench fight."

No couple is identical to any other, and there is a wide range of possibilities between a life of constant squabbling and one of mutual boredom. Disagreements are bound to crop up between any two people in close and constant contact.

Some apparent quarrels between husbands and wives are not really quarrels at all. They are simply a form of elaborate love play, with no more harm in them than the pretend-fights of a couple of puppies.

But true quarreling is a negative act, and not one to encourage. The fact that people do quarrel does not make quarreling a desirable or admirable way of life, any more than the fact that nations do wage wars makes warfare a condition to aspire to.

The saddest part of an oversimplification such as "couples who fight together stay together" is that a few unfortunates will take it seriously and really let themselves go. The result will be a few more needlessly broken homes.

So if you must squabble, at least don't let anyone, however many degrees he holds in psychology, persuade you that you are performing a virtuous act, and should make it a habit. The deeper the differences between two people are, the more imperative it is to talk sense about them. Rational discussion requires more discipline than screaming, and is not nearly so dramatic, but in the long run it is much more likely to do some good.

The only positive thing to be said for quarreling is that at least it may be preferable to indifference. Indifference— the sort experienced by Ruth and John at the restaurant— is emotional death.

SMALL TALK AT HOME

I do not assert that husbands and wives should always be talking. A relaxed silence can itself be an agreeable form of communication. There can be no greater bore, no more abrasive irritant, than the man or woman who never knows when to shut up.

"I believe in the discipline of silence," said George Bernard Shaw, "and could talk for hours about it."

But the silence of indifference, the silence of repressed anger, the silence of punishment, the deep-freeze silence— these have no place in the home. They are negative silence, which G. K. Chesterton called "the unbearable repartee."

Some people are more silent than others by nature. I know couples so attuned to each other that they communicate contentedly and effectively with almost no words at all.

Still, the extent to which husbands and wives talk together just for the fun of it is a pretty good index to the success of most marriages.

The talk need not be on a lofty level. It may amount to little more than a signal of availability—"I am here, I am with you"—like the dial tone of an empty telephone wire. Even the most trivial topics can make pleasant fare— especially if they are offered up by someone you love.

Indeed, what is said may have little, if anything at all, to do with what is actually conveyed.

You have probably heard a man, shaking hands vigorously with another, say something like, "Harry, you old bastard, it's good to see you again!" Harry knows that the word "bastard" is not pejorative; it is an expression of affection. Similarly, exchanges in marriage often take place in a sort of code, the real significance of which is known only to the husband and wife involved.

I am all for small-talk in the home. Its content is unimportant. The important thing is that it is the product of a shared intimacy, a relationship that has no duplicate anywhere in the world.

"Nothing," I read once, "lives on so fresh and evergreen as the love with a funny bone." Laughter doesn't have to cease when you enter the door of your own home. George G. Nathan said well that a sense of humor—a feeling for fun—the ability to laugh together—is a priceless ingredient giving pacing to the rhythm of life.

But Ogden Nash said it funnier:

> One would be in less danger
> From the wiles of the stranger
> If one's own kin and kith
> Were more fun to be with.

THE EMPATHY HOUR

There is no law saying *when* a husband and wife should talk. Talk when you feel like it, whether you are at the table, in bed, in the living room, or strolling across town. In many lives, however, there is one time of day when conversation can be especially rewarding—and especially tricky. That is when the working day has ended and the evening has not yet begun. It used to be called tea-time. Some today call it the cocktail hour. I noticed a sign outside of an Evansville, Indiana, motel cocktail lounge that expressed it better: "Attitude Adjustment Hours, 5–7 P.M."

Consideration for the other person is more important than ever in this twilight period. And consideration is not always easy to maintain. When you are tired and perhaps upset yourself, it is natural to want your wishes to take precedence over your mate's for at least a few minutes.

Nonetheless, this is a moment for particular sensitivity to the other person's mood and needs. Let's call it the Empathy Hour. The time may not be ripe for real communication until you have both had a chance to relax. But thereafter, your conversation can be a kind of reunion, a mutual refreshment.

Be prepared for that time. Make a habit of having a few pleasant conversational items to serve up. They need not be personal. Something you heard on the five o'clock news, or saw on the street, could be enough to get your evening together off to a running start. Squirrel away odd bits of information for your Empathy Hour. It is an easy habit to get into, and it pays a high dividend of freshness and variety. Hundreds of topics, if you watch for them, are available to brighten the interval when most husbands want to let down and most wives want to be lifted up.

REMEMBER:

- ◄ Love, honor—and keep the dialogue going. Do your share!
- ◄ Don't just sit there—*say* something!
- ◄ Don't escalate an argument into a war.
- ◄ Smile talk can help—even at home.
- ◄ Empathize—don't antagonize.

14.   Be the Host with the Most —
The Hostess with the Mostest

Sweet courtesy has done its most
If you have made each guest forget
That he himself is not the host.
—THOMAS BAILEY ALDRICH

The glow that comes from hosting a successful party lingers pleasantly for days—and it is a feeling that any of us can experience. It is easy to be a successful host or hostess, and to guarantee a happy evening for yourself and your guests. A few simple precautions, a little imagination, and careful attention to detail is the whole of the recipe, whether your party is given to repay social debts, to help a charity, to pay a business obligation, or simply to have fun. If you follow that recipe, the party will be fun—for everyone—whatever your reason for giving it.

THE GUEST LIST

The first ingredient for a successful evening is a well-chosen guest list. Do the same faces show up again and again at your parties? Are they likely to be a cross section of your country club membership, or of your business acquaintances? Can each guest tick off on his fingers in advance who the others are likely to be? If so, the chances are that the golfers will talk about their golf; the lawyers will talk law; the men will talk to the men, and the women will talk to the women. Discouraged guests call these "monotone parties."

"What's on the chair is more important than what's on the table," said W. S. Gilbert of dinner parties. Filling the same chairs with the same guests party after party, however engaging and stimulating they may be individually, is as unimaginative and palling as to serve truffles—or any other delicacy—as the only course at every meal.

Vary your guest list from party to party. Experiment. Bring in unfamiliar faces. Offer your guests the possibility of discovery.

If you must invite deadheads, at the very least leaven the lump with as many guests as possible who will be entertaining.

You may not always have a completely free choice of whom to invite. Some people may have to be invited for business reasons. You have to consider such matters as the balance between men and women; unattached men are much in demand, and you may not always be able to get your pick of them.

Don't feel you *must* ask good old Joe to every party you give, just because he is lonely and perhaps has no place else to go, or you are used to having him around. Indeed, a moment's reflection may show that you are inviting some people to your parties simply out of habit.

INTRODUCTIONS

Introduce your guests around as soon as they arrive.

Surprisingly, even sophisticated hosts often become confused and self-conscious about how to make an introduction. The basic guidelines are easily fixed in your mind:

1. The man is introduced to the woman, if she is over eighteen:

"Mrs. Carillo, may I present Stephen Harding"; or less formally, "Mrs. Carillo, Stephen Harding."

2. The younger person is introduced to the older if both are of the same sex:

"Father, this is Joe White's son Robert"; or, "Father, Bruce Hackstaff."

3. Girls under eighteen are introduced to older people: "This is Edna Dorne, Mr. and Mrs. Alan Ross."

4. Either men or women are always introduced to a considerably older person, and often to a person of special distinction.

Some informal but correct introductions:

"Shirley Eder, do you know Lester Rondell?"
"Shirley Eder, have you met Lester Rondell?"
"Shirley Eder, I'd like you to meet Lester Rondell."

Try not to be flustered if in the tension of the moment a name you know perfectly well, and perhaps have known for years, disappears completely from your mind. Remember that everyone has had the same experience. Admit frankly, "I just got one of those awful name blocks on you, after twenty years. *You* say it!"

A useful device for preventing such a block, when introducing one person to a group, is to go from one name to another in a kind of easy rhythm, not giving the block a chance to surface.

Introduce newcomers all the way around, unless so many people are present that this is totally impracticable. Too many hosts, perhaps out of a compulsion to be on the move, abandon them after half a dozen introductions.

When you have to leave a new guest with a group he has just met for the first time, tell them enough about each other so that the conversation will have a starting point. "Roy is just back from the Pacific Northwest," you might say, "and he almost didn't make it. His engine conked out while he was crossing the Columbia River bar . . ."

SEATING ARRANGEMENTS

The way you seat your guests at a formal dinner could make or break your party. Work this out carefully, well in advance, host and hostess comparing opinions. Then put the names on table cards, so that there is no possibility of your arrangements going awry. Juggle the cards in advance until the combination is exactly right. Mix and match.

Compare notes on each guest's interests, personality, conversational abilities. Should John, whose hobby is stamp collecting, be seated next to Alice, who is an expert on modern art? Is giggling Gladys a suitable table companion for booming Bill?

But do not cluster your guests simply according to the mutuality of their backgrounds or interests, putting all the pomegranates at one table and all the pears at another. On the contrary, upset the fruit basket. I recently attended a dinner party where the host—a psychiatrist, who should have had some knowledge of social dynamics—ignored this rule. He set up four tables, each with six places. At one sat doctors; at another, lawyers; at a third, friends of his wife's mother. The fourth table was made up of those who could not be fitted into any of the other categories. Each table was an isolated island, and the dinner was a disaster.

Use several tables, when possible, instead of one. It makes getting acquainted easier. And round or oval tables are preferable to rectangular ones. This does not mean that if you own a rectangular dining room table you should put a match to it, but in buying a new table bear in mind that a curved shape makes for warmer communication. It makes it easier for everyone sitting there to see and talk with everyone else.

The host was right in having tables of six. Six is an ideal number for warmth and informality. There are enough people for variety, and few enough so that each guest has a chance to talk with all the others. Mrs. Lyndon Johnson brought the small round table concept to White House luncheons and dinners. I list this as one of the achievements of the Johnson Administration.

In sum, having gone to the trouble of bringing a variety of people together, seat them so as to encourage conversational cross-pollination. Let each share the riches the others have to offer.

SHOULD YOU PUT HUSBANDS AND WIVES TOGETHER?

Usually not—unless, of course, they are honeymooners, and cannot be pried apart. You may wish to make exceptions also for possessive spouses who resent it if their mate, however faithful, is seated next to an attractive person of the opposite sex.

Sometimes a wife may be quite justified in wishing to keep within quick interrupting range of a husband with a roving eye. (Or vice versa.) If you wish to play Solomon, separate that husband and wife, but keep them in full view of each other.

PLEASE PASS THE CONVERSATION

Even the best-balanced seating arrangement cannot insure relaxed and enjoyable conversation. From where you sit, keep a weather eye on what is going on. If you see a table becalmed, you may have to go over and give the conversation a fresh start, even at a cost of leaving your own dinner unfinished. But don't bother them unless you are really needed. A good host, like a good waiter, does not get in the way.

Keep conversation-revivers in reserve: topics likely to arouse interest and discussion. A review of a book or motion picture in the morning paper, a local news item, or a diverting anecdote may turn the trick.

As a host, your responsibilities are not unlike those of the chairman of a panel discussion. You must pace the talk; spark it; see that all sides have a chance to get into the act.

TALK AFTER DINNER

I know a host—of sorts—who assumes that once dinner is over, his responsibilities are over too. He disappears
into the television room, and that is the last anyone sees
of him. The discourtesy is obvious. At a huge gathering,
run by a trained staff, it may be possible for the host or
hostess to disappear without damage, but not at a party
given by you or me.

A generation ago, Lady Asquith held a reception in
London. She received the guests graciously, and then retired upstairs to play bridge. Next day in a restaurant a
woman at the next table said, "Lady Asquith, I was at
your party last night." Lady Asquith smiled and bowed;
but under her breath she murmured, "Thank God I was
not."

A present-day host cannot permit himself such idiosyn-
crasies. When the guests settle down in the living room
after dinner, your responsibility is still very much alive.
By this time, most people will know whom they want to
talk to; but it is up to you to see that no one is left out.

If the party is small enough so that everybody can sit,
arrange your living room chairs in advance to facilitate
conversational groupings, even at the expense of disarrang-
ing the decor of the room. If, by chance, there is one
guest whom all the rest are sure to want to hear, go even
further; arrange all the chairs in one arc or oval.

No matter how the guests arrange themselves, continue
to be the quiet chairman. Move about, but don't interrupt.
Supervise, guide, nudge, point, direct, but only as necessary—and then without seeming to. If someone's toes
(conversational toes, that is) are being stepped on, rush
to the rescue. If voices are beginning to sound irritated,
create a diversion.

If someone is putting his audience to sleep with an endless story about his dog, as the lawyer was a few pages
back, give him the hook: Ask the mother of five at his

right whether she thinks sex in motion pictures has become too explicit, or whether she considers Beverly Sills as great a singer as Maria Callas.

"A host," said the Roman poet Horace, "is like a general; it takes a mishap to reveal his genius."

Sound like a strain for you? Well, in one way it is. A host can no more relax completely than a horseback rider can. At any instant the horse might shy. But if you have prepared your party carefully; if you have carried it forward with organization and consideration; if you have prevented the men from forming into one group and the women into another; above all if you have kept the conversation alive and lively—then when it is all over you, as well as your guests, will have had a wonderful time. They will remember a sparkling evening—and you will be the one who put the spark in the sparkle.

That, sir or madam, is hostmastery.

REMEMBER:

- ◄ Take time to plan everything about your party with care. You'll find it's worth the trouble.
- ◄ Vary your guest lists.
- ◄ Don't slight introductions.
- ◄ Mix and match your guests at the table.
- ◄ Keep the conversation going.
- ◄ Remember—the evening is not over until the door closes on the last guest.

15. The Golden Guest

Here lies Bill Beggs, so rare a guest
That God hath summoned him to feast.
——OLD EPITAPH

The delight of every host and hostess is the golden guest. He arrives on time; he knows when to leave. He comes not simply to be entertained, but to do his share of entertaining. He knows the Ten Secrets of Conversation: He stimulates others to express themselves; he edits his own conversation; his talk does not revolve forever around himself; he does not interrupt gratuitously; he does not bore; he does not offend; he does not gossip; he does not quarrel; he includes others; he listens.

The golden guest goes out of his way to interest others and draw them out. He may not bring flowers or a bottle of bourbon for his host, but he brings an abundance of food for the conversational pot.

DRESS UP YOUR MIND, TOO

When you are perking up your appearance for the evening, dress your mind in its best bib and tucker, too. Remind yourself of tidbits that might make for interesting discussion. Recall things you have read, seen, or experienced that others might enjoy hearing about. Think of something new and stimulating to say about a newspaper editorial, the business world, or current crises. Prepare yourself on some issue—higher rents perhaps, or longer skirts—that might lead to general discussion. Do you have an opinion of the chances of the Baltimore Colts against the Green Bay Packers? Be prepared to discuss it. If you expect to tell an anecdote or a joke, rehearse it—especially the punch line. How often we hear someone telling an involved story and then mangling the point, or forgetting it altogether!

If you know that one of the guests is a specialist in some activity, learn in advance about both the activity and the person. Find common ground. If business people will be there, keep an eye out for business news. Get a stockbroker started talking on the market—a weekend sailor talking about boats. If one of the guests is a well-known golfer you may want to learn in advance the difference between a Number One wood and a putter.

One of the most popular party guests I know is an eighty-year-old woman, fragrant with lavender sachet, who is regularly trailed by admiring men, some far younger than she. Her secret is that she makes a point of talking intelligently and entertainingly about the topics *they* like to discuss. She arrived one evening directly from the races. "I despise horses," she chuckled, "but I was invited by a couple of old beaux who love them. So yesterday I read up on the records of the horses and the riders. This afternoon I knew more about them than my escorts did. Won more, too!"

Before going out for the evening, I habitually tune the radio to a local conversation station. It puts topics on my tongue by keeping me abreast of the latest news. (It keeps me reminded of the time, too, and provides a countdown toward the moment when I have to leave the house. With the radio to time them, women can allot so many minutes to their hair, so many to their lashes, so many to their mascara.)

The first step toward a successful evening, then, is to prepare yourself with something interesting to say. The second is to leave for the party on time; for

> Lateness has ruined many a roast,
> And a silent guest is a party ghost.

MAKING YOUR ENTRANCE

Entering a room full of strangers may be as routine for you as dropping a coin into a parking meter. For some more timid people, however, it can be as nervewracking as the moment between your first jump from an airplane and the opening of your parachute.

Eleanor Roosevelt overcame her youthful shyness by pretending, as she entered a room, that she was a queen advancing toward her subjects. You might produce a similar result for yourself by imagining you are Prime Minister Trudeau of Canada, Richard Burton, Elizabeth Taylor, Senator Percy, Nancy Dickerson, or whoever may be your idol of the moment.

One of my pupils was a gym teacher, a little sparrow of a woman with a rapid, high-pitched, squeaky voice. She dreaded meeting anyone she did not already know. "Pretend you are Princess Grace," I suggested. "You have arrived in your coffee-colored Rolls-Royce, with a chauffeur liveried to match. You have come here from an interview for a *Time* cover article. An hour from now you are to dine with the President, so you are wearing your $50,000 emerald earrings and your $33,000 diamond solitaire."

The description was caricatured, but she caught its purpose and played the game with a will. By donning a mantle of assurance and charm, she was able to lift herself from the depths of feelings of inferiority to feelings of equality. Her sparrow-like hopping became a graceful glide. She entered the room with gracious poise, paused a moment to survey the scene, and then started with her host on the path of introductions, tranquil and interested, the friendly equal of her fellow men.

WHAT WAS THAT NAME AGAIN?

It is said that James Farley never forgets a name. Few of us, though, are James Farleys.

When you are introduced to someone, you are not likely to forget his face, at least not at once, since it is right there before you. His name, however, is another matter. A common embarrassment is to fail to catch a name, or instantly to forget it. To overcome that problem:

◄ If you are not sure you heard the name right, ask to have it repeated.

◄ If you are still in doubt then, ask to have it not only repeated but spelled.

◄ Check any uncertainties immediately. If you let the moment pass, it becomes awkward to ask the person's name later on—though I certainly would rather do that than go through the evening groping for clues.

(Friends of mine belong to a luncheon club that frowns on introductions. All the members eat at the same long deal table. Some have chatted with other club members for a quarter of a century without ever learning their names. Don't let that happen to you, even for one brief evening.)

◄ Repeat the name to yourself, perhaps seven or eight times.

◄ Address your new acquaintance by name at once, and continue using his name until it gets a grip on your mind.

◄ Try word associations. If Miss Smith had black hair, think of blacksmith. (You might suppose you would be in danger of calling her Miss Black, but that won't happen.) You can remember Miss Smiley's name because she smiles —or, just as effectively, because she doesn't. Form these mental associations, with no concern for their possible lack of logic, and you will be astonished at how the name you want leaps to your mind. I remember using association mnemonics when I was introduced at lunch to eighteen strangers; within a few moments every name was fixed in my memory. I was able to chat with first one and then another, certain of exactly who he was.

You don't have to pause in your conversation to make these name associations. Our brains are as clever as the little boy who could pat his head with one hand and stroke his stomach with the other at the same time.

"YOU DON'T REMEMBER ME, DO YOU?"

I am a one-woman lobby against this dreadful barbarism. It should be listed as a Federal, state, county, and municipal crime. It puts the other fellow on a spot that is intolerable.

The criminal ordinarily means no harm; he is simply thick-skinned. But that does not help his victim. It is hard to blame those who fail to turn the other cheek. Alexander Woollcott replied to such a question, "No, I can't remember your name, but don't tell me." Groucho Marx said, "I never forget a face, but in your case I'll make an exception."

If someone to whom you have been introduced fails to remember you, don't call the lapse to his attention. Simply reintroduce yourself. And if your host forgets to introduce you, there is nothing to prevent you from handling the chore on your own. Simply say—with a smile: "I am George Culver Brown, from Dallas," or "I am Dorothy Sarnoff. I persecuted your husband for six weeks in speech class."

SHAKING HANDS

It seems to me that people shake hands more than they used to. (Perhaps it is part of an increasing cult of flesh contact. Cheek-to-cheek embraces and kissing hello and goodbye, too, seem far more common than they were a few years ago.)

If you enjoy shaking hands, take the initiative. Formerly the man was supposed to wait for the woman to offer her hand, but that rule went out with the one-horse shay.

But know when to stop. I have seen two people shaking hands on and on, neither knowing how to let go. Their problem was like that of the two pedestrians, approaching each other, who keep sidestepping in the same direction until they finally bump into each other.

Don't be a knuckle crusher, and don't go to the other extreme, extending your hand like a limp mackerel. Instead, give the other hand a light pressure or squeeze, a sort of hand-hug. Let your hand, as well as your eyes and your voice, register, "I'm glad to meet you."

ARE YOU AT A LOSS?

Most people take pleasure in chatting with new acquaintances, once the ice is broken. Often, however, they are at a loss for an icebreaker. You see a man standing by himself, holding tight to his rapidly emptying glass, staring morosely at the portrait of someone's grandmother. His face tells exactly what is going through his mind: "I wish I knew how to get off the ground" . . . "Wish I could hold attention like Bill Hornaday over there" . . . "Wish I could join that group" . . .

Notice the constant wishing, the emphasis on "I." He is one of the persons we have mentioned whose shyness is really I-ness. The fact is that the only difficulty about taking a plunge into conversation is making up your mind. Simply say to yourself, "There is someone who looks interesting; I am *going over* to speak to her." Or, "I am *going* to find out the meaning of the ribbon that plump fellow is wearing in his lapel." Or, simply, "I am *going* to start a conversation." Then do it. GO!

OPENERS

A moment ago I mentioned the need for an icebreaker in starting a conversation. Perhaps I should have said an ice *melter*, for warmth of personality and interest in others will eventually thaw almost anybody. This is what I called "Smile Talk" in Chapter 11. I cannot overstress the importance of sincere and simple compliments: "What a happy color you are wearing!" Or, "I have heard about you, and I am half in awe. Would you un-awe me?" (I don't recommend that opener if you are a man.)

Don't be effusive, and don't make a statement that has no core of truth to it at all. If a man praises my hazel eyes, I may not be convinced that he means it, but at least I am pleased that he knows what color they are. If he praises my beautiful *brown* eyes, though, I become suspicious.

So don't be fulsome about a bushy Edwardian mustache if you prefer a clean upper lip, or go into ecstasy over a brightly polka-dotted bow tie if it makes the wearer look ridiculous. But if you do think that the mustache or the polka dot tie flatters, say so to the man who is wearing it.

If you are on the receiving end of a compliment, assume it to be sincere and accept it graciously.

ODDS AND ENDS

◄ Don't ask a new acquaintance for free advice in his business field unless he has given some clear indication that he would not mind. Whether he is a broker, doctor, lawyer, tennis professional, writer, or any other kind of specialist, you have no right to tap his brains without pay.

◄ Stay where you are if you are enjoying yourself, but if you aren't, don't hesitate to move on. Murmur an excuse—but not abruptly!—and ease out of the group.

◄ If you find yourself buffeted from all sides by loud, high-pitched, ear-shattering voices, and feel as though you're in the midst of exploding big guns, move from the center of the vortex to the outer edge, or to a quieter spot in some other part of the room.

◄ Sometimes you will find yourself caught with a taciturn person who seems, like an Alaskan mammoth, to have been encased in ice for thousands of years. (A Washington woman, seated beside President Coolidge at one of the elaborate luncheons he hated so, said to him, "Mr. President, I have bet my husband that I could get you to say more than two words." "You lose," replied Coolidge.)

If you meet one of these mammoths, don't try to melt him out of his ice with a conversational blowtorch. A pleasantly warm sun may be more effective. Show you are interested. Smile. Try a few conversational gambits. He may melt. If he does not, remind yourself that mammoths are extinct for a good reason—and turn to the person on your other side.

SAYING GOODBYE

Lovestruck Romeo told Juliet, "Parting is such sweet sorrow that I could say goodnight till it be morrow." That may have been all right for Romeo, but not for you. When the time comes for departure, say your goodbyes pleasantly and appreciatively to your hosts and the guests you have had most to do with (you don't have to circle the whole room again), shake hands if you like—and leave. Don't oo-ooo-oo-oooze out, so that fifteen minutes elapse between the announcement of your going and the time the front door closes behind you.

There is nothing difficult about any of the suggestions in this chapter. Follow them—and when the door closes behind you, your host and hostess will think, "There goes a golden guest!"

REMEMBER:

◄ As you dress for the party, dress your mind too. Take topics to talk about.

◄ If you are nervous as *you,* pretend you are George Plimpton, Raquel Welch, Eric Sevareid, Jackie Onassis, or any other person whose poise you admire.

◄ Don't be a knuckle crusher (or a limp mackerel) when you shake hands.

◄ Bring along some icebreakers to open conversations.

◄ Say your goodbyes in twenty-five words or less!

16. Be the Squire of the Wire — The Belle of the Tel

Spoken words are your masters.   —MOORISH PROVERB

The average American spends at least an hour a day on the telephone. That means seven hours a week, thirty hours a month, three hundred and sixty-five hours a year. During the next twenty-five years, you may spend the equivalent of a full year in telephone talk.

For most of us the telephone has become indispensable. "I'd die," confesses Jimmy Durante, "if the telephone stopped ringing." Theodore Granik, founder of "The American Forum of the Air," was being wheeled down a hospital corridor for a critical operation. He seized a desk telephone as he passed; he had to make one last telephone call.

It is said that Robert Finch, Secretary of Health, Education and Welfare, would feel more naked without a telephone than without his trousers. "He can't live without one," says one of his friends; "it's a permanent part of his physical equipment."

Most of us are body servants to the telephone. We would no more shut it off or bury it under the pillow than we would stop brushing our teeth. Wherever we may be—in the bathtub, climbing a tree, mowing the lawn—the first ring of the telephone brings us running, filled with fear lest the caller hang up before we arrive.

WHY NOT USE IT WELL?

Considering the amount of time you are likely to spend on the telephone before you die, why not learn to use it well? The principles for good telephone conversation are basically the same as those for any other conversation. All the suggestions in previous chapters apply to the art of telephone talking. The major difference is that on the telephone your speech has to stand by itself. You cannot distract attention from its defects by the dimple in your cheek or the twinkle in your eye. Your telephone voice is your only ambassador.

Nearly every day, strangers telephone me to arrange speech lessons. In twenty or thirty seconds, their speech sketches in a personality image. Often, when I meet them face to face, the true picture turns out to have been quite different from the sketch they have sent ahead. The man who sounded like a mobster or perhaps a descendant of Frankenstein's monster may turn out to be a pleasant, educated person, intelligent and interesting. His ear picture and the eye picture do not match. His speech is telling a lie about him.

Since your speech must stand on its own on the telephone, make it stand tall. The next time you answer the telephone (*never,* incidentally, answer it with food in your mouth—swallow before you pick up the receiver), ask yourself how you sound to the other person: Do you think that you come over the wire clear, vital, colorful, interested, and to the point?

Clarity. A salesman reporting to the home office by telephone knows he has to speak clearly so that there can be no confusion about what he is reporting. He spells out names, and asks to have them repeated. He makes sure the letters of the alphabet cannot be mistaken: " 'S' as in Samuel," " 'A' as in apple," " 'F' as in Frank." If you are conveying facts on the telephone, even socially, be sure that you are accurately understood.

DON'T SHOUT!

Think of the telephone as an ear, not an ear trumpet. Talk into it with enough projection for a telephone, not an auditorium.

Not long after World War I, the country fell in love with a very funny phonograph monologue, called "Cohen on the Telephone." Cohen, talking over a bad connection, is trying to explain to his landlord the damage done to his house by a storm. "No, no," he shouts in a fury of frustration, "I didn't say *shut up;* I said the wind blew down the *shutters!*"

In those days he had reason to shout. Telephone service, by today's standards, was rudimentary. Completing a telephone connection involved as much patient work and as quick reflexes as cranking a Model T Ford and then keeping it from running over you.

On a party line, first you held the receiver to your ear to learn whether anyone was on the line. Usually someone was; with as many as three dozen subscribers sharing a single wire, the wire was seldom disengaged.

When it was finally free, you cranked the number you wanted—say two longs and a short—and kept on cranking until your party answered. Then you tried to communicate over wires that hummed, whistled, buzzed, and occasionally collapsed under a falling tree in the midst of your conversation. At one moment the voice at the other end of the line might boom; at the next it would become a ghostly, indecipherable wail. Nobody objected to wire tapping in those days; the favorite diversion of lonely farm wives was to pick up the local gossip by listening in whenever the telephone rang. Sometimes these eavesdroppers served a useful purpose by relaying messages that failed to make it all the way on their own.

Farm wives no longer have party lines to provide gossip, and it is only on transoceanic telephone calls that the conversation is occasionally lost in howling static. To call anywhere in the United States or Canada is as easy today as to step across the hall and rap on the door of the next apartment. The current in the wire and the instruments at each end do all the work; there is no need to raise your voice to be heard.

Vitality. But even in the quietest telephone conversation, you must support your voice. Use as much breath support as Eliza Doolittle took to blow Professor Higgins' candle at ten inches. Remember, too, to speak with energy, vitality, and enthusiasm. Otherwise you may sound dreary, defeated, negative.

If your voice has a tendency to sag over the telephone, use the pencil trick we talked about before. Hold a pencil ten or so inches from you, and speak *at* it. If your voice tends to rise, hold the pencil lower than the mouth of the telephone, perhaps at table level, to remind you to lower your pitch and your resonance too.

Color and interest. The color of some birds' plumage changes to signal when they are interested in attention from the opposite sex. A firefly indicates availability for mating by blinking his (or is it her? only a firefly can be sure) light. Have you ever thought about the message conveyed by your "hello?" It can set the whole tone of your conversation. It announces your mood. It may be casual and relaxed, indicating that you have all the time in the world. It may be friendly but brisk, meaning, "We'll have to move right along; I'm busy." It may be brusque, warning of a storm on the horizon.

Make your "hello" say what you want it to. Some people who sound reserved, indifferent, chilly, even hostile over the telephone do so entirely unintentionally. If your "hello" seems cold, inflect down. Stay on the "o" an extra beat. Roll it around; warm it up a bit like brandy in a glass—"hell-oh-oh." (But don't make an aria of it.)

HOW DO YOU LOOK ON THE TELEPHONE?

Though the person on the other end of the telephone wire cannot see you, your voice will give him a picture of you. It is difficult to sound warm on the telephone if you are scowling. By the same token, if you smile as you talk, the wire will transmit that smile. Your telephone voice reveals your physical demeanor to an astonishing degree. The listener may even be able to tell if a woman is wearing her false eyelashes; since they give her a lift, they give a lift to her voice. Your telephone voice tells clearly whether your mouth is turning down, or up. The friendlier you feel, the friendlier you will sound; and friendliness, whether in social or business situations, is a useful tool. Put a mirror by the telephone, and check your expression when you talk.

The American Telephone and Telegraph Company used to advertise "the voice with a smile." Somehow such voices seem more rare these days—which only makes them more appreciated when one does hear them. We more often hear "the voice with a snarl." If you spend the night in a hotel, what a lift you receive if a voice with a smile takes your breakfast order over the telephone! How delightful to know that someone on the other end of the line feels a special responsibility to pull up the window shade on the new day for you, and let the sunshine in! How soul-satisfying to find that someone seems to take a personal interest in whether you like your eggs once over lightly or sunny side up!

In personal and business conversations, too, the telephone can transmit either an agreeable or a disagreeable picture of you. So be vital. Be warm. Be sincere.

Posture can affect voice clarity, intensity, and vitality no less when you are telephoning than when you are addressing a directors' meeting. Don't slump when you are talking on the telephone. If your body sags, so will your voice. Tuck in your vital center. Straighten up and support the small of your back against your chair.

Editing. A telephone extension in my apartment has a twelve-foot cord which permits me to wander about the room, doing odd chores, while I give much-needed telephone time to a few shut-in friends. While lifting someone's spirits by listening, I can sew, rearrange bureau drawers, and file cards.

It is sometimes rewarding and helpful—at least for women—to engage in this sort of long, essentially aimless but necessary telephone talk. Telephone conversation can substitute for a visit to a sick friend. It can help him or her pass the time of day. Generally, though, telephone talk should be brief and to the point, for the sake of both participants. Ration your telephone time—and even more the other person's—as if it were costing money. It is.

Quentin Reynolds was once sitting with Franklin D. Roosevelt in the White House when a call came through from Winston Churchill. Reynolds was astonished to hear the President say after a bit: "Okay, Winston—your three minutes are up. Better hang up, or you'll have to pay overtime." President Nixon, after his 1969 call to the astronauts on the moon, remarked, "The toll charge must have been high—I hope it was collect!"

Women can help themselves hold down their verbosity by pretending they are calling not from home but from a telephone booth, and have just deposited their last dime.

If you are the person called, be courteous; but that does not mean you have to be the helpless victim of a telephone rambler. If the telephone has been ringing all day, or if you are involved with things which require your attention —such as a family dinner on the stove, or the continuity of an article you are writing, or a meeting with a client— don't hesitate to say you can't talk just now. Tell the caller when you expect to be free, and say, "Mary, I'd love to talk with you when I can take my time. Right now it's impossible." Or "I'm terribly busy. Could I call you between nine and ten tomorrow morning?"

If you are the caller, remember that you take the other

person's time no less by keeping him on the telephone than by sitting across the desk from him. So if you are telephoning for an idle conversation, say so at once, and give PL 2-3453 the option of telling you that your call is untimely.

THE CALLER

To introduce yourself by telephone, say, "This is Tom Bell," or, "Good morning. This is Tom Bell calling." If the person you want is not the one who answers, say, "May I speak to Mr. Taylor? This is Thomas Bell calling."

Are you bothered, as I am, by this kind of opener: "What are you doing tonight?" Perhaps I am doing nothing, and an invitation from you is just what I have been hoping for. On the other hand, I may wish to keep on doing nothing. Or I may be eager to do something—but not with you. So tell me what you have in mind straight out *before* you ask what I am doing. "Can you join us for dinner? A visitor from Karachi whom I thought you might enjoy will be there." Give me a chance to accept, reject, invent an excuse, or check with my husband, knowing exactly what you have in mind.

(I'll probably say "Yes.")

INTELLIGENT LISTENING

Samuel Rogers, a man with a reputation for venomous wit, had a friend, Knight, who was a great talker and a bad listener. When Rogers was told that Knight was going deaf, he remarked: "It is from lack of practice."

Many of us are psychologically deaf on the telephone. *Listen.* It is hard enough to be sure you have not misunderstood someone when the two of you are face to face, so that you can be helped in determining his meaning by his body attitudes and gestures as well as his speech. It is even harder to be sure you are getting the right message in telephone talk, where hearing has to carry the load for all the listener's other senses.

So don't half-listen. Keep a pencil and notebook handy to jot down any salient facts. (This is particularly necessary in business calls.) Listen not just to what is being said, but to how it is said. What added information does the caller's tone give you? When William Shirer was broadcasting from Berlin prior to World War II, his talks were censored; but the tone of his voice gave the warnings that his words could not.

You can fill in an amazingly detailed and accurate picture of a telephone caller's physical and emotional state simply by listening between and under the words.

WHEN TO INTERRUPT

Use the same criteria for interrupting as you would if the conversation were face to face. Try not to cut in unless it becomes inescapably clear that otherwise the call may never end. There are times when you may have to disregard this guideline to preserve your sanity, but as a matter of telephone courtesy, at least bear the guideline in mind.

I do not hesitate to cut off, say, a salesman who is touting some product that does not interest me. Indeed, I think of my interruption as a form of kindness to him. "Pardon me," I say, "but I don't want to waste *your* time." And I get off the telephone fast—with a smile.

ONCE MORE—STICKERS!

If you know you have a bad speech habit, put stickers on the base of your phone to correct it. If you are addicted to clearing your throat, "you know"ing, rambling, or any

other distractor, the reminders will help you rid yourself
of them in short order.

Let the best of you do your talking on the telephone.

REMEMBER:

- ◄ Your voice on the telephone gets there before you do.
- ◄ The telephone is an ear—not an ear trumpet.
- ◄ Keep your telephone voice vital.
- ◄ Edit!
- ◄ Your telephone tone has a message of its own.
- ◄ Introduce yourself politely and clearly.
- ◄ Listen—and learn.
- ◄ Know when to interrupt.
- ◄ Know when to hang up.

17. Upping Your Interview Image

Interview, n., a meeting face to face.
—WEBSTER'S SECOND INTERNATIONAL DICTIONARY

The interview is a specialized conversation—one aimed at a limited and specific goal.

Suppose, for instance, that a reporter is interviewing a trustee. The reporter wants to learn the trustee's stand on college riots. The trustee wants to bring out facts about student unrest which he thinks have been neglected, as well as to present his own point of view.

Or say a personnel manager is interviewing a young man just out of college. He wants to discover whether the young man has the right qualifications for employment by his company. The young man, for his part, wants to persuade the personnel manager that he does have the right qualifications, and at the same time to learn whether the job is one he would like to have.

A successful interview involves a high degree of sensitivity on both sides. Each has to consider the other's interests and attitudes, as known before, or as shown during the interview. "When I'm getting ready to reason with a man," said Lincoln, "I spend a third of my time thinking about myself and what I am going to say, and two-thirds of my time thinking about him and what he is going to say."

If you are a job applicant, try to see yourself and what you have to offer through the interviewer's eyes, in order to help him see your qualifications through yours.

Samuel F. B. Morse, inventor of the telegraph, was justly proud of his painting skill. He once asked a physician friend to pass judgment on a painting of a man in his death throes. "Well," asked Morse impatiently, after his friend had examined the painting for several minutes without saying anything, "what do you think of it?"

"Pneumonia," replied the doctor.

IMAGE MAKING

So try to find out what the interviewer wants—and then to show him you have it. It is the same principle that an actor uses when auditioning for a part in a play.

Shortly after my first Broadway play closed, I wanted desperately to do the role of the Colombian Indian girl in *Magdalena*. This was a musical play to be produced by Ed Lester, head of the Los Angeles Civic Light Opera, for whom I had worked in several shows. The music was by Villa Lobos; Bob Wright and Chet Forrest, who had adapted the Grieg music for *The Song of Norway*, were preparing the musical arrangements and lyrics.

I called Ed from New York to tell him I was dying to play the part. An hour later he called back to report sadly that Wright and Forrest did not think I was the type. They had seen me on Broadway as Rosalinda, sophisticated and blond, and they could not envisage me as a Colombian Indian peasant.

"But Ed," I protested, "I look wonderful as an Indian!"

"Prove it," he said. "Send me some pictures I can show them."

I called the Colombian consulate and asked how peasants dressed. Did they wear shoes? "Señora!" said the man on the other end of the line indignantly; "we have no peasants—and of *course* they wear shoes."

A rental company provided me with a south-of-the-border blouse and dirndl skirt, brilliantly colored and with intricate designs, left over from the motion picture *A Walk in the Sun*. I darkened my skin, put on a long black-brown wig braided in Indian pigtails, dressed in the blouse and skirt, and posed barefoot for mood pictures.

Dino Yannopoulis, a Metropolitan Opera director and an old friend, directed me and supervised the photography. He posed me sitting cross-legged in a marketplace, eating an apple; carrying a jug on my shoulder to the well; shrinking back in a tent from a sombreroed, menacing shadow. (To make the shadow, we cut a silhouette from cardboard and put it in a frame over the spotlight.)

The pictures turned out like studies for *Life*. We air-mailed a number of them to Ed, who took them in to his associates without revealing who the model was. "Here is a possibility," he said; "what do you think of her?" "Perfect type" was the reply; "who is she?" When he told them, they said, "Send Dorothy our apologies—and a contract."

The trick was to make Wright and Forrest see in me the characteristics they were after. You have to do the same thing when interviewed by a potential employer.

I was engaged for *The King and I* after much the same sort of approach. The call for an audition reached me in Chicago, where I had just finished a concert. My manager called at one in the morning. By 8:00 A.M. I was back in my New York apartment, and Lina Abarbanel, my beloved coach, was at the door with the script.

In this case my job was to look and sound like the head wife of the King of Siam. I hid most of my blond hair under a black velvet cap, and the rest of it behind huge sunburst earrings. My oriental accent was a reasonable facsimile of the sounds of waiters I had heard in Chinese restaurants. To achieve that chopped, dry quality I fashioned my speech after the sound of a woodblock, tapped by a drumstick: "I am head-wife—to my lord—king of Siam—and bore him son—Crown Prince." The image I brought to the audition was the one Rodgers and Hammerstein wanted, and I got the role.

Just as an actor must audition for a play standing on a bare stage, in an all but empty theater, under one naked, unflattering bulb, with no set to help him create mood or atmosphere, you must sell yourself to the interviewer with nothing to help you except your confidence in your own qualifications and your skill in presenting them.

PREPARING FOR YOUR BUSINESS AUDITION

Start to prepare yourself for your job interview by learning all you can about the nature and history of the company. What parts of its activities are appropriate to your experience? What can you find out through phone calls, news stories, magazine articles, and books? Next, learn all you can about your interviewer. What is his background? Do you have anything in common? Do you know people who may know him?

Ask yourself:

◄ Do I understand the requirements of the job?
◄ Can I answer convincingly if I am asked, "Why do you want to work for us?"
◄ Am I prepared to answer the interviewer's questions frankly and comfortably?
◄ Can I not only show him my qualifications and background but convince him of my capacity to grow?

Consider yourself from the point of view of the interviewer. Which of your specific experiences, qualifications, and interests match his needs and project the image you think he is looking for? Have these ready for orderly presentation.

Try to think of all the questions you might be asked, and to come up with satisfactory answers for them. This is a technique that is used even by Presidents. On the eve of a press conference, President Nixon receives from his advisors lists of the questions most likely to be asked, together with summaries of the information from which his answers can be developed. He studies this material until he knows it thoroughly. Even the language of the answers he gives may have been worked out in advance.

You may not have all the President's resources at your disposal, but you should go to your interview as thoroughly prepared as possible.

REHEARSE

Don't underestimate the value of a rehearsal. Begin rehearsing well in advance. Put on paper the questions you anticipate and your answers to them. The evening before the interview, or even earlier, ask a friend or relative to play the part of the interviewer. Give him the questions you anticipate; ask him to think of more. Make sure he asks thorny as well as friendly questions. Listen to his criticisms. Then reverse roles. Put yourself in the interviewer's shoes, and begin questioning your friend. You may find that questions that had not occurred to you come unexpectedly to mind, and his answers may provide you with new insights.

Finally, tape-record both questions and answers, if you can. Play back the tape to see where and how your replies might be improved. This technique works for other than business interviews. A woman of my acquaintance went to court to fight what she considered an unjustified charge of traffic violation. Her lawyer husband made up a list of all the questions the judge was likely to ask. She carefully prepared her replies (and rehearsed them in the bathroom). She went to court with small hope; but she was acquitted.

EVERYTHING ABOUT YOU SPEAKS

1.   Are you pleasing to the eye?

Clothing for an interview should be your normal business attire, unless what you consider normal is inappropriate for the firm to which you have applied or the work for which you are being considered. If you hope to become secretary to the president of Pennsylvania Pothole Covers or Los Angeles Leggings, Inc., don't arrive at the interview looking more affluent than the president's wife. Leave your mink and diamonds at home. Don't have your hair piled high as though you were going to a ball at Buckingham Palace.

Hemlines. Women, watch your hemlines; others do. Bathing-suit-length hemlines will certainly get you attention, but not necessarily a job. (But styles keep changing; when I walked into an office last year the generation gap widened for me by about twelve inches. If you arrive at an interview with a hemline that is unfashionably long, or short, you will look like a relic from another generation.)

Alexander Pope's advice remains pertinent here:

> Be not the first by whom the new are tried,
> Nor yet the last to lay the old aside.

Hair length. A man with a hippy hairdo may fit into the creative art department of an advertising agency. Long hair looks groovy behind a guitar, but behind a desk it can distract as you try to persuade the company's client to think your way. If you are looking for a job with a square employer, go to the barber before you go to your job interview.

Don't cling to a beard or long hair just to assert your personality. The pertinent question is: Will the image you present help you or stand in your way when you are interviewed for a job? Images often depend on the time and place.

For seventy-two years no President of the United States wore a beard or mustache. Then after the Civil War there came the bearded countenances of Grant, Hayes, Garfield, and Harrison. Cleveland, Theodore Roosevelt, and Taft wore mustaches. The present smooth-shaven era began with Woodrow Wilson. Our only bald-headed presidents were John Quincy Adams and Dwight D. Eisenhower. (Bald heads were out socially, too, until Yul Brynner came along and gave them sex status.)

2.   Are you pleasing to the nose?

Go to your interview smelling like a country breeze on a newborn spring day. You will be fresh from the shower that morning and will have made use of the deodorant and mouthwash in your medicine cabinet. Equally important, protect your nose appeal by avoiding onions, alcohol, and garlic at the meal just prior to the meeting, and the latter even at dinner the night before.

If you use perfume, make it light; cloying, musky scents can be disagreeable, even overpowering, in a close room.

Don't smoke a cigar immediately before your appointment; the melody lingers on.

WHEN TO ARRIVE

Give yourself plenty of time to reach the location of your interview. The ultimate discourtesy is to arrive late; if that happens, you may as well turn right around and go back home. There is virtue in arriving a few moments early. It gives you an opportunity, while you are waiting, to adjust yourself to the office atmosphere, gather your thoughts, and compose yourself physically as well as mentally. If you feel nervous, sit in Executive Posture and play the Silent Steam Kettle game. Think positively: "I am confident, composed, compelling, and convincing," or "I am persuasive, powerful, positive," etc.

CURTAIN TIME

Meeting your interviewer. If you have not been announced, introduce yourself naturally, using your given name as well as your surname—Sue Brady, not Miss Brady. Use that famous Brady smile, that shows in the eyes as well as the mouth. And let your handshake be as natural as your smile.

How to sit. Try to pick an upright chair. If you have no choice but an overstuffed sofa or chair, resist the temptation to lounge, or to sag like a used sleeping bag. Do not cross your legs, girls, even if they have been much admired. Sit straight, the lower part of your spine against the back of your seat. Kings and queens, we are told, do not cross their legs on thrones; imagine yourself on a throne, with a crown on your head. Hold yourself not stiffly, but composedly. Good posture will help you to command yourself and the situation.

Avoid physical distractors—fidgeting, ear-pulling, leg-swinging, etc. If you are still nervous, fold your hands in your lap, and divert your tension by pressing your thumb nail of one hand hard into the palm of the other. You may end up with a scar, but meanwhile you will look calm, collected, and confident.

Extend your antennae. Be sensitive to the impression you are making. Avoid tentativeness or indecisiveness, but watch and be guided by the interviewer's reaction to what you say and how you say it.

Don't be so dynamic that your interviewer feels overpowered. Remember the image that he wants, and stay within that framework.

A little light talk is fine at the beginning, but it should not last too long or stray too far from the reason you are there. If it does, bring it back on track.

Be serious; be earnest; but show that if you do get the job you will be not just efficient but a pleasant person to have around. Listen thoughtfully. Pay attention. Ask pertinent questions of your own, but in a non-provocative manner. When answering questions, speak concisely, but don't leave out essential information. Shun monosyllabic replies, hard luck stories, tragedies, apologies, and recitals of illness. Don't leave negatives around for the interviewer to remember you by.

The Ten Hints for Conversation apply full force to interviews. Indeed, with an important decision at stake, they are more essential than ever. It may be regrettable to ramble in cocktail party conversation, but rambling on a job interview is *disastrous,* since your success in getting the job depends on the impression you make. Non-edited talkers are not wanted in business; they cost the company too much time and money. Have you ever waited in a department store while the sales people finished some long personal interchange before serving you? The store is losing not only sales but customer good will as well.

Know when to leave. Pace yourself. Think ahead. Don't let the conversation lose its way or die. Recognize the peak moment of the interview and be ready to conclude soon after. When you have said all you have to say, stand, smile, give the interviewer your hand, thank him, and go—leaving a positive impression behind.

THE INTERVIEWER

Your responsibilities as interviewer are the obverse of the interviewee's. You too must be interested and empathetic. You should learn in advance as much about the job applicant as you can. Applications, letters, and telephone inquiries help. The interview is only the fleshing out of all these.

◄ While you are interviewing someone, give him your whole attention, and let him realize that is what you are doing. It is inexcusable to rearrange your papers, glance at correspondence, pause for a chat with a colleague, or otherwise indicate that the interview is an interruption of other things on which you would rather be spending your time.

◄ Be as cordial as is fitting; don't retreat into your deep freeze and make the applicant sweat to thaw you out. He is your guest; put him at ease. Don't be one of those executives who are sent to me for help by the hundreds each year because their superiors find their executive personality with peers and subordinates too aloof and severe.

◄ Clarify to whatever extent you can the nature of the

job for which the applicant is being considered. Will the applicant and the job be compatible?

◄ Be prepared not only to ask questions, but to answer the questions you are asked.

◄ When the interview has accomplished its purpose, bring it politely to an end.

After the interview, try to make your decision at once, while facts and impressions are still fresh in your mind; or, if you feel you will need time to think your decision over, say so, so the applicant will know where he stands. Leave him cordially, even if you do not plan to employ him; but don't be so overwhelmingly cordial that he thinks he has the job when he hasn't.

THROUGH THE CAMERA'S EYE

Authors who are at no loss for words when writing them on paper, have sought me out in terror when the time came to promote their books in lectures and in TV and radio interviews. Though they may have written potential best-sellers, they could not project their personalities on the air.

The fault is sometimes the interviewer's. It is the responsibility of a professional radio or television interviewer to bring out the best in his guests. Many interviewers fail to do their homework. They don't know what questions to ask. The interviewer should be thoroughly familiar with the background, accomplishments, and some opinions of the person he is interviewing, and have a stock of questions that elicit stimulating and informative answers.

If your interviewer lets you down on the air, you may have to steer the conversation around to the message you wish to convey.

Presidents and lesser politicians are experts in news conferences at taking advantage of a question on an entirely different subject to bring out a point that they would like to leave in the public's mind.

You too can do this. You might say, "One question I am often asked, which I should like to answer here, is . . ."

Or, "Yesterday, a lawyer wanted to know . . ." Have a card with notes of points you want to cover to refer to unobtrusively.

In any radio or television interview, it is important to speak naturally, almost intimately, so that the listener or viewer feels you are talking expressly for him. This is what is meant by warm communication. Watch viewing panels and interviews on television—especially on Sundays, when the most intelligent fare seems to be served. Analyze the qualities of the best speakers. Emulate them. What is wrong with those who come over poorly?

If you have availed yourself of the suggestions for voice, speech, preparation, and delivery in this book, television and radio appearances should hold no terrors for you. But as insurance, bear these points in mind:

1.   For television, wear a colored shirt if you are a man, and color with design, if possible, if you are a woman. Do not wear black and white.

2.   Avoid glasses that reflect light (you can buy specially treated glasses now that don't), and wear no glasses at all if you can possibly get along without them.

3.   Check yourself on the monitor for unflattering shadows, poor makeup, disarranged hair, and the like. You may have to press the director hard before he will let you do this, but you owe it to yourself to protect your image before you go on the air. It pays.

4.   Use Executive Posture. Don't look like a rumpled old suit. Slumping looks even worse on television than it does in a living room.

5.   Remember that the camera with the lighted red eye is the one that is focusing on you. Talk to that camera as though it were a person—include it, but don't favor it too much.

6.   Don't read your remarks. A good politician learns this prohibition early. Voters want to give their votes to a man they feel they can trust; they like to see in his eyes that *he* believes all he says, even though *they* may not. Those of you whose business futures will include meetings

on closed circuit TV, please note. Make a habit of speaking eye to eye.

REMEMBER:

- ◄ Learn in advance what the interviewer wants of you.
- ◄ Find out how you would fit into the picture.
- ◄ Establish a favorable image of yourself.
- ◄ Rehearse the interview, and role-play the interviewer.
- ◄ Check your appearance.
- ◄ Arrive on time.
- ◄ Keep your finger on the pulse of the interview.
- ◄ Know when to leave.
- ◄ The interviewer's responsibilities.
- ◄ Successful TV interviewing.

PART III

THE SPEECH

18. Preparing the Speech

Nothing is a greater impediment to being on good terms
with others than being ill at ease with yourself.
—HONORÉ DE BALZAC

The most common complaint of people who come to me
for help in speechmaking is that nervousness overcomes
them whenever they have to give a talk. One may call it
stagefright; another, the yips; a third, nerves or butterflies;
but whatever the name, for them speaking in public is a
more painful experience than having a tooth removed
without novocaine.

Yet few attainments are more gratifying than the ability
to speak acceptably and confidently. "There is no other accomplishment that any man can have," said Chauncey
Depew, "that will so quickly make for him a career and
secure recognition."

Tens of thousands of people dread having to make a
speech. Once they have committed themselves to stand up
and talk, they start to lose sleep, appetite, and weight. They
wake up in nightmares of dreadful anticipation. Instead of
enjoying the speech while it is going on, they are in mortal
terror until it is over.

If you are one of these unfortunates, the day on which
you are committed to speak looms like your hanging day.
You would give all you own if only you could cancel out
and run the other way. When at last you are seated on the
platform with all those rows of faces before you, your
heart pounds; there is a knot in your stomach, a lump in
your throat, perspiration on your brow. Your hands may

tremble so that you dare not even lift your glass of water, and your lips are so dry that they stick to your teeth. When you rise to speak, your knees may knock and your voice quiver.

These manifestations generally subside with experience. Nonetheless, many professional performers continue to suffer from stage-fright all their lives.

Before Lily Pons sang, she often took an injection to calm her nerves. Nat King Cole, arising to accept an award, was so flustered that he said he had five sons when he meant five daughters. Yul Brynner was as tense before the curtain of the five hundred and fifty-seventh performance of *The King and I* as he was before the first.

General U. S. Grant found it harder to face an audience than the cannons of the Confederate Army. Benjamin Disraeli's maiden speech before the House of Commons failed—because he was terrified. Lloyd George confessed that in his first public speeches his tongue stuck to the top of his mouth from fear.

Ethel Merman, on the other hand, when asked whether she was nervous before the opening of *Annie Get Your Gun,* replied, "I know my lines; what is there to be nervous about?"

And therein lies a clue.

KNOW YOUR LINES

A certain amount of nervousness is natural, even inevitable, before you speak. It would be a poor racehorse, after all, who felt no nerves before the gate opened.

But that kind of nervousness only stimulates the racehorse to run his fastest. Destructive nervousness, stemming from insecurity, is a horse of a different color.

Isn't it astonishing that a man who gladly spends hundreds of hours and dollars to learn how to hit a golf ball will not invest one-hundredth of that time, money, and energy to find out how to deliver a talk, something of much greater importance to his career and self-confidence? Knowing he does not speak well, he is almost destroyed by panic from the moment he agrees to speak right through the speech itself. Suddenly he realizes he is putting up for public judgment his personality, his thinking, his worth as a person. To speak in public is to unveil a picture of yourself and you wonder, "Will I have their respect for what I have to say and the way I handle myself?"

Nervousness is caused by the fear of looking ridiculous to others. We look ridiculous if we are not well prepared and if we do not deliver our message well.

The elimination of paralyzing stagefright involves two separate steps: preparing your material—thoroughly; and preparing yourself—thoroughly. Speech confidence comes from knowing that you have something worth saying, and that you can say it in a way worth listening to.

PREPARING YOUR MATERIAL

1. What is expected of you?

When you have agreed to give a talk, whether to a dozen fraternity brothers, a PTA meeting, or a political rally of thousands, decide on your topic, and then learn exactly what your responsibilities are.

What do I wish to accomplish?

a. To inform?
b. To persuade?
c. To amuse or entertain?

Your answers to these questions will determine the selection and interpretation of your material.

Then check on the circumstances of the meeting, this way:

a. What kind of audience will I have?
b. How much time has been allotted me?
c. How am I supposed to dress?

    d. What are the physical arrangements: a dais or a stage? A table-lectern or a standing one? Will there be a microphone?

    e. Who are the other speakers, and what are their topics?

At a dinner given by the electronics industry, listeners spent an agonized twenty minutes while a leading executive repeated the talk just given by another speaker. He should have checked with the program committee in advance. Failing that, he should have been flexible enough at least to alter his opening remarks to something like: "Mr. X has saved me a great deal of trouble by making exactly the points I had in mind. Perhaps, though, I might add a few observations off the cuff . . ."

Chauncey Depew, a tremendous wit, once found himself in a similar situation. He was to speak just after Mark Twain. Twain received enthusiastic applause. "Ladies and gentlemen," said Depew, when his turn came, "Mark Twain and I agreed to trade speeches tonight. He has delivered mine very well, and I am grateful. Unfortunately, I have lost his and I can't remember a word of it." And he sat down.

YOUR AUDIENCE

The nature of your audience should determine the treatment of your speech. Are they mostly old or young? Men or women? Liberal or conservative? Cultivated or unlettered? What kind of sense of humor do they have? Are there topics you should avoid?

A usually sensitive comedian was asked to address a luncheon for an outstanding Jewish philanthropy. In an unusual display of bad judgment, he heaped borscht-circuit, chopped-liver jokes on some of the brightest women and most distinguished scientists in the United States. He had not researched his audience enough in advance. One does not give the same kind of talk to a horticultural club as to an advertising association.

The size of the audience must be considered, too. As J. M. Barrie once remarked, you do not speak the same way to a number of girls as you do to one. "To tell you the truth," he said, "I'd much rather talk one thousand times to one girl, than to talk one time to a thousand girls."

Orson Welles, speaking before a sparse audience in the Midwest, is said to have begun: "I'm a director of plays, a producer of plays. I'm an actor of the stage and motion pictures. I'm a writer and producer of motion pictures. I write, direct, and act on radio and television. I'm a magician and painter. I've published books. I play the violin and the piano." At this point he paused, surveyed his audience, and said, "Isn't it a pity there's so many of me and so few of you!"

TIMING YOUR SPEECH

A certain number of minutes has been allotted for your talk. Honor your time limit. Do you have ten minutes? Twenty? The limit is more than a casual matter, because the schedule of a meeting is like the bed of Procrustes. Procrustes was a highwayman of ancient Greece who forced his unwilling guests into a bed. If they were too long for it, he loped off their extremities. If they were too short, he stretched them to fit.

If the talk you have in mind would run too long, it must be lopped off. If it would run too short, you must fill the needed minutes. Remember the request that any intelligent chairman makes: a speech should fit the occasion and fit the schedule.

If you speak, say, at 130 words a minute, you will need about ten minutes to deliver 1300 words, twenty minutes to deliver 2600, and so on.

I use a device popular with car owners: one of those key-chain timers that remind you when the parking meter

is about to show a violation. (You can pick one up at a
stationery store or specialty cutlery store.) Set the timer
to go off five minutes before the scheduled end of your
speech, and it will buzz to tell you it's time to move into
your conclusion.

WHAT SHOULD YOU WEAR?

Ask what kind of dress is appropriate. You will be embarrassed if you arrive in a business suit to address a group
in black tie—and even more embarrassed if you come in
black tie and find your audience in its shirt sleeves. Women
should make an extra check about the color of the backdrop, if there is one. If the backdrop is red and you are
wearing orange, you two won't get along. Your dress
should enhance your talk—not take minds off it.

An alert and attractive young woman, creative vice-pres-
ident of an advertising agency, addressed one of my classes
wearing a skirt which ended twelve inches above her knees.
The talk was excellent, but her legs upstaged her message.
I doubt whether most of her male listeners took in much
of her presentation.

DO HECKLERS RAISE YOUR HACKLES?

Before a talk in Boston, I was told that a dowager in the
audience made a habit of baiting the speakers. Sure enough,
I had barely begun my second sentence when she shouted,
"Can't hear ya! And you're supposed to be a speech con-
sultant!" I replied, "I want you of all people to hear every
word. So whenever you have trouble hearing, won't you
please raise your hand, and I'll raise my voice?" Her hand
stayed down, and she was well behaved for the rest of the
evening.

One woman, an editor of a rather conservative magazine,
had been booed off the stage by a group of students at

Berkeley. Since she was scheduled to give several more talks on campuses around the country, she asked if I could help her deal with hecklers. We arranged to have her rehearse her speech in a large ballroom set up with about a hundred chairs, empty except for a few occupied by her friends, whom we had asked to act as hecklers. They baited her with questions which she had to answer on the spot. Thus, she had a rehearsal in a negative atmosphere. After her next college appearance she wrote in triumph to report that she had been able to turn hostility into a standing ovation.

Some speakers feel themselves more than the equal of any heckler, and even relish heckling as a source of amusing interchange. When a voice called from the balcony to George Bernard Shaw, "Come, Shaw, you know all this stuff is balderdash," the playwright replied good-naturedly, "I quite agree with you, my friend, but who are you and I against so many?"

There is no sure way to safeguard yourself from heckling. Your best protection is careful preparation. Your information should be irrefutable, your facts and examples unassailable. Your manner should combine authority and control with friendliness and tact—and a sense of humor helps.

SOMETHING WORTH SAYING

When you have learned all you can about the circumstances of the meeting, lay the groundwork for your talk.

Only the time and attention you devote to preparation justifies the time and attention your audience will have to devote to listening. Use *your* time to make *their* time worthwhile.

It has been said that "the reason there are so few good speakers in public is that there are so few good thinkers in private." Thinking takes time.

If a topic was not assigned to you, decide on one as early as possible—preferably one with which you already

have some familiarity. Give yourself ample time to gather
your material and develop it.

The point of giving yourself plenty of time to prepare
your talk is so that you can think it through. You cannot
give birth to a full-fledged speech the first night. A speech
and an unborn baby have this in common: they both need
considerable development before they are delivered.

My favorite time for speech gestation lies just between
sleeping and waking. My mind seems to be most creative
in those twilight or dawn moments. It focuses on the job
to be done. Deliberately, before dropping off at night or
coming to full wakefulness in the morning, I mull over
ideas for a talk on which I may be working.

My approach floats around at first in my subconscious,
shapeless and quiescent. During the day, I consider the
possibilities in odd moments, avoiding all sense of pressure.
Then suddenly, often when I least expect it, I feel a little
mental kick that means something is beginning to stir. The
kick may signal an idea for any part of the talk—beginning, middle, or end. If the kick comes during the night,
I grope for the pad on my nightstand, and scribble some
summary words as best I can, without turning on the light.
Usually I can manage next morning to make out what I
have written; and, in any event, I have not wakened my
husband.

GATHERING YOUR MATERIAL

First you collect your material. Then you organize it.

Begin by jotting down what you already know of a subject. Add personal experiences or observations illustrating
the points you wish to make. Interview people who have
information you may lack.

Sometimes a telephone call to the library or to a specialist in your topic will bring out the facts you are after.
Sometimes you will need a personal interview. If you require incontrovertible evidence of some arguable point, get
it in writing.

Add to your information from newspapers, magazines, and books. Under no circumstances include as a fact any statement that is not backed by an unimpeachable source.

Your speech is divided into opening remarks, body, and conclusion. Let's look first at the opening remarks.

THE INTRODUCTION

The varieties of opening remarks are as limitless as your imagination. Begin, if you wish, with a reference to the immediate locale . . . or the chairman . . . or the weather . . . or the train service. You may ask a question ("How many of you were caught in the New York blackout of 1965?"); you may make a dramatic statement; you may cite an incident from the day's news, history, or your own experience.

Quotations and anecdotes can make good introductions. (You will find some examples of openings and conclusions in the Appendix section, "Readings for Color and Effectiveness." They will give you an idea of different styles, and practicing them aloud will help your delivery.)

"Quotations have great service for speeches," said Aristotle, "because audiences are commonplace. People are pleased when a speaker hits on a wide general statement of opinions that they hold in some partial or fragmentary form." But use them only if they are *appropriate*. Nothing is more pitiable than a story or joke dragged in, like a stray dog, by the scruff of its neck, and tied into your talk against its will.

Anecdotes and jokes told on the platform require a different form from those written for the printed page. Rehearse yours until you know you have the pacing and the punchlines right, or they will neither amuse your audience nor buttress your point.

Once you begin watching for quotations, you will find them popping up all over the place. Dozens of books (some listed in the Appendix) are fine sources of anecdotes, quotations, and jokes suitable for speakers, chairmen, and toastmasters. When you see a line worth quoting in a newspaper or magazine file it on a card.

You may enjoy quoting *epigrams*—brief, witty commentaries on some particular circumstance, like this epitaph for Charles I of England:

> Here lies our sovereign lord and king
> Whose word no man relies on;
> Who never said a foolish thing,
> And never did a wise one.

Or you may prefer *aphorisms*—trenchant sentences which bring out universal truths. "The voice of the people is the voice of God" is an aphorism.

One of the most common, delightful, and dangerous introductions is *humor*. Nothing can warm up an audience like a good joke *well told*—but do not venture on a joke unless you know how to make it come off. Truly gifted raconteurs are few and far between.

A joke should be short, crisp, pruned. If your jokes fall flat when you tell them to your friends, do not delude yourself that somehow they will fare better when a hundred or a thousand people are listening. If you have a joke that seems appropriate, practice it aloud until you are confident that you have the timing and the punchline just right. Then try it on a friend or two. If their laughter is perfunctory, file the joke in the wastebasket.

THE BODY OF THE SPEECH

At the beginning of a speech, you make friends with your audience and state your proposition. At the end, you nail down your proposition. But the body is the heart of your speech. It is there that you develop your theme and convince your listeners.

A speech should be organized as carefully as a sentence is parsed. The main idea and the supporting ideas should take their due positions and receive their due share of time.

Talks should be either *informative, persuasive, amusing* or a little of each. An *informative* talk adds to the listeners' knowledge, but is not intended to change or strengthen their opinions. In effect it may be simply the extended and orderly answer to some factual question: "What can computers do to help a business?"; "How do you make a candle from an empty milk carton?"; "What will it be like to live on the moon?"

A *persuasive* talk, on the other hand, presents a problem, proposes solutions, and, through a progression of carefully reasoned steps, rouses the listeners to action.

Your talk should not go around and around like a leaf in a whirlpool, until it is finally sucked under. Make sure it has forward movement. See to it that each step reinforces the previous one and leads logically to the next.

It is natural to prepare, or at least organize, the body of the speech before deciding how to introduce it, since there is no point to developing an introduction before you know the idea you are introducing.

However, some people preparing a talk prefer to begin at the end. Somerset Maugham said he always wrote the end of his stories first; once he knew where to go, all he had to do was find a way to get there.

PREPARE A TALK, NOT AN ESSAY

Lincoln used to say that he liked a talk to be as personal and familiar as a chat between two people riding along in a buckboard. Though you should write out your speech to fix the organization and the key phrases in your mind, employ the familiar spoken language of person-to-person conversation. Make every sentence so plain that no listener can find an excuse for failing to get your meaning Your listeners may never have heard of Disraeli, but by instinct they will agree with his statement that "I make it a rule to believe only what I understand." As Emerson said: "Speech is the power to translate a truth into a language perfectly intelligible to the person to whom you speak." A speech,

whether to thirty people or to three thousand, should have
the quality of speaking not *at* or *to,* but *with.* Each time
you rewrite, say the sentences aloud first to test them on
your tongue. Be sure they sound as good as they look.

Avoid technical language where it will not be understood. Use images that sharpen your point, not fuzz it. Use
words that say exactly what you mean. Be colorful if you
can. In any event, see to it that your listener goes away
knowing exactly what your message was.

Be specific. "Any talk," said Louis Calhern, "without a
specific example is weak." If you use a generalization, back
it up with a specific the mind's eye can see. "Ten times the
size of an office building elevator" gives you the picture
faster than "640 square feet."

If your subject is abstract or complicated, take particular pains to present it in concrete terms, avoiding techni-
calities and statistics. Inflation comes to life for a listener
not in billion-dollar terms but in terms of the cost of a
loaf of bread or a quart of milk.

As Elizabeth Barrett Browning put it:

> A red-haired child
> Sick in fever, if you touch him once,
> Though but so little as with a finger-tip,
> Will set you weeping; but a million sick . . .
> You could as soon weep for the "rule of three,"
> Or compound fractions.

VERBAL TRICKS

Skilled speakers cast magic spells through devices of
rhetoric. The beginning speaker will profit by close attention to the choice of words and word structures in famous
speeches.

I have just mentioned one of these devices—*concrete-
ness,* which puts otherwise difficult concepts into terms that
are familiar, easy, and often touched with emotion. *Simplicity* is itself a device.

A simple statement, however, does not always of itself evoke an emotional response. It is strengthened if placed in *context:* "They drove to the village often for supplies and always stopped at the post office, a frame building that had once been a Catholic mission." Knowing that the post office (described by L. Woiwode in *What I'm Going to Do, I Think*) was a frame building, and that it once had been a Catholic mission, makes it seem more real to the reader.

Sensual images are highly effective: "Then they all left the room," writes Kafka; "the door was shut; the singing stopped; clouds covered the moon; the bedding was warm around me; the horses' heads in the open windows wavered like shadows." Note how one sense after another takes over: sound; sight; warmth.

Here is how Woiwode evokes smell:

"The smell was so toxic that when he held his face close to the stove, his eyes began to water, his nose and lungs burned, and he felt lightheaded." And again: "The sheets . . . were damp and clinging and smelled of naphthalene. He'd fallen asleep to the smell and waked to it in the night and now, as he looked out at the meadow overlaid with moonlight, the smell seemed responsible for the silver color of the grass and the silver color of the trees encircling it, and for their unnatural stillness."

A sentence of O. Henry's shows what the imagination can do with the sounds heard from a Manhattan hotel in summertime:

"The pleasing distant roar of Broadway is transformed in the imagination of the happy guests to the noise of a waterfall filling the woods with its restful sound."

There are images, too, that evoke the sensations of physical activity, called *kinaesthetic*. Ernest Hemingway was a master of kinaesthetic images: "I slapped the Roman on the back and we went through the thumb pulling again; me pulling his thumb too. I embraced the Wanderobo-Masai and he, after a thumb-pulling of great intensity and feeling, slapped his chest and said very proudly, "Wanderobo-Masai wonderful guide."

Slang can add vividness to a talk, but must be used with great care, since it may either offend or baffle some listeners. "Attaboy," "do your thing," "that's his bag," "blew his top," "what a jerk," "up tight," "don't put me down"— all are appropriate in some situations.

Figures of speech, if not labored, add greatly to the color of a talk. We all use figures of speech, often without even realizing what we are doing; if you say "Wall Street is in trouble," you don't really mean a street, you mean the stock market in general.

There are many types of figures of speech.

A *simile* is a comparison of one thing to another: "My luv is like a red, red rose."

A *metaphor* is a comparison in which one thing is described as if it were another: "the starry canvas of the night."

Irony says one thing to convey another: "To prove his devotion, he beat her soundly."

Hyperbole is the use of exaggeration for emphasis: "He stood tall as a mountain."

Other speech devices:

Rhyme ("courtly" and "portly"; "earning" and "learning," etc.) can tickle the ear, but should be used sparingly.

Anaphora is the repetition of words at the beginning of successive clauses or sentences, as in these lovely lines from Corinthians: "Charity suffereth long, and is kind; charity envieth not; charity vaunteth not itself, is not puffed up."

Balance can be equally effective: "Love beareth all things; believeth all things; hopeth all things; endureth all things."

Assonance is the deliberate repetition of a vowel sound, but in combination with a different consonant, so that it is not what is normally thought of as a rhyme: "old oak," "mad hat," "top notch," "mad as a hatter," "time out of mind," "free and easy."

Consonance is the repetition of final consonant sounds, as in "tip top," "knick-knack," "ding-dong."

Alliteration is the repetition of initial consonant sounds: "lonely, low-lying lands," "tried and true," "rhyme or reason," "sighted sub, sank same."

Word repetition pounds an idea home, as in this paragraph from President Kennedy's inaugural address: "There is an old Chinese proverb saying that each generation builds a road for the next. The road has been built for us, and I believe it is incumbent upon us, in our generation, to build our road for the next." Notice how the words "road" and "generation" are repeated to provide a harmonious integration of thought.

Cadence is rhythm combined with inflection; the melody of the phrase: "Give me liberty or give me death"; "I saw him wounded, bleeding, and dying."

There is much overlapping among these categories and terminologies, and the important thing is to grasp their function rather than to worry over what they are called.

THE CLIMAX

The most popular climax is the strong conclusion. Arrange your ideas in a series that climbs to a crescendo. As in some symphonies, the talk should seem to build of itself. One instrument after another comes in until the entire orchestra is speaking. A speech on a great theme may deserve the rising thunder of such a finale as this:

"Others may hesitate, others may procrastinate, others may plead for further negotiations; but as for me, I am ready to act now. And for my action I am ready to answer to my conscience, my country, and my God."

DISSOLVE ENDING

An opposite, equally effective form of climax is the diminuendo, or dissolve ending. I call this "iris-ing out." Perhaps you've heard it in the last movement of a symphony where the orchestra diminishes and the instruments drop out section by section, even instrument by instrument, until the final passage ends with the cello on a single, long-drawn-out sigh.

In night-club songs that involve deep emotions and end

in low key, the song seems to fade away while the light on the singer shrinks gradually to a smaller and smaller circle until it lights only the face, then the eyes. Finally, it is a pinpoint, and disappears with the last note of the song.

Here is a speech conclusion that iris-es out:

"I saw him bear the burden of a nation's destiny. I saw him implore divine guidance. I saw him wounded, bleeding, dying. For you . . . and for me." The final words fade like the spotlight, leaving the audience emotionally drained.

Climaxes, whether crescendo or diminuendo, require skillful handling. When overdone or inappropriate, they only make the audience uncomfortable and the speaker absurd. Say the sentences aloud before you put them down. Underact them in delivery. Rehearse until you know your cadence is right and your emotion convincing.

OTHER HINTS

For closer communication, use the words "you" and "we"; balance statistics with graphic images; and pause for effect.

Questions can also strengthen a speech. They are of three kinds: those the speaker asks the audience to answer aloud; those he asks the audience and answers himself; and those which are entirely rhetorical, implying their own answers.

Be sparing with statistics and visual aids—flipcharts, blackboards, or slides. Use them only if there is no other way to make your point clear. Most statistics and visual aids are like lampposts drunks lean on, more for support than for light.

If your speech requires a blackboard or easel, do not display the information on it until the time has come to use it. It distracts your listeners' attention.

If you are using a blackboard, don't scribble on it; write clearly, so that your audience will have no difficulty reading your words. Keep talking to your audience and eye contacting them on your way to the board. Otherwise you are apt to cut off your connection.

If you are using slides, rehearse first with the technician, to be sure they are in focus. Be certain he understands your change-slide signal. Try to arrange for a screen with a mat finish, to avoid glaring.

If you are using a projector, don't put it in the middle of the audience. That irritates. Put it in the back of the room.

Don't let your visuals get in the way of your message.

A chief petty officer was teaching about bulletin board displays in a navy instructor's training course. He held up a calendar bearing a stunning picture of a scantily clad young lady. After the class had had time to inspect it carefully, he put it away. Then he asked, "What was the month showing on the calendar?"

When no one could answer, the instructor drew this moral: "Don't make your teaching aids so attractive that they draw attention away from the message they are intended to present."

HOW JFK DID IT

Theodore Sorensen in his book *Kennedy* gives us the guidelines by which he and the President prepared speeches.

The relevant section is reproduced here, with my marginal comments. Note the basic principles the President followed: short speeches, short clauses, short words; points or propositions in logical sequence; simplicity and clarity; anecdotal emphasis tailored to the need of the speech. These principles will work for you too.

FROM KENNEDY

By Theodore C. Sorensen

He would never blindly accept or blandly deliver a text he had not seen and edited. We always discussed the topic, the approach and the conclusions in advance. He always had quotations or historical allusions to include. Sometimes he would review an outline. And he always, upon receiving my draft, altered, deleted or added phrases, paragraphs or pages. Some drafts he rejected entirely.

The Kennedy style of speech-writing—our style, I am not reluctant to say, for he never pretended that he had time to prepare first drafts for all his speeches —evolved gradually over the years. Prepared texts were carefully designed for an orderly presentation of their substance but with no deliberate affectation of any certain style. We were not conscious of following the elaborate techniques later ascribed to these speeches by literary analysts. Neither of us had any special training in composition, linguistics or semantics. Our chief criterion was always audience comprehension and comfort, and this meant: (1) short speeches, short clauses and short words, wherever possible; (2) a series of points or propositions in numbered or logical sequence, wherever appropriate; and (3) the construction of sentences, phrases and paragraphs in such a manner as to simplify, clarify and emphasize.

The test of a text was not how it appeared to the eye but how it sounded to the ear. His best paragraphs, when read aloud, often had a cadence not unlike blank verse—indeed at times key words would rhyme. He was fond of alliterative sentences, not solely for reasons of rhetoric but to reinforce the audience's recollection of his reasoning. Sentences began, however incorrect some may have regarded it, with "And" or "But" whenever that simplified and shortened the text. His frequent use of dashes as a means of separating clauses was of doubtful grammatical standing—but it simplified the delivery and even the publication of a speech in a manner no

Abridged from pp. 60–65, *Kennedy* by Theodore C. Sorensen. Copyright © 1965 by Theodore C. Sorensen. Reprinted by permission of the publishers.

comma, parenthesis or semicolon could match.

Words were regarded as tools of precision, to be chosen and applied with a craftsman's care to whatever the situation required. He liked to be exact. But if the situation required a certain vagueness, he would deliberately choose a word of varying interpretations rather than bury his imprecision in ponderous prose.

AVOID

For he disliked verbosity and pomposity in his own remarks as much as he disliked them in others. He wanted both his message and his language to be plain and unpretentious, but never patronizing. He wanted his major policy statements to be positive, specific and definite, avoiding the use of "suggest," "perhaps" and "possible alternatives for consideration." At the same time, his emphasis on a course of reason—rejecting the extremes of either side—helped produce the parallel construction and use of contrasts with which he later became identified. He had a weakness for one unnecessary phrase: "The harsh facts of the matter are . . ."—but, with few other exceptions, his sentences were lean and crisp.

No speech was more than twenty to thirty minutes in duration. They were all too short and too crowded with facts to permit any excess of generalities and sentimentalities. His texts wasted no words and his delivery wasted no time. Frequently he moved from one solid fact or argument to another, without the usual repetition and elaboration, far too quickly for his audiences to digest or even applaud his conclusions. Nor would he always pause for applause when it came.

AVOID

He spoke at first with no gestures, though he gradually developed a short jab to emphasize his points. Often his tone was monotonous. Often his emphasis was on the wrong word. But often when his audiences were large and enthusiastic—particularly indoors, if the hall was not too vast—an almost electric charge would transmit vitality back and forth between speaker and listeners.

AVOID

He used little or no slang, dialect, legalistic terms,

contractions, clichés, elaborate metaphors or ornate figures of speech. He refused to be folksy or to include any phrase or image he considered corny, tasteless or trite. He rarely used words he considered hackneyed: "humble," "dynamic," "glorious." He used none of the customary word fillers (e.g., "And I say to you that is a legitimate question and here is my answer"). And he did not hesitate to depart from strict rules of English usage when he thought adherence to them (e.g., "Our agenda *are* long") would grate on the listener's ear.

The intellectual level of his speeches showed erudition but not arrogance. Though he knew a little French ("very little," he commented in 1957 after a somewhat halting telephone conversation with the King of Morocco on the North African situation), he was most reluctant to include any foreign words in his addresses.

He was not reluctant, however, particularly in those pre-1960 days, to pack his speeches with statistics and quotations—frequently too many for audiences unaccustomed to his rapid-fire delivery. While I learned to keep a *Bartlett's* and similar works handy, the Senator was the chief source of his own best quotations. Some were in the black notebooks he had kept since college—some were in favorite reference books on his desk, such as Agar's *The Price of Union*—most were in his head.

He would not always be certain of the exact wording or even the author of a quotation he wanted, but he could suggest enough for his staff or the Library of Congress to find it. Preparing his brief, effective statement against the isolationist Bricker Amendment to the Constitution, for example, he told me, "Someone—was it Falkland?—gave the classic definition of conservatism which went something like 'When it is not necessary to change, it is necessary not to change.' Let's include the exact quotation and author."

He also liked on occasion—especially with college

audiences which he enjoyed—to include humorous illustrations and quotations in the body of his speeches. An excerpt from a particularly abusive debate between earlier Senators and statesmen always delighted him, possibly because it contrasted so vividly with his own style of understatement.

Humor in the *body* of a prepared speech, however, was rare compared to its use at the *beginning* of almost every speech he made off the Senate floor. While here, too, he preferred historical or political anecdotes, both the quality and the sources of this introductory material varied widely. He believed topical, tasteful, pertinent, pointed humor at the beginning of his remarks to be a major means of establishing audience rapport; and he would work with me as diligently for the right opening witticism, or take as much pride the next day in some spontaneous barb he had flung, as he would on the more substantive paragraphs in his text.

Successful stories told by a toastmaster or by another speaker would be jotted down for future reference. Collections of Finley Peter Dunne and Will Rogers, current newspaper columns and quotations, the works of writers who liberally sprinkled their thoughts on history and government with amusing expressions or examples (such as Denis Brogan and T. V. Smith) were all carefully mined. Standard joke-books were never used, nor would he ever say, "That reminds me of the story of . . ." as a bridge to some irrelevant and lengthy anecdote, but many an old saw was adapted to modern politics and to a particular audience.

No laugh-getter once used or even considered was ever discarded. A large "humor folder" in my files grew continuously. Omitting all anecdotes from the texts that were distributed to the press usually avoided their being publicized, and thus made possible their use in another speech in another part of the country. Audiences watching him scribbling away during dinner often thought he was rewriting his speech, as at times he was. More often he was jotting down the opening lines most appropriate to that audience, working in many cases from a typewritten "humor list" of one-line reminders.

Except for joking about the political liabilities of his own religion, he avoided all ethnic references as well as all off-color remarks in public (although not in private). The only joke which backfired was told early in his Senate career. "The cab driver did such a good job rushing me to this luncheon," he told a Washington audience, "that I was going to give him a big tip and tell him to vote Democratic. Then I remembered the advice of Senator Green, so I gave him no tip and told him to vote Republican." The Associated Press solemnly reported the story as though it had actually happened, and a storm of letters from cab drivers and their wives caused the Senator to think twice about his choice of humor in the future.

He liked to poke fun at politics and politicians, his party, his colleagues and himself. He liked humor that was both topical and original, irreverent but gentle. In his eight years in the Senate no speech assignment worried him longer or more deeply than his role as Democratic jester for the Washington Gridiron Club Dinner in 1958. His successful ten-minute talk on that occasion was drawn from several hours of material gathered from many sources and tried on many "experts." Thereafter he tended more and more, except perhaps on the 1960 campaign circuit, to use that kind of political, more subtle and self-belittling humor, for it was naturally consistent with his own personality and private wit.

His best humor, of course, was spontaneous, and his increasing confidence on the platform brought increasing numbers of spur-of-the-moment gibes. Candor and humor, when combined, can be dangerous weapons politically, and at times he had to restrain his natural instincts in this direction.

In addition to the humor file, we kept a collection

of appropriate speech endings—usually quotations
from famous figures or incidents from history which,
coupled with a brief peroration of his own, could
conclude almost any speech on any subject with a
dramatic flourish. On many of the hectic precampaign
trips of 1957-1959, he would leave one community
for the next with a paraphrase from a favorite Robert
Frost poem:

> Iowa City is lovely, dark and deep
> But I have promises to keep
> And miles to go before I sleep.

He soon knew all these closings by heart; and while
the standard closings, like the humorous openings,
were almost always omitted from his release texts
in order to facilitate their continued use elsewhere,
his own reading copy (prepared in extra-large type)
would have merely a word or a phrase to indicate
the appropriate close: e.g., "Candles," "General Marshall," "Rising or Setting Sun."

Obviously the Senator was capable of selecting and
remembering his own peroration without the help of
these few words. But he looked upon his text and
each part of it as insurance. Should the pressures of
the moment or the fatigue of the trip benumb his
brain as he stood on his feet, he wanted a complete
text in his hands which he could follow or at least
take off from. He would often deviate from his text
or delete passages previously approved and sometimes discard it entirely. But—particularly in earlier
days, when he knew his extemporaneous remarks
were likely to be less organized, precise and grammatical than a more carefully prepared text—he
wanted the reassurance a manuscript gave him.

GHOSTWRITERS

President Nixon is said to have an even more elaborate stable of ghostwriters than Kennedy had. One of them specializes in humor, another in the poetic touch, a third in economics, a fourth in crime, and so on.

If you use outside help in preparing your speech, be sure to make your own decisions about what you want to say. Then work as closely with your writer as Kennedy did with Sorensen. Let the preparation be a mutual enterprise—but make sure the resulting speech bears the stamp of your own thoughts and personality. It has to reflect *you*.

A ghostwriter, who had been doing a series of articles for Samuel Goldwyn, fell ill, and one of the pieces was written by a substitute ghost. Goldwyn, reading this article, expressed dismay, "This," he said, "is not up to my usual standard."

Some men come to my first speechmaking class and read speeches that obviously have been manufactured for them by someone else. Their talks fit their personalities about the way my husband's golf shoes would fit my feet. One of the first things a speaker must learn is to choose a ghostwriter who understands him and will work closely with him. If you and your writer do not operate on the same wave length, get another ghost!

EDIT!

When the draft of your talk is ready, the time has come to edit, edit, edit. Check it against the following list:

1. Have I honored all requirements of the talk? ☐
2. Have I researched the topic enough? Investigated all sources? ☐
3. Have I taken into account the nature of the audi-

ence—its economic level, sophistication, culture, age, sex, experience, etc.? ☐

4. Have I rechecked to make sure the talk fits the allotted time? ☐

5. Have I "boiled down" the scope of the topic for the time allotted? ☐

6. Have I constructed the talk so it has a clear purpose and makes a point at the end? ☐

7. Have I enough strong ideas in the body and have I developed them sufficiently? ☐

8. Have I arranged them in good order? ☐

9. Have I asked questions, used "you" enough? ☐

10. Have I an appropriate introduction? ☐

11. Have I a strong conclusion? ☐

12. Have I enough variety, specifics, and continuity? ☐

13. Does my language appeal to sight, sound, smell, taste, and touch? ☐

14. Have I used too many statistics? ☐

15. Have I familiarized myself with the locale, its idioms, news, etc.? ☐

16. Have I prepared the speech in *spoken*, not written language? ☐

Harry Emerson Fosdick once commented that a half hour of writing time is needed for every minute of speaking time. Mark Twain said it takes three weeks to write a good ad-lib speech. Be sure you have taken all the time you need to prepare your speech well.

REMEMBER:

◄ Thorough preparation lessens nervousness.

◄ Check the requirements of the talk: what your audience is like; the time limits; the proper clothing, etc.

◄ Make sure you have something worth saying—and listening to.

◄ Gather your material intelligently.

◄ Prepare your introduction for immediate impact.

◄ Convey your message in the body of your speech.

◄ Make your conclusion memorable.

◄ Edit, *edit*, EDIT.

19.   Preparing the Speaker — You

YOUR FRIEND THE TAPE RECORDER

By now you are ready to try aloud not just single sentences or paragraphs, but the speech as a whole. Ask relatives or friends to lend you their ears. They can help you analyze the structure and delivery of your speech.

But your best friend and severest critic is your tape recorder. Deliver your talk into it. Listen objectively to the playback, pretending, as in earlier checks, that the speaker is someone you do not know. Make notes and edit again, adding or deleting as necessary. Repeat, re-edit, over and over until you are satisfied. Listen for faulty structure, errors of logic, poor usage, irrelevant examples and quotations. Are some of your words stoppers, either because they may be unfamiliar to your audience or because you find them difficult to pronounce? Do you conclude three or four times instead of once?

When you are satisfied with the organization of your talk, sit down and write it out once more, preferably typing it in triple space.

You are now ready for cue cards.

HOW TO USE CUE CARDS

Television actors use teleprompters or reminder cards as fail-safes in case they forget their lines. These latter are called idiot cards—and most professionals would rather use idiot cards than appear to be idiots.

I began synopsizing my talks on cue cards after seeing how beautifully they worked for Bob Hope, who was filming a show at Madison Square Garden. He kept giant-size cards in various locations where his gaze could pick them up without seeming to. He used the cards so skillfully that his chatter seemed entirely spontaneous and unrehearsed to television viewers.

If you want to sound spontaneous to your audience, buy a 6″ × 9″ looseleaf notebook with some file cards to match, and a punch. Punch the cards the long way for insertion in the book, so that they can be flipped up, like a wall calendar—not opened from side to side like a book.

Your talk by now is on paper. Go over it. Strike out such small words as "the," "and," "but," "for," "by," "with," "at," and "in." Also drop self-evident verbs, and abbreviate other words—but be sure that when the time comes you will recognize instantly what the abbreviations mean.

Next, transcribe this shortcut version of your talk onto your cards. Look at the sample on the next page. Notice that it is written with a felt tip pen, not in script but in print. Each letter is about a half inch high, so that an entire sentence can be scooped up in a single peripheral glance. It has been proven in our classes that print is easier to read than your own handwriting, even the clearest, or typing. So, resist the temptation to write script. It may be faster, but it also is harder to read. Don't use a typewriter either, unless it has jumbo type.

Read the first sentence of the unabridged paragraph in the following sample three times aloud. Then cover it with your hand, and go to cue-card abbreviation No. 1. You will find that the cues enable you to re-create the whole text of the sentence without hesitation. Try it.

In using cue cards, remember to:

1. Number each card.
2. Number each sentence and start each at left margin.
3. Leave plenty of white space between sentences.

A—FULL TEXT

No one can say that morale is high in America today. The President, in his State of the Union Message in January, spoke of "a certain restlessness" in the land. This is the understatement of the century. The "restlessness" looks dangerously like nothing less than a widespread loss of faith in America, in our political institutions, and in our whole middle class, technological civilization.

Editorial writers say that everywhere we look, something is wrong. But they usually point to the war in Vietnam and the Negro poverty problem in our cities as the causes of most of our troubles.

B—THE CUE CARD ABBREVIATION

1   NONE CN SAY MORALE HIGH AMER.. T'DAY.

2   PRES. JONSON... ST. OF UNION MESG., JAN...CERTAIN
        RSTLESNESS IN LAND

3   UNDERSTATMNT... CENTURY

4   RESTLESNESS...DANGROUSLY... NOTHNG LESS WIDE-
        SPRD LOSS FAITH AMER.
            IN PLITICAL INSTUTIONS
            IN WHL MIDDLE CLASS...TECNOLGICAL CIVILZA

5   ED. WRTRS EVRYWHR.. LOOK SOMTHNG WRNG.

6   BUT... USLLY POINT WR VIET...NEGRO POVRTY
        PROBLM... CITIES...CAUSES... MST TRUBLES.

Cue cards will give you the confidence that comes from knowing you will not falter even if some synapse in your mind short-circuits while you are speaking. They will enable you to speak more freely, almost conversationally. They will also free you to look at your audience. This is important, because that interchange of looks is the first step toward rapport. If you have to read your speech, your eyes are preoccupied with your text. With cue cards to back you up, you can look at the audience almost all the time.

Rehearse with cue cards as many times as is required to use them naturally. For me the magic number is generally eight. Your magic number may be two, or twenty, or anything in between. In any event, practice ALOUD as though in an actual speech situation—on your feet, not at your desk—and don't be satisfied until the speech seems almost to come by itself.

DON'T MEMORIZE—FAMILIARIZE!

"He who speaks as though he were reciting," says Quintillian, "forfeits the whole charm of what he has written."

The purpose of your rehearsals is not to memorize what you are going to say, but to become thoroughly familiar with the key expressions and the flow of ideas. If you memorize, your eyes are lack-luster, focusing inward, trying to remember words. If you read your speeches, you are communicating with the text instead of the audience; they see the top of your head instead of your eyes. (Nothing will make a bald-headed man switch from a full text to cue cards faster than to see himself on a television playback in which his polished pate instead of his animated face holds center stage.)

When young Abraham Lincoln was on a speaking tour, his roommate reported that the effectiveness of the future President's presentations was invariably in direct ratio to the amount of time he had spent rehearsing them—aloud, and on his feet. Simply looking over what you plan to say does not substitute for saying it, any more than looking over a swimming pool substitutes for a swim. I cannot say too often: Rehearse as if you were on the platform with an audience before you. On your feet. Aloud.

Now you are on the last lap of familiarization. Use that tape recorder again. Do you sound attractive? Vital? Self-confident? Warm? Knowledgeable? Informed? Vibrant? Sincere? Relaxed? Amusing? Clever? Check your ending. Do you strengthen it by pausing for effect? Is it strongly delivered?

Or do you sound dull? Tired? Cold? Uncertain? Monotonous? Affected? Tense? Confused? Perhaps even a little bit stupid? Do you conclude weakly and more than once?

Practice and check, practice and check, until you feel that you are the kind of speaker you would like to hear if you were in the audience.

D (FOR DO IT) DAY

You have arrived at D-Day. Last-minute preparations are in order.

First, the matter of dress. Remember—wear nothing that will distract your listeners from what you are saying. (One of the worst enemies a woman speaker can have is dangling, dancing earrings or a hat that hides half her face so people wonder what she looks like from the nose up.)

If you have time, go through one final tape recorder session. If there is not enough time for that before you have to leave for your talk, at least use the recorder for a last-minute check on the beginning and end of your speech.

ON THE SPOT

Be prepared to spend from one half to an hour checking the physical arrangements of the meeting place before the audience arrives. If possible in small meetings, and particularly in business meetings, ask to have the chairs arranged amphitheater style, in arcs rather than straight across. The more the audience can see of each others' reactions, the better it is for the speaker.

PROXIMITY BREEDS CONTENT

Get as close to your audience as physical conditions permit. I have at times had the lectern and microphone moved from the stage to the floor, or even sat on the edge of a platform stage dangling my legs, or moved my chair and sat among the group if it were small enough. A yawning chasm between speaker and audience is a psychological as well as a physical barrier.

LET THERE BE LIGHT

At a recent meeting in a New York hotel ballroom, the guest of honor sat on a dais beneath an overhanging balcony. Spotlights, fastened to the balcony rim, illuminated the tablecloth, the silver, the crystal, and the speakers' hands. Yet every face was left in shadow. Nobody had checked to see if the lights would illuminate the speakers' faces.

In Texas, before a concert, I found there was no spotlight in the hall. "We keep our eyes closed," said the chairwoman haughtily; "singers are to be listened to, not looked at." My accompanist was Josef Blatt, now head of the Opera Department of the University of Michigan. Joe was the most talented conductor and accompanist I ever had, and also the most conscientious and considerate. He refused to accept the chairwoman's verdict. Instead, on his own, he searched the city, and arrived finally at the concert hall with two borrowed spotlights which he had found illuminating the display sign on the lawn in front of a funeral home and attached them to the balcony rail. After the concert, the chairwoman agreed that the spotlights had added to the evening. "I had no idea," she said, "how much it adds to the enjoyment of a concert to be able to watch the singer's facial expression. Just think what we have been missing all these years!"

THE LECTERN

Make sure the lectern is the right height for you. Carlos Romulo, Foreign Minister of the Philippines, is an outstanding speaker but unusually short—just a little over five feet tall. To be seen, he always asks to have a box to stand on behind the lecturn.

Incidentally, Mr. Romulo says that as a young man his lack of height caused him agonizing feelings of inferiority until one day, in Paris, he visited Madame Tussaud's wax museum.

When he found that he was fully a half-inch taller than the life-size figure of Napoleon Bonaparte, he started to gain confidence. He knew the worst was over when he found himself on a platform in Houston, surrounded by tall Texans. One of them asked him how it felt to be a man of his stature "among us Texas giants." "Well," replied Romulo thoughtfully, "I guess you might say that it's rather like being a dime among nickels."

Back to the lectern: it is important to check the light. Often it not only lights up your notes, but also your Adam's apple or double chins. If you would rather have attention focused on your face than your Adam's apple, clip or Scotch-tape a sheet of paper or a napkin over the light to soften and diffuse it. I make a habit of keeping Scotch tape with my lecture book for this purpose.

MICROPHONE—FRIEND OR FOE?

Check the position of your microphone. Generally it should be not more than eight inches from your mouth. If it is in the wrong position, you may have to lean forward or stretch up to it in an awkward manner. If the microphone is wrong for you, adjust it until you are comfortable. The closer you are to the mike, the more intimate the sound. The more forcefully you project, the farther away from it you should be. I prefer the most conversational sound possible, and keep the microphone about six inches away, at chin height. Now and then I come closer for emotional effect.

You may have to ask for a gooseneck extension to bring the microphone closer.

If the microphone squeals or screeches, you may be touching it. Some mikes, like some dogs and babies, don't like to be touched by strangers. Take your hand off, and the squealing will stop.

Sometimes the sound "p" comes from the mike with a loud pop. If so, talk into it not straight on but at an angle.

THANKS, FRED!

If there is a sound engineer—Fred, for instance—make a point of meeting him and learning his name. It can forestall crises and help you make the mike your friend. Ask him to test the mike with you and to adjust it so the tone is warm and the volume does not blast. If you are a woman, you may want him to turn the tone control knob so there's less treble and more bass. Some added bass flatters a woman's voice, an overdose of treble results in a pinched, metallic sound. Get the right sound mix for you.

Without knowing Fred's name, in a minor crisis you could be a voice crying in the wilderness. If, despite arrangements, you cannot be heard by the audience, simply call, "Fred, can you please turn up the volume? I don't think they can hear me." You are apt to get prompt action. Fred, who has probably forgotten completely to turn up the sound, and is happily munching on a hamburger as he reads the racing form, will leap to his feet, feeling the hundreds of disapproving eyes fixed on his booth, and in a moment the volume will be restored.

Fred can help in another way. If the room is too close and hot, so that you see people fanning themselves or nodding, ask him to turn up the cooling system. Nothing defeats a speaker more than a room that is too hot.

POST TIME

While you are waiting to go on:

◄ Don't drink anything alcoholic—or, if you must, limit your intake to one drink. Pilots would be allowed to drink before flights if alcohol did not lessen their ability to have complete control of themselves and the plane. Competence cannot be preserved in alcohol. It will not make you a better speaker; it will only make you think you are better.

◄ Be moderate in your eating. There is more than meets the palate to the old saw that a full belly makes a sluggish mind.

◄ Study the audience while others are speaking. Do they respond quickly? Slowly? Negatively? Do they laugh easily? Is their reaction different from what you had expected? If so, you may wish to amend some statement you had intended to make; modify an argument; add a joke, or omit one. (Unless you are fully confident of your mastery of the situation, though, do not make a last-minute change in the basic structure of your speech.)

◄ Listen to the other speakers. This is a courteous gesture, and the audience will like you better for it. Moreover, you may hear something you want to acknowledge or that bears on what you are about to say.

◄ Confirm that your notes are in order. I have seen inexperienced speakers lose their place and go into a panic. Your notebook of numbered cue cards insures you against ever becoming confused in this way. Dog-ear the cards for quick flipping.

◄ Set your key-chain timer, now attached to the ring of your notebook, for five minutes less than the length of your talk plus the estimated time of the chairman's introduction of you.

BYE, BYE, BUTTERFLIES

However thoroughly you have prepared yourself, even if you are an old speaking hand the chances are that adrenalin is now pouring into your blood stream. Don't worry about a slight case of nerves; it only shows, as I said earlier, that you are a race horse rather than a truck horse. Below are prescriptions to combat butterflies. Memorize the steps and follow them while you are waiting to go on:

1. Sit in Executive Posture, doing a silent version of the steamkettle exercise. Press against the chair with your lower back, directing your tension into your vital center. Keep your upper abdominal muscles taut. This leaves the butterflies no place to flutter around in.

2. Permit *only* positive thinking. Avoid succumbing to the negative by repeating to yourself any one of these positive catch statements:

I am:

◄ Poised, prepared, persuasive, positive, powerful.

◄ Composed, confident, convincing, commanding, compelling.

◄ Effective, energetic, enthusiastic, enjoyable.

◄ Imaginative, informative, instructive, inspirational, impressive.

◄ Zestful, zippadeedoo, zing and zowie!

Or make up your own positive energizers. The words don't matter, as long as you saturate yourself with positive, upbeat feelings. Refuse to be negative or apprehensive.

3. Keep running your opening remarks through your mind. Have them literally on the tip of your tongue. You should know them well enough so that you can deliver your first four or five sentences smack into the eyes of your listeners without looking at your cards at all. (This should also be true of your concluding remarks. Say the last two or three sentences right into their eyes—no looking down here.)

Every speaker has his own butterfly net. Winston Churchill overcame his early fear of audiences by imagining that each of them was sitting there naked. Franklin D. Roosevelt is said to have pretended they all had holes in their socks.

I hope you won't have to go that far. Your audience is not a jury that has already found you guilty and is about to decide on your sentence. They want to like you. All you have to do is make it easy for them.

REMEMBER:

◄ Use cue cards. Don't memorize—familiarize.

◄ Rehearse aloud, on your feet, at least six times, editing after each playback. Make your tape recorder your editor.

◄ Check the physical arrangements on the spot—the lectern . . . the microphone . . . the sound engineer.

◄ Reinforce your confidence while waiting to speak. Banish those butterflies.

20. Delivering the Speech

> Without effective delivery, a speech of the highest mental capacity can be held in no esteem, while one of the moderate abilities, with this qualification, may surpass even those of the highest talent. —CICERO

ON YOUR WAY

And now, after all those hours and days of preparation, the chairman has introduced you, and you are on your way to the speaker's stand. Look happy as you make the journey. Look as though you would rather be there, about to speak to this particular group, than any place else in the world.

You may not really feel so joyful. William Lyon Phelps, for example, used to describe the speaker's table as "the pillory of torment."

"Having to speak at a public dinner in Chicago," he once recalled, "I found my place at the pillory of torment, the speakers' table; and there, seeing a magnificent man in evening dress, I gave him my name and grasped his hand with what cordiality I could command.

" 'I'm the headwaiter, sir,' said he.

" 'Shake hands again, old man,' I cried; 'you don't know how I envy you!' "

But it is fair to assume that Dr. Phelps, a relaxed and accomplished speaker, was not serious in that remark. Even if you still have a few nervous twinges, act enthusiastic, and you will be enthusiastic. Don't grin like a politician trying to please, but do smile. As the Chinese saying goes, "If you don't have a ready smile, don't keep a shop." In a speech you have to sell yourself before you can sell your message.

Even if you start with the audience entirely on your side, don't be quite as obvious as a cruise ship's social director ("Is everybody happy? Ha, ha, ha!"). Use what Madison Avenue calls "soft sell." But if the audience is not on anybody's side—if you are speaking to stockbrokers, for instance, on a day when the Dow-Jones average has dropped twenty points—be particularly chary about a hard-sell approach. It will only irritate them. Instead, present your message simply and warmly, until you arrive at the wonderful moment when the sun comes up over the horizon, and smiles at last appear on their faces.

The blossoming of those smiles, as seen from the platform, is a sight as beautiful as the first buds of spring. Suddenly your audience is receptive and relaxed; you *see* their approval. They look years younger—and you, in your relief, feel years younger yourself.

AT THE LECTERN

Take time to get yourself set. Deliberateness adds to your appearance of poise and confidence. The audience respects this kind of control.

Put your notes as high as possible on the stand. (You may have to tape your cue card book to the lectern so that it will stay where you want it.) This gives your eyes the shortest possible distance to travel between your cards and the audience.

Adjust the microphone to the right height for you. The previous speaker may have raised it to match his six feet three inches, while you are only five feet nine.

Now that your notes and microphone are set, set your body. Stand chest up, stomach in; weight, almost evenly distributed on the balls of both feet. (Do not lean on the speaker's stand; do your resting at home.) Look, and be, in command of yourself and the situation.

For perhaps six beats (a beat is the time it takes to say "one hundred and one"), eye-sweep the room, looking from one side to the other, from front to back, eye-clasping as many individuals as you can. Like a horse with a nervous rider, if they sense fear in you they will become nervous themselves; let your eyes communicate not "I'm scared to death," but "I'm glad *you're* here, I'm glad *I'm* here."

Your eyes make the first electrical connection with your audience. They turn on the current. The current is strengthened by an animated smile. Don't just look *at* people; look into their eyes. Give them, in turn, a few moments to take you in with *their* eyes before they have to put their ears to work.

ESTABLISHING RAPPORT

My good friend, Max Rubin, former president of the New York City Board of Education and currently a member of the New York State Board of Regents, illustrates the importance of attention-getting with this story:

A teacher herded an unruly child into the principal's office. "This boy," the teacher explained, "is absolutely unmanageable. He is constantly causing trouble in the classroom; he talks back; he . . ."

"Please," the principal interrupted, "he is only a child. You must show him love, patience, and understanding."

At that moment the boy took the principal's inkwell and threw it against the wall, where it splintered and spattered. The principal instantly seized him, turned him over his knees, and paddled him until he howled for mercy.

"But you just finished telling me," said the horrified teacher, "that we must show children patience, love, and understanding!"

"Oh yes," replied the principal, "but you have to get their attention first!"

When Judy Garland played the Palace, here is how she "got their attention first" and guaranteed herself a warm reception: In her opening number each night, she would start to sing, interrupt herself, glance down at her skirt, and exclaim, "Oh dear, my hem is undone! Does anybody have a safety pin?" Few of her fans were so equipped, but that was immaterial, since the pin was always supplied by the orchestra leader. She had accomplished her purpose— she had established complete and instant rapport with her audience.

BEGINNING YOUR TALK

I hope your first words won't be a cold, impersonal, old-fashioned salutation—a dreary list of the people around you: "Mr. Chairman, Mr. President, Mr. Secretary, distinguished delegates, fellow citizens . . ." Everyone knows who is there; a cordial "Good evening" will be much more appreciated.

Thank the chairman for his introduction. Comment, informally perhaps, about something you may have thought of or observed—perhaps a bit of local color—while waiting to speak. What it is doesn't matter as long as it strikes a sympathetic note with your audience. (Actually, you should have scribbled it on your top cue card sometime during the pre-speech period.) Then go into the body of your talk.

Never—but never—apologize. Follow the positive road all the way. "An apology," said Oliver Wendell Holmes, is only egotism wrong side out." It starts the audience looking for the shortcomings in you and your message. All the things you may be tempted to apologize for should have been taken care of, and would have with a little planning, long before D-Day. If you failed to take the time needed to research, develop, and rehearse your talk, or if you did not know, or learn, enough about your subject, you won't improve matters by pointing this out. Instead, you will lessen the audience's interest and put them on the lookout for anything about you or your talk that may be deficient.

NO POMP IN THIS CIRCUMSTANCE

The elaborate oratory of Daniel Webster, the fireworks of Patrick Henry, do not jibe with our times. We have traded oratory and fireworks for warm, personalized communication. The informal, conversational style is best suited to the fast-paced spirit of our age. As I said before, speak *with* your audience; don't talk *at* or *to* them. Project an impression of give and take, of interchange, as though it would be perfectly natural for one of the audience to reply to you in kind.

You call attention to any nervousness you may still feel if you fidget with pencils or jewelry, scratch your nose, pull your hair, grimace, weave, roll your head, or indulge in other distracting gestures. If gestures come naturally to you, use them moderately; but if you have to choreograph them, if they look wooden, skip them. Pockets are off limits; don't put your hands into them. If by some chance your hands do end up there, don't jingle coins or keys.

By all means keep your eyes up for the opening sentences and the conclusion of your talk. During these key periods, try not to look down at your cue cards at all.

Eye-sweep throughout the talk. Let the audience see as well as hear your sincerity; let your eyes do some of the talking. After the initial eye-sweep, continue to look briefly, personally, from one person to another, even the one farthest away. Remember, as an actor does, to make the man in the last row of the balcony feel that you want to communicate with him as much as with the woman in the first row of the orchestra.

Be on the lookout for your listeners' reactions. Your eyes can pick them up instantly. The life or lack of life in their expressions, their fidgeting or their whispering, their alertness or their nodding, will give you all the clues you need.

When Carl Sandburg fell asleep at a young playwright's dress rehearsal, the dramatist was outraged. "How could you sleep," he asked, "when you know how much I wanted your opinion?" "Young man," replied Sandburg, "sleep *is* an opinion."

Don't let your eyes stay glued to your notes, or drift out the window, or contemplate the ceiling or floor, or flit and flutter about the walls. And while we are on the subject of eyes, try to avoid wearing glasses unless they are part of your public image, or unless you are nearly blind without them. If you must wear them, don't put them on until you have started your talk. The light reflecting on your glasses may cut off your eyes from your audience; and the connection between your eyes and theirs is the lifeline which holds you and them together.

Keep your ears open to the way you sound, just as you did when you played back your voice on the tape recorder. If you hear monotony creeping in, give your voice a shot of added energy and enthusiasm.

Pause at appropriate intervals for emphasis and effect. Signal ahead to the audience by your cadence, pacing, and pauses when you are nearing your conclusion. The kind of punctuation Mary Martin taught me for signaling applause with my hands—letting them know for certain the song was ending—has its counterpart for a speaker. Let the audience know you are slowing to a halt.

TIME TO RETIRE

All the while you have been talking, the timer in your pocket or on the lectern has been moving toward its buzzing point. When it sounds, you have five minutes in which to ring down the curtain on your talk. You should have passages in mind that can be dropped without damage, if necessary, to meet your deadline in case you fell behind. Remember to give your last thoughts—like the first ones—right to your listeners' eyes without looking down at your cards. After your last word, hold your look for two beats, and murmur a quiet "thank you." You have crossed the finish line.

Let it never be said of you, "I thought he would never finish." Follow the advice I was given when singing in supper clubs: "Get off while you're ahead; always leave them wanting more." Make sure you have finished speaking before your audience has finished listening. A talk, as Mrs. Hubert Humphrey reminded her husband, need not be eternal to be immortal.

To paraphrase the Toastmaster's Manual:

> Stand up to be seen;
> Speak up to be heard;
> Wind up to be appreciated.

QUESTIONS AND ANSWERS

When first in opera, I was approached by a most distinguished-looking gentleman who introduced himself as a claque master. His group, he explained, provided applause to singers, under stated conditions and for a certain recompense, plus free seats for the claque.

The claque would applaud to order: when the singer entered; when she exited; when she hit her highest note; as her aria faded away. Or they would bring the applause back as it faded; start the bravos early or late; applaud to heighten excitement or to create it. You could order an infinite variety of audience reactions as if by catalogue. The new singer who had no claque would, by comparison, seem an utter failure in a performance where all the other singers had themselves protected by these showers of applause.

To protect yourself in the question-and-answer period, if one follows your talk, you should ask the committee to place three or four preselected questions in the audience. While these questions are being answered, others of the audience will be gathering their courage to ask questions of their own. It gives them time to get started.

If, however, a lull does set in, you can fill it by putting forward questions yourself, this way:

"The other day someone asked me . . ."
"People often wonder whether . . ."

Questions show the interest and involvement of the audience in what the speaker has had to say, just as applause shows approval of the singer. In effect your planted and reserve questions create the momentum. They involve your audience. This is not cheating; you are helping your listeners to start a process they often do not know how to start by themselves.

Make a point, by the way, of repeating the questions you are asked, to be sure that all of the audience has heard and understood them. If a question is too long, or simply a cover-up for a speech by the questioner, do not let your impatience show. Cut him off if necessary, but do so with friendliness, poise, and good humor.

When you feel that you have hit the peak of the question-and-answer activity, and interest is just beginning to wane, bring the whole session cordially to an end, before it goes into a decline, and thank the audience warmly for their attention.

Remember:

◄ You must get attention at the lectern *before* you speak. Use your eyes, and a posture of authority.
◄ Eye-sweep throughout the talk.
◄ Watch for the reactions of your audience in their eyes, and adjust as required.
◄ Finish on time.
◄ Use the claque approach if necessary to get the question-and-answer period started.

21. Don't Be Chairman of the Bored!

With words we govern men.   —BENJAMIN DISRAELI

"The winds are always on the side of the ablest naviga-
tors," said Gibbon. In these days gatherings tend to be
less formal than they once were, but the functions of
the navigator—the chairman or the toastmaster—is as essential as ever. Often the two posts fall into the lap of the
same person. We are dealing here with a general list of
responsibilities for an average program. The responsibilities
of the chairman or toastmaster are similar for almost every
type of program.

As chairman, your concerns include casting the characters, timing the meeting, making it interesting, and seeing
to it that everything goes smoothly. Many of these chores
can and should be delegated. Nonetheless, you are going
to have to take care of innumerable details, some of them
boring, without overlooking or neglecting any.

Sometimes the speaker is chosen first, sometimes the
topic. If you have decided on a topic, select speakers who
will throw light on it, whether or not they throw heat. A
little of both is desirable.

SCHEDULING THE TALKS

In arranging the order of speakers, remember that, since you want your program to build in interest as it goes along, the most important speaker should be the last, and he should get first choice of the subject matter.

Make clear to each speaker exactly how much time has been allotted to him. This point cannot be stated too vigorously; he has to know you mean it.

A speaker was told he was to begin his talk to a businessmen's luncheon at 1:15 P.M. He asked how long he should talk.

"As long as you wish," was the reply. "We all leave at one-thirty."

To make the warning on time limits still more emphatic, explain to each speaker what your cut-off signal will be—and tell him it has to be observed.

Even your principal speaker should not talk more than twenty minutes, and his forerunners' talks should be briefer. The most fascinating speaker has trouble holding an audience for more than thirty or thirty-five minutes. Few indeed should speak for more than half that time—unless they are the only speakers or are lecturers.

Remember—forty-five minutes of varied, well-paced, sparkling talks is vastly preferable to a dull and dragged-out hour.

If you are chairing a luncheon—especially a women's luncheon—bear in mind that many of the women in attendance may have to pick up children at school or at least be home when their children get there. If your audience needs to be on its way by two-thirty, anyone who starts to speak at two-twenty is murdered—and you, as the chairman, are accessory after the fact.

So plan your meeting backward from the two-thirty deadline. Let us say you have allotted an hour for speeches, which is quite enough. Luncheon must be over, then, not later than one-twenty to allow ten minutes for introductions. Even a large gathering can be fed in fifty minutes, bringing you to your one-thirty starting time. Take care of your unimportant announcements and acknowledgments, door prizes, etc., during the meal. They are seldom so transcendentally important that they must be heard in rapt silence. They can stand the clink of spoons.

For an evening affair with dinner and no music, serve cocktails at seven, and dinner at eight. Start the speeches (no more than three, of varying lengths) at nine. The guests can be on their way home by ten.

Any schedule is only as good as your insistence on abiding by it. If the schedule says the meeting is to open by twelve-thirty, don't open it at twelve forty-five.

INSTRUCTIONS AND EQUIPMENT

Though the ultimate responsibility is yours, enlist as many helpers as you need. One may arrange for the flowers; another for the catering; a third for the tickets. Delegate your most reliable assistant to see to it that the stage is properly lighted and that the chairs and tables are placed properly (often they are too far apart, giving a cold atmosphere), leaving space in the back of the room but closing in the front for intimacy. He will make sure that there are enough microphones, that there is a glass of water for the speaker (no pitchers, please). At a meeting I spoke at not long ago, there were lozenges on the lectern—a considerate though unnecessary touch.

While I am on the subject of physical furnishings, I urge you to rent a spotlight if the meeting is large enough to justify its use. The few pennies it costs to throw a light on the speakers will be returned many times over in the increased attention they will get. Rent the best possible amplifying equipment, too.

TREAT YOUR SPEAKERS WITH TLC
(tender loving care)

Have someone confirm the speaker's plane or train schedule and his accommodations at least a week in advance. He should be met at the station or airport, and taken to the hotel or home where he is to stay. Ask him first, though, if he would like to check the meeting place on the way to make sure that the lights, microphone, reading stand, and other arrangements are satisfactory. Often there is a supper or reception after the meeting. Ask him if he wants to attend. (He may feel like Elbert Hubbard, who, asked what he charged for a speech, said, "Two hundred dollars—two hundred and fifty if I am to be entertained afterward.")

Advise the speaker exactly when he should arrive at the meeting. If possible, send a car for him.

BE WARM BUT NOT WASTEFUL IN YOUR WELCOME

Begin the program with spirit. Your welcome should be brief and to the point: "We are happy to have you all here. Now we will sing the national anthem (I wish someone would write an anthem *everybody* could sing!) and then the Reverend John Miller will give a brief invocation." (Make sure in advance that the Reverend Miller understands *he* is to be brief, too. An invocation should not turn into a sermon.) After the invocation, it is enough to say, "Now—enjoy your dinner!"

YOU'RE OFF!

To start the program, tap firmly on the microphone with your finger, or on the lectern with a gavel. (There is no use rapping if the gavel is not within microphone range so adjust the microphone to angle in and pick up the sound.)

Rap with authority—once, twice, three times. Don't scold if your guests do not fall instantly silent; people do like to finish their sentences. I once heard a chairwoman alienate an audience by saying, "Now, if you are not going to be quiet, we are just not going to give you the program." What a silly thing to say. Obviously, she was going to give them the program. If you speak to an audience as if they were naughty children, you can expect them to respond like naughty children.

But say a forceful word or two; this is no time to be a mouse. Be direct and authoritative. You need only say into the microphone (but con brio!): "Ladies and gentlemen!" It may take a moment or two, but they will fall quiet.

It is gracious, either before or after the speeches, to thank the people who have worked to arrange the meeting. Don't belabor this. For the sake of crispness, give a blanket acknowledgment when you can: "Our thanks to all who have worked so hard to make this meeting a success." If, however, the situation requires individual acknowledgments, make them in a bundle, quickly, permitting applause only at the end rather than after each name.

Introduce the notables on the dais crisply, thus:

"Since time is short, and we want a full opportunity to hear our guest speakers, I am going to introduce the distinguished ladies and gentlemen at the head table rather quickly. Each one will stand and show himself to you as I give his name, but please withhold your applause until they have all been presented."

Then reinforce the request by the rhythm of your introductions. If you pause for a beat between one name and the next, the audience will think they should applaud anyway. Zip right along: "The dynamic Miss Lena Horne→Mr. Arnold Neustadter, brilliant young president of Zephyr American who has made Rolodex an office-hold word→Mr. Milton Raymond, wizard of the stock market and the golf course→Mr. Ernest Wolff, internationally famous financier." Your pacing, tone, energy, and drive must say, "This is an express→no local stops."

But your introductions must also be enthusiastic. Speak each person's name as if it were the most important in the world. To him it is. And don't fail to identify him, preferably with a colorful adjective or phrase.

The amount of time you give to introducing the main speaker depends partly on how important he is. It would be a rare person indeed whose introduction required more than three minutes. That's for heroes! Half that time is generally enough.

Your introductions should reflect a warm anticipation and a sense of genuine excitement over the person and the message the audience is about to hear. Do not be effusive, but certainly be complimentary. Don't make him the greatest thing since air conditioning, but do make him almost the greatest. Don't give away what he is going to say, but do pique the audience's interest.

The Reverend Harry Emerson Fosdick graciously accepted one chairman's send-off this way: "There isn't a word of truth in those kind remarks but thank God for the rumor." After another chairman's glowing introduction, the speaker smiled and said, "After such an introduction, I can hardly wait to hear what I have to say."

Be the brief, smiling transition between one speaker and the next. If you are going to comment on a speaker's remarks, make notes while he is talking. Your thanks should be complimentary if possible, but above all brief:

"We are grateful to Irving Mitchell Felt for giving us his insights into the problems of our community. Certainly we'll want to pass on these new facts to our friends who have not had the good fortune to be here today."

Sometimes, unfortunately, there is not much of a

complimentary nature that can be said about a talk. It does not help, in that event, to pretend to an ecstasy you don't feel. I once heard Leonard Bernstein take care of this problem, backstage after the opening of a particularly poor play, by exclaiming, "What a show!" And then there is the story of Mrs. Moran, who met a friend pushing a singularly unattractive baby granddaughter in a carriage in the park. "What a baby!" exclaimed Mrs. Moran tactfully. To which the proud grandmother replied, "Ah, but you should see her picture!"

Thank the last speaker and summarize briefly. Remain upbeat. Be dynamic; be enthusiastic; praise the speakers; praise the audience. But don't waste time. Half a minute is plenty:

"You have been a rewarding audience. Our thanks to you, and we look forward to seeing you next year."

If you have followed the suggestions in this chapter, they will look forward to seeing *you* again, too.

REMEMBER:

◄ Plan your agenda painstakingly.
◄ Assign responsibilities.
◄ Check equipment in advance.
◄ Pace your introductions.
◄ Treat your speakers with tender loving care.
◄ Watch your time, and stick to your schedule.

A Parting Word

If you have read this book with care and followed the suggestions conscientiously, by now you are well on the way to becoming a more effective, confident speaker, to having better speech habits and a more attractive voice. You are already beginning to derive benefits like these:

◄ A new sensitivity to others. You feel a connection with them. You consider their feelings and needs in what to say. You have learned not just to speak better, but to listen better.

◄ A new awareness of yourself. You see and hear yourself as others see and hear you. You are in command of yourself. You say what you want to say in the way you want to say it.

◄ A new self-confidence. You move through your business and social life knowing that people enjoy listening to you and respect what you have to say.

◄ A new sense of power. You know you can persuade and convince.

Nearly a century ago, Prime Minister William Gladstone remarked that "the time and money spent for training in speech and voice is an investment that pays greater dividends than any other." His Tory rival and successor, Lord Salisbury, agreed: "In these days," he said, "whether we like it or not, power is with the man who can speak."

So it remains today. Your ability to communicate warmly and persuasively determines the image others have of you—and that you have of yourself.

Let me make one parting request. Even if you are confident that you have now whipped your major speech difficulties, do not tuck this book away and forget it. It is easy to slip back into old, bad habits. Keep this book where you can refer to it conveniently. Recheck your speech at intervals, using the tape recorder that I trust you bought even before you finished the first chapter. If you catch any trace of the old distractors—if you find yourself again experiencing difficulties in conversation, speeches, or presentations—return to the hints that you found helpful before, and practice until those speech detractors are gone for good.

Keep your speech image in focus—from now on!

APPENDIX

APPENDIX

A. Speech Cosmetics

1. Stand in Executive Posture, chest up, stomach in, weight evenly distributed on balls of both feet.

2. Do *not* take big breaths; a quick sip through the mouth is adequate.

3. Feel vital center constantly tucking in as you exhale and as you talk. Do not hold it rigid.

I. PRACTICE TWO OR MORE OF THE FOLLOWING FIVE MINUTES DAILY:

a *Steam Kettle.* Hiss out, as long as you can on one breath.

b *Numbers.* 1. Count fast on one exhalation (1, 2, 3, 4, 5, 6, 7, 8, 9, etc.) to 60 or 70.

2. Do the same as above with "uh" between the numbers.

c *Candle.* Pretend your finger is a candle. Blow at it with a thin stream of air on one exhalation in three positions at 10″, 16″, and arm's length. Your vital center should be pulling in toward your back.

II. DO ALL OF THE FOLLOWING WITH

V itality
E nthusiasm

E nergy
V igor
as if:
  a on the telephone
  b to someone ten feet away
  c to a group thirty feet away.

(1) I was born an American, I shall live an American, I shall die an American!

—DANIEL WEBSTER

(2) As a citizen of this great country, you must count your blessings and exercise your rights!

(3) A situation like this demands strong minds, courageous hearts, abiding faith and ready hands!

(4) We are fighting by ourselves alone, but we are not fighting for ourselves alone.

—WINSTON CHURCHILL

(5) I am ready to act now, and for my action I am ready to answer to my conscience, my country, and my God.   —J. THURSTON

(6) Arise then ye people of the earth, arise, ye sorrow stricken and oppressed.

—RICHARD WAGNER

(7) We need dreamers, thinkers, doers—we need *you!*

(8) Zion, O Zion, O Zion, that bringest good tidings, get thee up into the high mountains; O Jerusalem, that bringeth good tidings, lift up thy voice with strength; lift it up, be not afraid; say unto the cities of Judah, Behold your God!   —ISAIAH 40:9

FLOWING SPEECH *(also aid to pacing speech)*

1. First say each capital letter phrase by itself on one flowing breath.
2. Then say two phrases (connected with and) on one flowing breath.
3. Then the whole sentence smoothly flowing.

4. If you are a speed talker, drag out the phrases.

5. If a slow talker, tighten them up.

I. SENTENCE EXAMPLES

(He was) ROUNDING THE BEND (and) TURNING THE CORNER.

(He was) ROUNDING THE BEND AND TURNING THE CORNER.

HE WAS ROUNDING THE BEND AND TURNING THE CORNER.

A. 1. (He will) BOARD THE BUS (and) FIND A SEAT.

2. (I shall) BUY THE BOOK (and) STUDY IT WELL.

3. (We like to) BUY FINE WINE (and) SAVOR ITS FLAVOR.

4. (You must try to) CHEW YOUR FOOD SLOWLY (and) LET IT DIGEST.

5. (He ought to) THINK HIS PLANS OUT WELL (before) PUTTING THEM INTO ACTION.

6. (She said) "IF I AM GOING TO GO SHOPPING (I ought not to) SPEND ALL MY MONEY."

B. 1. This brave new world has all too soon grown old and weary.

2. The moon was drifting among the clouds and the river danced below.

3. The woods are lovely, dark and deep. But I have promises to keep, and miles to go before I sleep.

—ROBERT FROST

4. Alone, alone, all alone, alone on a wide sea.

5. I wandered lonely as a cloud that floats on high o'er vales and hills.

6. The wind is blowing all day long, a weeping, wailing lover's song.   —WILLIAM WORDSWORTH

7. I am thy father's spirit, doomed for a certain term to walk the night.   —WILLIAM SHAKESPEARE

8. The smell of coffee freshly ground, of rich plum

pudding, holly crowned or onions fried and deeply
browned.   —CHRISTOPHER MORLEY, "Smells"

9. The Lord is my shepherd; I shall not want. He
maketh me to lie down in green pastures; he leadeth me
beside the still waters. He restoreth my soul.

II. ANTIDOTE FOR CHOP TALK, MUMBLING AND GONNA/WANNA

A. Swing through each phrase smoothly:

going to	going to speak well
going to think	going to go through
going to buy	want to
going to see	want to think
going to do	want to buy
going to win	want to see
going to improve	want to be
going to lose	going to say
weight	going to impress
	going to lose
	weight
	going to speak
	well
	want to accom-
	plish

B. Glide right through from beginning to end of each
sentence:

1. I'm going to call because I want to speak with
him.

2. He is going to ask for a raise and I don't want
to pay it.

3. She's going to do it if we want to have it done.

4. We're going to go to the office to see if we want
to go through with it.

5. They're going to make reservations because they
want to leave tonight.

6. If we want to do it, no one is going to stop us.

7. We want to see if they're going to go through with it.

8. Are you going to proceed even though you don't want to do it?

9. If I'm going to make a speech, I want to prepare it today.

10. If you want to try to look attractive, aren't you going to try to sound attractive too?

VOWEL SYMBOLS (*simplified*)

Symbols		Words
ah	as in	father, on, sergeant
ă	" "	add, laugh
ay	" "	ache, say, bait, break, vein
aw	" "	raw, all, thought, autumn
ee	" "	me, meat, people
eh	" "	met, head, any, said, bury
ih	" "	it, build, myth, pretty, business
oh	" "	bone, own, coach
oo	" "	food, move, shoe, truth, grew
ŏŏ	" "	good, should, put, worsted
uh	" "	up, trouble, alone, soda
uhr	" "	her, bird, church

DIPHTHONG SYMBOLS

aħih   as in   eye, height, like, rye, buy
aħoo   as in   cow, bough
awee   as in   coy, noise
yoo   as in   you, few, unit, beauty, Tuesday

(NOTE: We put a dash through ħ to indicate it is not pronounced.)

CONSONANT SYMBOLS

Unvoiced *Symbols*		*Words*	*Voiced* *Symbols*		*Words*
k	as in	kick, cat	g	as in	go
s	" "	soon	z	" "	zoo
th	" "	think	th	" "	the
sh	" "	she	zh	" "	azure
ch	" "	church	j	" "	George
eks	" "	excite	gz	" "	example
ksh	" "	luxury			
p	" "	pie	b	" "	buy
f	" "	fine	v	" "	vine
t	" "	toe	d	" "	dough

h	as in	hat
l	" "	let
m	" "	met
n	" "	net
ng	" "	sing
r	" "	red
w	" "	wed
y	" "	yes
z	" "	zoo

DRILLS FOR SOME OF THE MOST COMMONLY TARNISHED SOUNDS

"ah," as in father, art, hot

TO PRONOUNCE:

Tongue is relaxed and flat as a pancake in the mouth. Jaw is dropped lower than for any other speech sound.

Important and not only for itself but also because it is the key to producing attractive sounds in the diphthongs "ow" (which is a combination of the two vowels "ah" and "oo") and "eye" (a combination of "ah" and "ih," or "ee").

I. WORDS

1.	2.	3.	4.	5.
cot	cod	balm	are	barn
dot	God	calm	bar	charm
hot	hod	psalm	car	market
not	nod	qualm	far	garden
rot	rod	pond	chart	horror
sot	sod	don	heart	foreign
tot	wad	wan	part	chocolate

II. PHRASES

1.	2.	3.
not hot	fond of art	park the car
what yacht	calm contest	orange coral
ardent heart	contoured pond	moral quarrel
wash hard	Don Juan	foreign horror

III. SENTENCES

1. Demagogues, pedagogues, polliwogs, and hedgehogs indulge in monologues.

2. Opera is popular and Anna Moffo is boffo but rock is sock.

3. Almonds, large olives, and artichoke hearts are marvelous with cocktails.

4. Arguing harshly instead of discussing ardently and honestly is common.

5. Foreign products popular for import are caviar from Moscow, oranges from Lebanon, and tartans from Scotland.

6. Congressmen and politicians in Washington are constantly involved with parties.

7. Knotty problems are often like large rocks in a farmer's field; you solve them and promptly find larger ones underneath.

(Make up three sentences loaded with "ah" words, *saying each aloud* before you write.)

8.

9.

10.

IV. WORDS WHICH SHOULD BE PRONOUNCED PREDOMINANTLY "AH" BUT WITH A DASH OF "AW"

off	loft	boss	Boston
office	soft	loss	belong
cough	soften (t not pronounced)	frost	strong
coffee	often (t not pronounced)	cost	dog

ă as in apple, laugh

TO PRONOUNCE:

Lower front of your tongue.

Drop jaw so that there is about ½" between teeth.

Caution:

1. Do not allow sound to come through the nose (this can give you a twang).

2. Do not allow sides of mouth to pull back.

3. Do not pronounce a one-syllable sound in two syllables: "may-un" instead of "man" or "ay-und" instead of "and." Don't allow "Harry" to come out "hairy," "carry" to come out "care-y" or "marry" to come out "mare-y" or "may-ry."

I. WORDS

Bite into the "ă" vowel of apple and carry it over into all the other "ă" words as in the examples in Column 1 below:

1.	2.	3.	4.	5.
apple—at	add	as	an	and
bapple—bat	bad	gas	ban	canned
capple—cat	cad	mass	can	hand
happle—hat	dad	pass	Dan	land
mapple—mat	had	grass	man	candy
napple—nat	sad	plaza	ran	dandy

6.	7.	8.	9.	10.
am	cast	bask	answer	bath
dam	fast	mask	fantastic	after
ham	last	task	fancy	anxiety
lamb	past	clash	rampart	cancel
lamp	classed	crash	random	candid
camp	harassed	dance	scandal	castle

II. PHRASES

pass the glass	fancy pants
grand advantage	grand family
mass advance	bad analysis
band grandstand	half past
lamb sandwich	ran last
canned ham	stand fast
after class	can't stand

III. SENTENCES

1. Republican or democratic, there is often static in demanding practical and tactical actions—not to mention whim-wham distractions and flim-flam transactions.

2. An important factor for every actor is to act out romance and grand passion in a fashion that's smashin' and then he can cash in.

3. Analysts of habit, aptitude, and attitude can help stamp out bad management of companies and earn their gratitude.

4. Apples are handy but candy is dandy.

5. Madison Avenue advance advertising for new products can whet appetites, persuade the masses and woo the classes.

6. Haystack, haversack, horseback, and hackmatack all rhyme well with Hackensack.

7. In speaking don't exaggerate, exasperate, fabricate, or lacerate but try to captivate, animate, evaluate, substantiate, and fascinate.

(Make up three sentences loaded with "ă" words, *saying each aloud* before you write.)

8.

9.

10.

· *"aw" as in saw, talk, caught, bought*

TO PRONOUNCE:

The sides of the back of the tongue touch the sides of the upper back teeth. The back of the tongue is raised higher than "ah" of father. The lips are only *slightly* rounded.

I. WORDS

Words in Column 1 are used *only to illustrate relaxation* of lips. (Vowel sound in Column 1 is "uh" and in the other columns is "aw.") Words in Column 6 do not end with an "r" sound. If yours do, push the tongue tip against the lower gum ridge after pronouncing the "aw" to prevent this from happening.

1.	2.	3.
bus	ball	bought
cuss	call	caught
fuss	fall	fought
huff	hall	haughty
muss	mall	naught
pus	pall	sought
tough	tall	taught
crunch	crawl	wrought

4.	5.	6.	
dawn	oar	but	awe
pawn	core	"	claw
yawn	door	"	daw
pawed	floor	"	flaw
sawed	lore	"	law
toward	roar	"	raw
because	sore	"	saw
vault	thorn	"	thaw

(NOTE: Do not pronounce:

caught	as	cot
taught	"	tot
maul	"	moll
Paul	"	Poll
dawn	"	don
yawn	"	yon
water	"	wotta
daughter	"	dotter
awful	"	offal)

II. PHRASES

war talk	fought for causes	warm shawls
short form	corner store	all brawn
morning squall	ignore the horns	shorn lawn
walk tall	short pauses	pause for applause
taught courses	false yawn	long walk
pawn store	thwarted talk	sprawling crawl
autumn thaw	cautious call	appalling falls

III. SENTENCES

1. Automobile doors are sometimes too small for tall mothers-in-law.

2. Auctioneers should talk with wall-to-wall audibility.

3. Calling all morning can be appallingly boring.

4. Reporters abroad ought not to distort in order to write forceful stories.

5. Talk without thought is to be deplored, abhorred, ignored; with thought to be lauded, applauded, rewarded.

6. Law and order should be restored, supported, and enforced.

7. Sportsmen, authors, and lawyers mumble more than storekeepers, doormen, and exploring astronauts in orbit.

(Make up three sentences loaded with "aw" words, *saying each aloud* before you write.)

8.

9.

10.

"*eh*" *as in set*

TO PRONOUNCE:

Tongue: tip behind lower teeth, middle is slightly raised.

Caution:

"Eh" must not be replaced by "ih" in the "eh" words listed below. In pronouncing "ih," the tongue has more tension and the middle is higher. This guide is mostly for those who wish to lose the Southern sound.

I. WORDS

1.	2.	3.
bet	any	endless
beg	elm	entertain
bend	every	generation
less	engine	heavenly
mention	getting	immense

4.	5.
adventure	entire
expensive	mention
nonsense	pensive
September	sensitive
whenever	tentative

II. DISTINGUISH BETWEEN

"ih"	*"eh"*	*"ih"*	*"eh"*
bit	bet	bid	bed
mit	met	did	dead
pit	pet	lid	led
sit	set	rid	red

"ih"	—	*"eh"*
din		den
bitter		better
infliction		inflection
imminent		eminent

III. SENTENCES

1. The tender, sentimental gender annexes, perplexes, and vexes when compelling, retelling, or rebelling.

2. To be tremendously effective be selective, objective, and a little reflective but not introspective.

3. Many eminently successful men tend to be better spenders than lenders.

4. Tension, pent-up envy, and resentment rob you of contentment, mental well-being, and health.

5. Intensive dedication to extensive education brings splendid treasures and extra measures of exceptional pleasures.

6. Editors, commentators, and investigators should question events relentlessly and incessantly.

7. Senseless, excessive feminine expense offends and incenses the gentlest of men.

(Make up three sentences loaded with "eh" words, *saying each aloud* before you write.)

8.

9.

10.

"uhr" as in her, burn, search, bird

TO PRONOUNCE:
1. Start with "uh" and go into "r" sound: uh-r=uhr.
2. Do not go from "uh" into "ee": uh-ee=uhee.
3. Say "uh-er, uh-er, uh-er, uh-er, uh-er" over and over.
4. Think *UHR!*

I. WORDS

1.

sir	→ search	her	→ hurry
sir	→ serve	her	→ heard
sir	→ certainly	her	→ Herman
sir	→ circus	her	→ hurt
fir	→ first	burr	→ burn
fir	→ further	burr	→ bird
fir	→ firm	burr	→ burst
fir	→ furnish	burr	→ Burke
fir	→ fervent	burr	→ Burt

3.

cur	→ curve
cur	→ cursory
cur	→ curtain
cur	→ curse
were	→ word
were	→ work
were	→ word
were	→ worse
were	→ world

II. PHRASES

worse world	third church	learn and earn
earthly worth	thirty-first	work don't shirk
first word	thirty-third	turn don't burn

III. SENTENCES

1. If the early bird shirks and does not turn he will not be there to catch the worm.

2. The smell of coffee on the burner perking wakes you up to feel like working.

3. The purpose of urban services is to furnish help for those with reverses.

4. A wordy preacher on his perch makes you want to doze in church.

5. Waitresses should serve with verve to earn the tips they think they deserve.

6. A man of virtue and of mirth is certainly worth a lot on this surly earth.

7. Girls with curls
> Like ermine and pearls
> But should curb their urge
> To splurge and splurge.

(Make up three sentences loaded with "uhr" words, *saying each aloud* before you write.)

8.
9.
10.

The diphthong, "aĥih" or "aĥee" as in eye, by, high, tie

TO PRONOUNCE:

"ah" as in "father" plus "ih" as in "it" (sometimes "ee" works better for people), mostly "ah" gliding into a dash of "ih" or "ee." (*ah → ih*)

Caution:

1. Tongue should remain flat as a pancake for the "ah" part of the diphthong.

2. If you have a nasal or tarnished "eye" sound, it helps to pretend you are very Southern.

3. Make certain that the corners of the mouth do not pull sideways and uglify the face.

4. Bite down as though into an apple, to make a big "ah" sound before the jaw comes up to end the diphthong with "ih."

5. If you're Southern and want to sound Northern, make sure you do not pronounce the "eye" diphthong as the "ah" vowel. The "ih" syllable *must* follow "ah."

I. HOW TO CONSTRUCT THE DIPHTHONG

A. Hold the first two "ah" syllables two beats each, so you force yourself to load the "eye" sound with "ah":

1.

naaħ,	naaħ,	naħih	—nigh
saaħ,	saaħ,	saħih	—sigh
maaħ,	maaħ,	maħih	—my
whaaħ,	whaaħ,	whaħih	—why
raaħ,	raaħ,	raħih	—rye

2.

baħ,	baħ	—buy
daħ,	daħ	—die
laħ,	laħ	—lie
paħ,	paħ	—pie
taħ,	taħ	—tie

3.

din	—don	—dine
win	—wan	—wine
hid	—hod	—hide
rid	—rod	—ride
tip	—top	—type

(NOTE: Where the ħ is marked with a dash it is not to be pronounced.)

B. Cover Columns 2, 4, and 6, and read the words from our spelling in Columns 1, 3, and 5.

1.		2.	3.		4.
aħih	—	I	knaħihf	—	knife
baħih	—	buy	raħihf	—	rife
haħih	—	high	waħihf	—	wife
maħih	—	my	maħihn	—	mine
vaħih	—	vie	vaħihn	—	vine
applaħih	—	apply	waħihn	—	wine

5.		6.
raḣihd	—	ride
saḣihd	—	side
waḣihd	—	wide
craḣihd	—	cried
diḣnaḣihd	—	denied
riḣsaḣihn	—	resign

II. WORDS

Write out the following words in our spelling, saying each syllable aloud as you write.

1.			2.		
fine	—	faḣihn	nine	—	naḣihn
time	—		mine	—	
high	—		design	—	
climb	—		divine	—	
crime	—		combine	—	
grime	—		refine	—	

3.		
devise	—	diḣvaḣihz
exercise	—	
realize	—	
surmise	—	
surprise	—	
tantalize	—	

III. PHRASES

my eye	I try styles
fine time	my nine lives
buy wine	fine dividing line
applied design	stifles sighs and cries
divine kind	life of high times
right size	surprising devices and exercises

IV. SENTENCES

Because the "eye" sound is one of the most tarnished, here is a large dose of sentences.

1. Isometric exercises are designed to refine you to tiny sizes.

2. Strive to be alive in divine design on the bright side of life.

3. Trying to incite to riot and violence is a crime.

4. Mankind unites as of one mind behind the plights of pining nations!

5. Keep thy friend under thine own life's key.

—SHAKESPEARE

6. Idly sighing, sometimes crying, slightly mystifying, woman decides to bide her time.

7. Apply my ideas and do not resign yourself to signs of the times.

8. In times of trial, kindness triumphs in sublime style.

9. If my friends are one-eyed, I try to look at them in profile.

—JOSEPH JOUBERT

10. Rise and shine, the climate's fine, the air's like wine, the day divine, and all of it's mine!

(Write five more sentences of your own, saying "eye" words aloud as you write.)

11.
12.
13.
14.
15.

The diphthong "ow" as in how, bout

TO PRONOUNCE:

"ah" as in "father" plus "oo" as in "zoo" (ah→oo).
Caution:
Tongue should remain flat as a pancake for the "ah" part of the diphthong. Do not contract sides of the mouth.

I. HOW TO CONSTRUCT THE DIPHTHONG

A. Hold the "ah" syllables two beats, loading the word with "ah."

1.

haah, haah — how
naah, naah — now
craah, craah — crowd
praah, praah — proud
taah, taah — towel
gaah, gaah — gown
braah, braah — brown

2.

baah, baah — bout
daah, daah — doubt
caah, caah — count
faah, faah — found
maah, maah — mount
blaah, blaah — blouse
haah, haah — house

3.

toot, tot, tout
shoot, shot, shout
root, rot, rout
cooed, cod, cowed
wooed, wad, wowed
dune, don, down
boon, bond, bound

B. Do not produce the "ow" sound by going from "ay" into "oo," like "dayoon tayoon" (down town). Go from "ah" into "oo."

1.

bahoo	—	bow
cahoo	—	cow
nahoo	—	now
plahoo	—	plow
sahoo	—	sow
bahood	—	bowed
crahood	—	crowd
prahood	—	proud
shrahood	—	shroud
dahoody	—	dowdy

2.

ahout	—	out
bahoot	—	bout
clahoot	—	clout
drahoot	—	drought
dahoot	—	doubt
ahool	—	owl
dahool	—	dowel
hahool	—	howl
tahool	—	towel
vahool	—	vowel

3.

baħoond	—	bound
faħoond	—	found
haħoond	—	hound
maħoond	—	mound
paħoond	—	pound

braħoon	—	brown
claħoon	—	clown
daħoon	—	down
gaħoon	—	gown
naħoon	—	noun

II. WORDS

1.	2.	3.
hour	about	allow
ounce	around	cow
our	count	endow
out	down	now
owl	gown	plow
outside	found	bough
outcast	doubt	eyebrow
outline	mouth	scowl

III. PHRASES

1.	2.
about now	loud mouth
count down	count the house
our flower	shouting, howling crowds
brown cow	vowel sounds
downtown	found out

3.	4.
bounce to the ounce counts	out of bounds
down and out	around the south
somehow doubt	shout out loud
pronounce noun	without foundation
now is the hour	plowed the ground

IV. SENTENCES

1. Out of sight, out of mind, out of town, out of bounds.

2. Doubts may crowd around you but never doubt yourself.

3. Don't mouth the vowels but sound them out and round them out.

4. The ground that a good man treads is hallowed.
—GOETHE

5. "No smoking allowed" makes an ounce of prevention worth a pound of cure.

6. We allow our friends to hold us to account and to counsel us.

7. Doubt is the mountain which the coward knows not how to move but the power of faith can.

(Make up three sentences with as many words as possible having "ow.")

8.

9.

10.

The diphthong "oy" as in boy, oil

TO PRONOUNCE:

"aw" as in saw, plus "ih" (or "ee"). "aw→ih" or "aw→ee". Say "aw-ee, aw-ee, aw-ee, aw-ee, aw-ee."

Caution:
"oy" should not sound like "uhr."

I. WORDS

1.		2.		3.	4.
awih	→ oil	mawih	→ moist	joint	destroyer
bawih	→ boil	nawih	→ noise	point	employer
cawih	→ coil	pawih	→ poise	anoint	cloister
fawih	→ foil	chawih	→ choice	appoint	oyster
sawih	→ soil	rejawih	→ rejoice	loyal	moisture
tawih	→ toil	annawih	→ annoys	royal	spoilage

NOTE: Distinguish between:

oil—earl	loin—learn	noise—nurse	choice—church
foil—furl	poise—purse	toys—terse	join—journey

II. PHRASES

1.	2.
boil oil	disloyal employees
noise annoys	destroy employers
royal doilies	pointed joints
noisy oysters	noisome poison

3.

appoint and anoint
choice of coins
joy in the voice
points on poise

III. SENTENCES

1. Teenagers toil and trouble, coil and cuddle, boil and bubble.

2. Some cloy and clutter, spoil and sputter, enjoy and utter.

3. Annoyance shown in the voice can destroy poise.

4. Moisture is fine for choice oysters but may cause spoilage in soy beans and boysenberries.

5. Female lawyers, though adroit, if they're coy do sometimes annoy.

6. Costly toys multiply joys but spoil little boys.

7. Women don't enjoy embroidering doilies anymore and rejoice at having a choice of employment.

(Make up three sentences with as many words as possible having "oy.")

8.

9.

10.

Sound of "d"

TO PRONOUNCE:

The tip of the tongue on the gum ridge behind the teeth should be like a feather tip touching lightly.

Caution:

Do not allow an explosion of air to follow, causing the sound to come out "dz."

It should resemble the gentle drip, drip, drip from a faucet, not a splash.

I. WORDS

1.	2.	3.
do	did	Daddy
day	dog	today
dear	door	Tuesday
dark	draw	ready
doll	dress	under
dig	dread	candy
done	drab	children
down	drown	hundred

4.	5.
body	and
building	did
radio	bed
modify	bad
ready	hand
louder	cold
under	loved
window	second

II. PHRASES

dreaded incidents	dented fenders
desired goods	drugged dentists
doubtful doodling	standard precedent
dainty dessert	addicted to candy
deserved delight	deductible dividend

decidedly dumbfounded
deserted dead-end
dutiful dieting daughter
doggedly defended freedom
determined debater

III. SENTENCES

1. Engaged in Dallas, married in Des Moines, honeymooned in Deauville, divorced in Denver.

2. A domain divided against itself definitely does not long endure.

3. Dauntless daredevils dangled dangerously and defied defeat.

4. Don't devote days and days to despair, dawdling, and delaying decisions.

5. Demoralizing, outmoded procedures denied democratic dividends and decisions.

6. Avoiding duty, details, and devotion definitely does not decrease domestic discord.

7. Old doddering daddies don't dance divinely with discothèque debutantes.

(Make up three sentences loaded with "d" words, *saying each aloud* before you write.)

8.

9.

10.

"l" as in lady

TO PRONOUNCE:

a) Thin tongue tip darts up and touches upper gum ridge. Say as quickly as possible, "la, la, la, la, la, la."

b) Note the position of the tongue for the "t" sound when finishing the words in Column 1 below. Use the same position to begin words with "l" in Columns 2 and 4.

1.		2.	3.		4.
hit	—	lit	hist	—	list
set	—	let	bode	—	load
tot	—	lot	tiffed	—	lift
hate	—	late	oft	—	loft
root	—	loot	aft	—	laughed
route	—	lout	apt	—	lapped
fast	—	last	short	—	lord

Caution:

The tongue should not feel heavy as in making a "w" but light and agile as in articulating "t." Contrast the following:

1.			2.		
wean	—	lean	wed	—	led
weep	—	leap	wet	—	let
week	—	leak	wag	—	lag
weed	—	lead	wap	—	lap

3.			4.		
wake	—	lake	wise	—	lies
wade	—	laid	wink	—	link
wait	—	late	winch	—	lynch
ware	—	lair	wisp	—	lisp

I. WORDS

1.	2.	3.	4.
locate	ball	blaze	able
like	call	blame	bubble
lake	bill	claim	capable
leave	hill	click	durable
lounge	wall	flank	edible
lunatic	will	flicker	inimitable
lily	tall	slack	lovable
lovely	tole	slick	manageable

II. PHRASES

(Sail through the "l"s fast, pronouncing half as much "l" as you think you need.)

1.	2.
alone at last	yelled for help
along a lane	tell a tall tale
laws of the land	fill lanterns with oil
looseleaf calendars	three million Italians
light loads	William won a medallion
lovable lasses	bleak and blustery
legs of lamb	plump and pleasing plums
plastic plaques	flock to the flag
flash and flicker	clever clowns
climb the cliff	licorice lollypops

III. SENTENCES

1. Be likable, lovable, and livable or you're liable to be leavable, left, and lonesome.

2. A little farm well tilled,
   A little barn well filled,
   A little wife well willed,
   Give me, give me.

—JAMES HOOK

3. If you want knowledge, you must toil for it; if good, you must toil for it, and if pleasure, you must toil for it. Toil is the law. Pleasure comes through toil and not by self-indulgence and indolence. When one gets to love his work, his life is a happy one.

—JOHN RUSKIN

4. In order to love people and to be loved by them, one must train oneself to gentleness, humility, the art of bearing with disagreeable people and things.

—LEO TOLSTOY

5. The money-getter who pleads his love of work has a lame defense, for love of work at money-getting is a lower taste than love of money.

—AMBROSE BIERCE

6. If you will think about what you ought to do for other people, your character will take care of itself. Character is a by-product, and any man who devotes himself to its cultivation in his own case will become a selfish prig.

—WOODROW WILSON

7. Applause waits on success. The fickle multitude, like the light straw that floats on the stream, glide with the current still, and follow fortune.

—BENJAMIN FRANKLIN

(Make up three sentences loaded with "l" words, *saying each aloud* before you write.)

8.
9.
10.

"ng" as in singing

TO PRONOUNCE:

The back of the tongue is raised almost to the soft palate and stays up there clinging like a suction cup, the sound comes out of the nose. Contrast this with "n" where the tip of the tongue touches the front upper gum ridge. In the mirror, observe that the back of the tongue and the palate meet on "ng."

Say "ng" followed by "ah"—do not say "gah"—over and over.

Caution:

The sound must end in a hum! Do not end it with the hard "g" or a "k" click, nor with a simple "n."

I. CONTRAST

Say "n", then "ng" several times until you can *distinguish* between them: n-ng, n-ng, n-ng.

A. Now:

front hum		*back hum*	*front*		*back*
sin	—	sing	taken	—	taking
sun	—	sung	lighten	—	lighting
ban	—	bang	ribbon	—	ribbing
tan	—	tang	cannon	—	canning
win	—	wing	bacon	—	baking

B. Watch for and practice the distinctions between the following words. See that the words with "ng" spelling do not have the "k" or "g" clicking sound:

1. **2.**

Click		*Click*		*Back Hum*			
bag	—	bank	—	bang		sink	—	sing
hag	—	Hank	—	hang		wink	—	wing
rag	—	rank	—	rang		rink	—	ring
tag	—	sank	—	sang		think	—	thing
sag	—	tank	—	tang		tug	—	tongue

3. **4.**

dog	—	dong	bagging	—	banging
log	—	long	rigging	—	ringing
lug	—	lung	gagging	—	ganging
brig	—	bring	rigging	—	ringing
wig	—	wing	wigging	—	winging

II. PHRASES

Practice the following. (Be sure that you do *not* carry the "g" over to the following vowel!) Southerners: pronounce the back hum sound of "~~ng~~" *not* front tongue tip sound of "n."

1.	2.
belon~~g~~ing out	swin~~g~~ing up
carryin~~g~~ off	gleamin~~g~~ eyes
amon~~g~~ us	goin~~g~~ over
thron~~g~~ing in	growin~~g~~ old
flin~~g~~ing at	brin~~g~~ing up
win~~g~~ing over	believin~~g~~ all
wron~~g~~ art	fallin~~g~~ out
clin~~g~~ing on	pourin~~g~~ out
comin~~g~~ at	Lon~~g~~ Island
wron~~g~~ing us	swarmin~~g~~ over

III. EXCEPTIONS

A. Although the "g" is not pronounced in long, strong, young, it is pronounced in the comparative and the superlative.

longer	longest
stronger	strongest
younger	youngest

B. Words in which the "ng" is in the middle and where, if the following syllable were cut off, the remainder would have no meaning to the full word.

See: anger (ang?) dangle (dang?)
      angry (ang?) jungle (jung?)
      linger (ling?) single (sing?)
      finger (fing?)
      hunger (hung?) length (leng?)—pronounced "k"
                      strength (streng?)— "   "

IV. A. 1. Adoring not boring, bugging not huggirg.
       2. Blaming not flaming, roaring not soaring.
       3. Chanting not panting, booming not zooming.
       4. Kissing not hissing, deceiving not believing.
       5. Dawning not morning, hurrying not scurrying.
       6. Angling not tangling, lingering not fingering.

    B. 1. Believing but grieving, craving but raving.
       2. Quivering but shivering, dating but waiting.
       3. Working but shirking, homing but roaming.
       4. Towing but rowing, winking but thinking.
       5. Raving but craving, rousing but carousing.

    C. 1. Shooting and looting and rooting and tooting.
       2. Dining and wining and eating and bleating.
       3. Brightening and whitening, enlightening and frightening.
       4. Gunning and sunning and running and funning.
       5. Giving and living or sinning and winning.

"r" as in red

TO PRONOUNCE:

Lift the tongue so that its sides contact the upper side teeth. Then the tongue tip should point upward.

Caution:

1. Do not purse lips as in pronouncing "w" consonant or you will get a baby sound as "wabbit" for "rabbit."

2. For foreign-speaking people: There should not be any gargling sound at the back of the tongue. It is very difficult for many Europeans to eliminate this trill. There should be no vibration of the tongue. The "r" sound in English is much higher in the mouth than in other languages. Say "no tongue tension" aloud before every "r" word.

I. WORDS

1.	2.	3.
er—rabbit	are	already
"—race	bear	around
"—ran	car	every
"—read	dear	harrow
"—ready	chair	morning
"—red	far	orange
"—ride	fur	parrot
"—right	hear	story
"—round	her	very
"—run	near	weary

4.	5.
berate	brag
carry	brim
deride	brother
glory	crew
horrid	crop
morrow	dress
perish	drink
pouring	group
terrible	grasp
tyranny	ground

II. CONTRAST

1.			2.		
weep	—	reap	wait	—	rate
week	—	reek	wail	—	rail
weed	—	read	ware	—	rare
weal	—	real	wide	—	ride
wed	—	red	wise	—	rise
wad	—	rod	wink	—	rink
watt	—	rot	wench	—	wrench
won	—	run	wake	—	rake

III. PHRASES

1.	2.
droopy group	through trials
pretty proud	cramped and crowded
print programs	cream of the crop
present problems	create a crisis
trim trees	creeping crocodiles

IV. SENTENCES

1. Reading, writing, and 'rithmetic aren't enough to turn the trick in these electronic days of computers.

2. There is nothing stronger and nobler than when man and wife are of one heart and mind in a house; a grief to their foes, and to their friends great joy, but their own hearts know it best.   —HOMER

3. Armstrong, Aldrin, and Collins, three men of courage, heroes of this world, explorers and discoverers of outer space.

4. Loving kindness is greater than laws; and the charities of life are more than all ceremonies.

5. Rioters and revolutionaries resolutely refuse to respond to recommendations.

6. Every generation tends to edit and correct the faults of its predecessors.

7. Grow to greatness by grappling with and overcoming your problems, going through not around them.

(Make up three sentences loaded with "r" words, *saying each aloud* before you write.)

8.
9.
10.

"s"

TO PRONOUNCE:

For Lispers: any or all of these hints can help you!

A. 1.   Head up to ceiling—let tongue fall back in throat.

2.   Make a hissing sound as though hissing a villain.

3.   Aim a thin breath stream through opening of the two upper front teeth close to the gum line.

4.   Tip of tongue points to upper gum ridge but doesn't touch anywhere, sides of tongue anchor lightly to upper side teeth, furrow tongue lengthwise.

5.   Check in mirror to see that you do not see the tongue at any time.

6.   Teeth held loosely together as though nibbling corn; upper teeth should overlap lower teeth.

B.   Lean chin on back of hand. Keep tongue retreated as in looking at ceiling. Hiss!

For Sibilizers:

The idea is to fuzz up or put whiskers on the "s" so it is not as piercing. To do this nestle tongue tip against lower teeth and aim breath stream low over tongue and lower lip. Try almost to lisp. Do Column 5 below which has the "th" sounds and let them influence the Column 6 words, leaving tongue in *almost* the same position for both.

I. WORDS

1.		2.		3.		4.
toe	—	sew		ssseen	—	sheen
tot	—	sot		ssseep	—	sheep
tat	—	sat		ssseek	—	sheik
too	—	Sue		ssseat	—	sheet
told	—	sold		sssad	—	shad
tame	—	same		sssop	—	shops
tub	—	sub		sssock	—	shock
tell	—	sell		sssod	—	shod
tip	—	sip		Swiss	—	swish
tight	—	sight		class	—	clash

5. (Contrast) 6.

thin	—	sin
think	—	sink
thank	—	sank
thaw	—	saw
thong	—	song
thick	—	sick
bath	—	bass
worth	—	worse
truth	—	truce
forth	—	force

7.	8.	9.
lapse	squeak	strike
crops	squat	stream
backs	square	straw
trucks	squint	strap
shocks	small	scram
cooks	smirk	scroll
stuffs	smart	script
roofs	smoke	scratch
puffs	skim	sprig
staffs	scant	spray

10.

lend(s)	—	sends
cat(s)	—	sats
cart(s)	—	starts
gate(s)	—	sates
torte(s)	—	sorts
mate(s)	—	states
rot(s)	—	slots
route(s)	—	suits
pate(s)	—	spates
short(s)	—	snorts

II. PHRASES

Read each phrase. Say each one in front of the mirror, watching to see that the teeth are together. (Retract the tongue.)

1.

sink or swim
spic and span
soft as silk
Mississippi
serve yourself and save
sin, sex, and sensuality

2.

stop, shop, and save
supersonic sports
serendipity swings
parsley, spinach, watercress
please pass the strawberries
scrimp and save

III. SENTENCES

1. Fashion forces us to face society with scanty skirts.

2. Suspicion centered on the southern senator's statements on taxes.

3. Superior wisdom certainly dominates the Supreme Court's decisions.

4. Sara serves watercress sandwiches and iced cider laced with cinnamon.

5. Spices and salt seem to spruce up simple recipes.

6. She substitutes saccharin for sugar sometimes.

7. The happiness of life is made up of minute fractions—the little, soon-to-be-forgotten charities of a kiss or

smile, a kind look, a heartfelt compliment—countless in-
finitesimals of pleasurable and genial feeling.

—SAMUEL TAYLOR COLERIDGE

(Make up three sentences loaded with "s" words, *saying
each aloud* before you write.)

8.
9.
10.

"t"

TO PRONOUNCE:

Tongue tip touches upper gum ridge lightly like a feather
tip. Take it away quickly.

Caution:

Do not overpronounce "t" so it comes out "tsoy" instead
of "toy," "tsime" instead of "time," "tsell" instead of "tell,"
etc. If you have trouble with "t" do the following like a
machine gun or a woodpecker or a dripping (not a splashing faucet: t-t-t-t-t-t. Also do the same with d-d-d-d-d-d.

I. WORDS

1.	2.	3.	4.
to	it	into	rotate
toy	out	after	totem
tie	got	until	lettuce
time	not	city	better
talk	late	pretty	sweater
town	soft	sometime	letter
took	want	beautiful	actor
tall	last	sister	octave
table	about	water	affectation
today	basket	wanted	expectation

II. PHRASES

1.

twenty trumpets
twice twelve
trunk for trinkets
trials and tribulations

2.

twenty-two times
true to Tony
triumphed and tripled
tribal treasure trove

3.

twin treatments
two Saturday nights
triplets tried
travel tickets

III. SENTENCES

1. To be addicted to candy or cigarettes is to taste purgatory.

2. The cost of theater tickets is too high for us to accept third-rate entertainment.

3. To test tranquility try to rest and to do without activity.

4. Respect the child. Be not too much his parent. Trespass not on his solitude.   —RALPH WALDO EMERSON

5. Television audiences are frequently irritated by interviewers who inflict stupid questions on their subjects.

6. Life is short, the art long, opportunity fleeting, experience treacherous, judgment difficult.

—HIPPOCRATES

7. In giving a talk, take advantage of the first twenty seconds to impress listeners with anecdotes or quotations.

(Make up three sentences loaded with "t" words, *saying each aloud* before you write.)

8.

9.

10.

"th" as in them (and "th" as in thin)

TO PRONOUNCE:

Tongue tip pushes against cutting edge of upper teeth.

Caution: Do not substitute "d" or "t" for "th." Memorize: the, this, that, these, them, those, there.

I. WORDS

1.			2.		
the*	not	duh	this	not	dis
they	"	day	these	"	deez
that	"	dat	there	"	dare
them	"	dem	those	"	doze

3.		
though	not	dough
with	"	wit
than	"	Dan
thy	"	die

*Pronounce "the" as "thuh" except before words beginning with a vowel where it is pronounced "thee."

II. PHRASES

1.	2.
another brother	smooth lathe
mother and father	bother breathing
without bother	feathers and leathers

3.

unclothes and bathes
other weather
gather together

4.   5.

the bonds   with deals
the closings   with gains
the debentures   with investments
the sales   with losses
the transactions   with profits

6.

without backing
without inquiring
without interviewing
without counting
without thinking

III. SENTENCES

1. Thatched or thorny, thick or scrawny, flabby or brawny, a man's a man for all that.

2. The thirsty, thwarted, and thoughtless thump tables, thunder and threaten until their thirst is thoroughly slaked.

3. Mathematicians and even theologists, theocrats and therapists are thankful for thoughtful theorems.

4. Things have their day and their beauties in that day.
—GEORGE SANTAYANA

5. The work of progress is so immense and our means of aiding it so feeble; the life of humanity is so long, that of the individual so brief, that we often see only the ebb of the advancing ways, and are thus discouraged. It is history that teaches us to hope.   —ROBERT E. LEE

6. Wise men say, and not without reason, that whoever wishes to foresee the future must consult the past; for human events ever resemble those of preceding times. This arises from the fact that they are produced by men who have been, and ever will be, animated by the same passions, and thus they must necessarily have the same results.
—NICCOLÒ MACHIAVELLI

7. The technique that protects the voice is the same that gives you the thrust of enthusiasm.

(Make up three sentences loaded with "th" words, *saying each aloud* before you write.)

8.
9.
10.

"v"

TO PRONOUNCE:
Bite the lower lip hard.

Caution:
Foreign-language-speaking people often confuse the "v" consonant and pronounce it as a "w." Distinguish between the articulation of each. For "w" the lips are completely rounded as in whistling or in pronouncing "oo" and the lip is not bitten.

I. WORDS

1.	2.	3.	4.
vast	view	valuable	avert
van	vine	villain	avoid
vat	valve	vitamins	avow
veto	virtue	volatile	event
vent	visit	volume	eventually
vote	vocal	vulture	evict

II. CONTRAST

vase	— ways	(oo)	ways
vane	— wane	(oo)	wane
vent	— went	(oo)	went
vine	— wine	(oo)	wine
veer	— weird	(oo)	weird
vile	— while	(oo)	while

III. SENTENCES

    1. Vivacity and verve are valuable for vocal variety.

    2. Volcanic revolutions provoke violence and often provide victims not victories.

    3. Vitamins of various vegetables vastly improve vitality.

    · 4. Voters vowed to evaluate the virtues and vices of the visiting candidates.

    5. Vim and vigor will vastly benefit your visage and verbalizing.

    6. Verily, verily wish, work and wait and never wonder.

    7. Avoid Venice and Virginia in very warm weather and Vladivostok in winter.

    (Make up three sentences loaded with "v" *saying each aloud* before you write.)

    8.

    9.

    10.

B. Readings for Color and Effectiveness

Following are some selections that have appealed to me enough, for their language or their message, so that I thought them useful and interesting for reading aloud. Obviously these are only a surface scratch on the numberless memorable passages of literature. I am sure you have many favorites of your own, and I hope you will add many more.

Study these passages to see how you can profit by their style and thinking. Notice the multifarious ways in which the authors add to their color, expressiveness, and power.

Read the excerpts aloud, not once but many times. On each reading, aim at some particular quality of delivery: pacing; emphasis; variety; sincerity; pauses. Bring out the full value of the words, but shun like the plague any impression of "giving a recitation."

Read sometimes as though you were talking to a small group, close at hand. At other times read as though you were addressing a crowd of hundreds. This practice will help you to strengthen your projection and to maintain audience interest some day when you are giving a talk of your own. The concepts and turns of phrase, too, will provide useful approaches to your own speech preparation. Also, some passages may serve as useful quotations in your own speeches.

Select your readings according to your needs. All of the

selections can be read aloud with great profit by anyone, no matter what the purpose.

OPENING—HUMOR

1. I appreciate very much your generous invitation to be here tonight.

You [newsmen] bear heavy responsibilities these days and an article I read some time ago reminded me of how particularly heavy the burdens of present-day events bear upon your profession.

You may remember that in 1851, the New York *Herald Tribune*, under the sponsorship of Horace Greeley, included as its London correspondent an obscure journalist by the name of Karl Marx.

We are told that the foreign correspondent Marx, stone broke and with a family ill and undernourished, constantly appealed to Greeley and managing editor Charles Dana for an increase in his munificent salary of £5 per installment, a salary which he and Engels labeled as the "lousiest petty bourgeois cheating."

But when all his financial appeals were refused, Marx looked around for other means of livelihood and fame, and eventually terminated his relationship with the *Tribune* and devoted his talents full time to the cause that would bequeath to the world the seeds of Leninism, Stalinism, revolution, and the Cold War.

If only this capitalistic New York newspaper had treated him more kindly, if only Marx had remained a foreign correspondent, history might have been different, and I hope all publishers will bear this lesson in mind the next time they receive a poverty-stricken appeal for a small increase in the expense account from an obscure newspaperman.
—JOHN F. KENNEDY

2. I recently read that the preamble to the Declaration of Independence contains 300 words. The Ten Command-

ments has 297. The Gettysburg Address comes in at 267, while the Lord's Prayer has less than 100.

However, a recent report from the Federal Government on the pricing of cabbages allegedly contains 26,911 words. I will confine my remarks to something between the Lord's Prayer and the pricing of cabbages.

—CHARLES L. GOULD

3. I won't make the same mistake this morning that I made at a speaking engagement last Saturday. I was at the Arizona State Penitentiary . . . with a round-trip ticket . . . to speak to a group of inmates. Without thinking, I began by saying, "It's good to see so many here this morning." In trying to correct my blunder, I made an even greater mistake. I said, "What I meant is, I'm pleased to speak to such a captive audience."   —KEITH L. FLAKE

4. When I say that we are both in the "security" business, there are some people who will say that I'm playing with words. That you from Wall Street and I from the Pentagon have a different view of security. Your security interest is bonds and stock; mine is bombs and shock.

Like most things today, we have our specialties.

—VINCENT F. CAPUTO

5. A well-known literary man objected to Lincoln's calling a certain Greek history "tedious." The man said to Lincoln: "Mr. President, the author of that history is one of the profoundest scholars of the age. Indeed, it may be doubted whether any man of our generation has plunged more deeply into the sacred fount of learning."

"Yes," said Lincoln, "or come up drier."

All too many people seem to plunge deeply into the sacred fount of learning, and still manage to come up quite dry. I don't understand this, for learning, scholarship, ought to be exciting, and when anyone makes it dull and dry, he has gotten off the track somewhere.

—CLIFFORD D. OWSLEY

OPENINGS—SERIOUS

1. In this symposium my part is only to sit in silence. To express one's feelings as the end draws near is too intimate a task.

But I may mention one thought that comes to me as a listener in. The riders in a race do not stop short when they reach the goal. There is a little finishing canter before coming to a standstill. There is time to hear the kind voices of friends and to say to oneself: The work is done. But just as one says that, the answer comes: "The race is over, but the work is never done while the power to work remains. The canter that brings you to a standstill need not be only coming to rest. It cannot be, while you still live. For to live is to function. That is all there is to living."

And so I end with a line from a Latin poet who uttered the message more than fifteen hundred years ago, "Death plucks my ear and says: 'Live—I am coming.'"

—OLIVER WENDELL HOLMES on his ninetieth birthday

2. Man's fascination with Tomorrow is as old as man himself.

From the dawn of his imagination, he has tried to peer behind the "curtain's magic fold" to where Bret Harte said "the glowing future lies unrolled."

He has speculated about the future for profit, for amusement, out of simple curiosity . . . and sometimes for reasons bigger than himself.

And sometimes, he has, indeed, looked into Tomorrow.

—ORVILLE FREEMAN

3. The habit of reading is one of the greatest resources of mankind; and we enjoy reading books that belong to us much more than if they are borrowed. A borrowed book is like a guest in the house; it must be treated with punctiliousness, with a certain considerate formality. You must see that it sustains no damage; it must not suffer while un-

der your roof. You cannot leave it carelessly, you cannot mark it, you cannot turn down the pages, you cannot use it familiarly. And then, some day, although this is seldom done, you really ought to return it.

But your own books belong to you; you treat them with that affectionate intimacy that annihilates formality. Books are for use, not for show; you should own no book that you are afraid to mark up, or afraid to place on the table, wide open and face down.   —WILLIAM LYON PHELPS

4.   My friends: No one not in my situation can appreciate my feeling of sadness at this parting. To this place, and the kindness of these people, I owe everything. Here I have lived a quarter of a century, and have passed from a young to an old man. Here my children have been born, and one is buried. I now leave, not knowing when or whether ever I may return, with a task before me greater than that which rested upon Washington. Without the assistance of that Divine Being who ever attended him, I cannot succeed. With that assistance, I cannot fail.

—ABRAHAM LINCOLN (Farewell to Springfield)

CONCLUSIONS

1.   Sure I am that this day now we are the masters of our fate, that the task which has been set before us is not above our strength, that its pangs and toils are not beyond our endurance. As long as we have faith in our cause and unconquerable will power, salvation will not be denied us.

In the words of the Psalmist: "He shall not be afraid of evil tidings, his heart is fixed, trusting in the Lord."
—WINSTON CHURCHILL before the United States Congress,
December 26, 1941

2.   In the elimination of war lies our solution, for only then will nations cease to compete with one another in the production and use of dread "secret" weapons which are evaluated solely by their capacity to kill. This devilish pro-

gram takes us back not merely to the Dark Ages, but from cosmos to chaos. If we succeed in finding a suitable way to control atomic weapons, it is reasonable to hope that we may also preclude the use of other weapons adaptable to mass destruction. When a man learns to say "A" he can, if he chooses, learn the rest of the alphabet too.

—BERNARD M. BARUCH

3. Let's tell them that the victory to be won in the twentieth century, this portal to the golden age, mocks the pretensions of individual acumen and ingenuity. For it is a citadel guarded by thick walls of ignorance and mistrust which do not fall before the trumpets' blast or the politicians' imprecations or even the generals' baton. They are, my friends, walls that must be directly stormed by the hosts of courage, morality, and of vision, standing shoulder to shoulder, unafraid of ugly truth, contemptuous of lies, half-truths, circuses, and demagoguery.

—ADLAI STEVENSON, 1952 acceptance speech

4. We are a nation of many nationalities, many races, many religions—bound together by a single unity, the unity of freedom and equality. Whoever seeks to set one nationality against another, seeks to degrade all nationalities. Whoever seeks to set one race against another, seeks to enslave all races. Whoever seeks to set one religion against another, seeks to destroy all religion.

—FRANKLIN D. ROOSEVELT

5. Neither let us be slandered from our duty by false accusations against us, nor frightened from it by menaces of destruction to the government, nor of dungeons to ourselves. Let us have faith that right makes might, and in that faith let us to the end dare to do our duty as we understand it.   —ABRAHAM LINCOLN, Cooper Institute

6. Where, after all, do universal human rights begin? In small places, close to home—so close and so small that they cannot be seen on any map of the world. Yet they are the world of the individual person: the neighborhood he

lives in, the school or college he attends, the factory, farm or office where he works.

Such are the places where every man, woman and child seeks equal justice, equal opportunity, equal dignity without discrimination. Unless these rights have meaning there, they have little meaning anywhere.

—ELEANOR ROOSEVELT

7. With malice toward none; with charity for all; with firmness in the right, as God gives us to see the right, let us strive on to finish the work we are in; to bind up the nation's wounds; to care for him who shall have borne the battle, and for his widow, and his orphan—to do all which may achieve a just and lasting peace among ourselves, and with all nations.

—ABRAHAM LINCOLN, Second Inaugural Address

8. God grant that not only the love of liberty but a thorough knowledge of the rights of man may pervade all the nations of the earth, so that a philosopher may set his foot anywhere on its surface and say: "This is my country."   —BENJAMIN FRANKLIN

9. Grant us a common faith that man shall know bread and peace—that he shall know justice and righteousness, freedom and security, an equal opportunity and an equal chance to do his best, not only in our own lands, but throughout the world. And in that faith let us march toward the clean world our hands can make.

—STEPHEN VINCENT BENÉT

10. It is not the critic who counts; not the man who points out how the strong man stumbled, or where the doer of deeds could have done them better. The credit belongs to the man who is actually in the arena; whose face is marred by dust and sweat and blood; who strives valiantly; who errs and comes short again and again; who knows the great enthusiasms, the great devotions, and spends himself in a worthy cause; who at the best knows in the end the triumph of high achievement; and who at the

worst, if he fails, at least fails while daring greatly; so that his place shall never be with those cold and timid souls who know neither victory nor defeat.

—THEODORE ROOSEVELT

11. Let our object be our country, our whole country, and nothing but our country. And by the blessing of God, may that country itself become a vast and splendid monument, not of oppression and terror, but of wisdom, of peace, and of liberty, upon which the world may gaze with admiration forever.   —DANIEL WEBSTER

12. A revival of integrity and character can mean a renewal of freedom. The nurturing of values that maintain society's moral tone is going on every day in the financial market place as in the classroom. These values manifest themselves more dramatically through what men and women do than through what they say, and they can never be any better than the generation that holds them in trust.

To some, this may seem an impossibly arduous burden; but others it will inspire to greatness.

—GEORGE CHAMPION

13. I believe that man will not merely endure; he will prevail. He is immortal, not because he alone among creatures has an inexhaustible voice, but because he has a soul, a spirit capable of compassion and sacrifice and endurance. The poet's, the writer's, duty is to write about these things. It is his privilege to help man endure by lifting his heart, by reminding him of the courage and honor and hope and pride and compassion and pity and sacrifice which have been the glory of his past. The poet's voice need not merely be the record of man, it can be one of the props, the pillars to help him endure and prevail.

—WILLIAM FAULKNER

MISCELLANEOUS READINGS

1. Those who compare the age in which their lot has fallen with a golden age which exists only in imagination, may talk of degeneracy and decay; but no man who is correctly informed as to the past, will be disposed to take a morose or desponding view of the present.

—THOMAS MACAULAY

2. Unceasingly contemplate the generation of all things through change and accustom thyself to the thought that the nature of the Universe delights above all in changing the things that exist and making new ones of the same pattern. For everything that exists is the seed of that which shall come out of it.   —MARCUS AURELIUS

3. Appearances to the mind are of four kinds: things either are what they appear to be; or they neither are, nor appear to be; or they are, and do not appear to be; or they are not, and yet appear to be. Rightly to aim in all these cases is the wise man's task.   —EPICTETUS

4. Men, by their constitutions, are naturally divided into two parties: 1. Those who fear and distrust the people, and wish to draw all powers from them into the hands of the higher classes. 2. Those who identify themselves with the people, have confidence in them, cherish and consider them as the most honest and safe, although not the most wise, depository of the public interests.

—THOMAS JEFFERSON

5. Behavior seemeth to me as a garment of the mind, and to have the conditions of a garment. For it ought to be made in fashion; it ought not to be too curious, it ought to be shaped so as to set forth any good making of the mind, and hide any deformity; and above all, it ought not

to be too strait, or restrained for exercise or motion.

—FRANCIS BACON

6. Anybody can become angry—that is easy; but to
be angry with the right person, and to the right degree, and
at the right time, and for the right purpose, and in the
right way—that is not within everybody's power and is
not easy.   —ARISTOTLE

7. Whenever you are angry, be assured that it is not
only a present evil, but that you have increased a habit,
and added fuel to a fire . . . If you would not be of an
angry temper, then, do not feed the habit. Give it nothing
to help its increase. Be quiet at first, and reckon the days
in which you have not been angry. "I used to be angry
every day; now every other day; then every third and
fourth day." And if you miss it so long as thirty days, offer
a sacrifice of thanksgiving to God.   —EPICTETUS

8. We are never so virtuous as when we are ill . . . It
is then a man recollects that there are gods, and that he
himself is mortal; . . . and he resolves that if he has the
luck to recover, his life shall be passed in harmless happiness.   —PLINY THE YOUNGER

9. For just as I approve of a young man in whom there
is a touch of age, so I approve of the old man in whom
there is some of the flavor of youth. He who strives thus
to mingle youthfulness and age may grow old in body, but
old in spirit he will never be.   —CICERO

10. You may not carry a sword beneath a scholar's
gown, or lead flaming causes from a cloister . . . a scholar
who tries to combine those parts sells his birthright for a
mess of pottage . . . when the final count is made it will be
found that the impairment of his powers far outweighs any
possible contribution to the causes he has espoused. If he
is fit to serve in his calling at all, it is because he has
learned not to serve in any other, for his singleness of

mind quickly evaporates in the fire of passions, however holy.   —LEARNED HAND

11. We seek an open world—open to ideas, open to the exchange of goods and people, a world in which no people, great or small, will live in angry isolation.

We cannot expect to make everyone our friend, but we can try to make no one our enemy.

Those who would be our adversaries, we invite to a peaceful competition—not in conquering territory or extending dominion, but in enriching the life of man.

As we explore the reaches of space, let us go to the new worlds together—not as new worlds to be conquered, but as new adventures to be shared.

     —RICHARD M. NIXON, Inaugural Address, 1969

12. Peace does not appear so distant as it did. I hope it will come soon, and come to stay; and so come as to be worth the keeping in all future time. It will then have been proved that among free men there can be no successful appeal from the ballot to the bullet, and that they who make such an appeal are sure to lose their case and pay the cost.   —ABRAHAM LINCOLN

13. . . . Not to destroy but to construct,
         I hold the unconquerable belief
         that science and peace will triumph over ignorance
             and war
         that nations will come together
         not to destroy but to construct
         and that the future belongs to those
         who accomplish most for humanity.
                                   —LOUIS PASTEUR

14. We have seen what the space program has already done to make America more secure, more comfortable, more prosperous, and, above all, more progressive. An invaluable stockpile of the required skills and techniques has been developed in recent years through the government-

industry partnership in defense, aerospace, and atomic
energy programs and under the incentives inherent in the
free world. I am optimistic about the future because we
have the resources needed to meet the immense challenges
of our era. The proper use of these will unlock the expand-
ing vistas of a bright future. But all of us must share the
responsibility of insuring the right balance among enthusiasm, imagination, and reality.   —JOHN R. MOORE

15.   We know that the only alternative to private competition is government monopoly of enterprise. We know
that when government monopolizes production, distribu-
tion, and employment, it is no longer the servant of men—
it is their master. And, therefore, we know that economic
liberty and political liberty are inseparable parts of the
same ball of wax—that we must keep them both, or we
shall lose them both.   —BENJAMIN FAIRLESS

16.   Newspapers give the impression that railroads are
dead or dying. Obituaries are not in order. Actually, we're
a growth industry. We're on the way up. Don't expect us
to spread our wings and fly. But believe me, gentlemen,
the railroads are emerging as a spirited industry—the best
that's roared down the track in quite a while. This nation
has long needed us. In the years ahead, we're going to
make it want us, too.

—THOMAS GOODFELLOW, Pres. Assoc. of Amer. Railroads

MISCELLANEOUS READING FOR LIGHT TOUCH

1.   The number of things a small dog does naturally is
strangely small. Enjoying better spirits and not crushed
under material cares, he is far more theatrical than average man. His whole life, if he be a dog with any pretensions to gallantry, is spent in a vain show, and in the
hot pursuit of admiration. Take out your puppy for a walk,
and you will find the soft little ball of fur clumsy, stupid,
bewildered, but natural. Let but a few months pass, and

when you repeat the process you will find nature buried in convention. He will do nothing plainly; but the simplest procedures of our material life will all be bent into the forms of an elaborate and mysterious etiquette.

—ROBERT LOUIS STEVENSON

2. So, 37 per cent of life is luck. We have to plan to accept the mystery of luck, but we keep in mind what Charlie Brown said one day too. Charlie and Lucy were playing marbles and Lucy was a humdinger. As she knocked agate after agate of Charlie's, and steelies as well, he kept saying, "Luck, luck, luck." In the second frame it was more of the same. In the third frame Lucy is going saucily down the street with all of Charlie's marbles and he is saying, "Luck, luck, luck." But when she gets around the corner he says, "Boy, that girl can really play marbles."

—JOHN P. LEARY

3. "Papa is a preferable mode of address," observed Mrs. General. "Father is rather vulgar, my dear. The word papa, besides, gives a rather pretty form to the lips. Papa, potatoes, poultry, prunes, and prism, are all very good words for the lips; especially prunes and prism. You will find it serviceable, in the formation of a demeanor, if you sometimes say to yourself in company—on entering a room, for instance—'Papa, potatoes, poultry, prunes and prism, prunes and prism.'"

—CHARLES DICKENS

4. There are members of Parliament so enamored of the spoken word that if waylaid, en route, to the House, an important speech in their pocket, they would, at the cry, "Your type-transcript or your trousers" (if hesitantly) part with the latter. A taxi and a tailor could save *that* situation; the other loss, nothing. Again, there are those sad persons we see, with next to nothing to say, and no hope of saying it without the paper, from which they lift reluctant eyes an anxious moment, for would-be human glances.

—A. P. ROSSITER

READINGS TO HELP THE LISTENER SEE

1. On the verge of the forest we paused to inquire our way at a log house, owned by a white settler or squatter, a tall rawboned old fellow, with red hair, a lank lantern visage, and an inveterate habit of winking with one eye, as if everything he said was of knowing import. He was in a towering passion. One of his horses was missing; he was sure it had been stolen in the night by a straggling party of Osages encamped in a neighboring swamp; but he would have satisfaction! He would make an example of the villains. He had accordingly caught down his rifle from the wall, that invariable enforcer of right or wrong upon the frontiers, and, having saddled his steed, was about to sally forth on a foray into the swamp; while a brother squatter, with rifle in hand, stood ready to accompany him.

—WASHINGTON IRVING

2. The general attention had been directed from himself to the person in the carriage, and he was quite alone. Rightly judging that under such circumstances it would be madness to follow, he turned down a bye street in search of the nearest coach-stand, finding that after a minute or two he was reeling like a drunken man, and aware for the first time of a stream of blood that was trickling down his face and breast.

—CHARLES DICKENS

3. PRESIDENT FRANKLIN D. ROOSEVELT (speaking of the Lend-Lease program prior to World War II): Suppose my neighbor's home catches fire, and I have a length of garden hose four or five hundred feet away. If he can take my garden hose and connect it up with his hydrant, I may help him put out his fire. Now, what do I do? I don't say to him before that operation, "Neighbor, my garden hose cost me $15, you have to pay me $15 for it." I don't want $15—I want my garden hose back after the fire is over.

READINGS—FOR SMOOTH, FLOWING SPEECH

1. The proverbs of all nations, which are always the literature of reason, are the statements of an absolute truth without qualification. Proverbs, like the sacred books of each nation, are the sanctuary of the intuitions. That which the droning world, chained to appearances, will not allow the realist to say in his own words, it will suffer him to say in proverbs without contradiction. And this law of laws, which the pulpit, the senate and the college deny, is hourly preached in all markets and workshops by flights of proverbs, whose teaching is as true and as omnipresent as that of birds and flies.   —RALPH WALDO EMERSON

2. No man is an island, entire of itself;
   Every man is a piece of the continent, a part of the
        main;
   If a clod be washed away by the sea, Europe is the
        less,
   As well as if a promontory were, as well as if a
        manor of thy friend's or of thine own were;
   Any man's death diminishes me, because I am in-
        volved in mankind;
   And therefore never send to know for whom the
        bell tolls; it tolls for thee.   —JOHN DONNE

3. Flowers have an expression of countenance as much as men or animals. Some seem to smile; some have a sad expression; some are pensive and diffident; others again are plain, honest and upright, like the broadfaced sunflower and the hollyhock.   —HENRY WARD BEECHER

4. Though I speak with the tongues of men and of angels, and have not charity, I am become as sounding brass, or a tinkling cymbal. And though I have the gift of prophecy, and understand all mysteries, and all knowl-

edge; and though I have all faith, so that I could remove
mountains, and have not charity, I am nothing. And though
I bestow all my goods to feed the poor, and though I give
my body to be burned, and have not charity, it profiteth
me nothing. Charity suffereth long, and is kind; charity
envieth not; charity vaunteth not itself, is not puffed up . . .
Charity never faileth . . ."

—I CORINTHIANS 13:1–4, 8

5.   To everything there is a season, and a time to every
        purpose under the heaven:
     A time to be born, and a time to die;
     A time to plant, and a time to pluck up that which
        is planted;
     A time to kill, and a time to heal;
     A time to break down, and a time to build up;
     A time to weep, and a time to laugh;
     A time to mourn, and a time to dance;
     A time to cast away stones, and a time to gather
        stones together;
     A time to embrace, and a time to refrain from
        embracing;
     A time to get, and a time to lose;
     A time to keep, and a time to cast away;
     A time to rend, and a time to sew;
     A time to keep silence, and a time to speak;
     A time to love, and a time to hate;
     A time of war, and a time of peace.

—ECCLESIASTES 3:1–8

6.   I asked God for strength that I might achieve,
          I was made weak, that I might learn to
               humbly obey;
     I asked for health, that I might do greater things,
          I was given infirmity, that I might do better
               things,
     I asked for riches, that I might be happy,
          I was given poverty, that I might be wise;
     I asked for all things, that I might enjoy life,

I was given life, that I might enjoy all things;
I got nothing that I asked for
But everything I had hoped for;
Almost despite myself, my unspoken prayers were
answered.
I am among all men, most richly blessed.
—AUTHOR UNKNOWN

7. Thinking cannot be clear till it has had expression. We must write, or speak, or act our thoughts, or they will remain in half torpid form. Our feelings must have expression, or they will be as clouds, which, till they descend in rain, will never bring up fruit or flower. So it is with all the inward feelings; expression gives them development. Thought is the blossom; language the opening bud; action the fruit behind it. —HENRY WARD BEECHER

8. You cannot pluck out the mystery of the human heart. Go placidly amid the noise and the haste and learn what peace there may be in silence. Speak your truth quietly and clearly; and listen to others, even the dull and ignorant; they too have their story . . . If you compare yourself with others you may become vain and bitter; for always there will be greater and lesser persons than yourself.

9. Enjoy your achievements as well as your plans. Keep interested in your career, however humble; it is a real possession in the changing fortunes of time. Exercise caution in your business affairs, for the world is full of trickery. But let this not blind you to what virtue there is; many persons strive for high ideals; and everywhere life is full of heroism.

10. Be yourself. Especially do not feign affection. Neither be cynical about love; for in the face of all avidity and disenchantment it is as perennial as the grass. Take kindly the counsel of the years, gracefully surrendering the things of youth. Nurture strength of spirit to shield you in sudden misfortune. But do not distress yourself with imaginings. Many fears are born of fatigue and loneliness. Beyond a wholesome discipline, be gentle with yourself. You

are a child of the universe no less than the trees and the stars; you have a right to be here.

> —AUTHOR UNKNOWN. Found at Adlai Stevenson's
> bedside after his death.

11.   When the conduct of men is designed to be influenced, persuasion, kind, unassuming persuasion, should ever be adopted. It is an old and true maxim that "a drop of honey catches more flies than a gallon of gall." So with men. If you would win a man to your cause, first convince him that you are his sincere friend. Therein is a drop of honey that catches his heart, which, say what he will, is the great high-road to his reason, and which, when once gained, you will find but little trouble convincing his judgment of the justice of your cause, if indeed that cause really is a good one.   —ABRAHAM LINCOLN

12.   May the road rise to meet you,
    May the wind be always at your back,
    May the sun shine warm upon your face
    And the rains fall soft upon your fields,
    And, until we meet again,
    May God hold you in the palm of his hand.
                                            —GAELIC PRAYER

13.   Give us grace and strength to persevere. Give us courage and gaiety and the quiet mind. Spare to us our friends and soften to us our enemies. Give us the strength to encounter that which is to come, that we may be brave in peril, constant in tribulation, temperate in wrath and in all changes of fortune, and down to the gates of death, loyal and loving to one another.
                                    —ROBERT LOUIS STEVENSON

C.   Punchliners

Ability
The university brings out all abilities including incapability.   —CHEKHOV
Skill to do comes of doing.
> —RALPH WALDO EMERSON

We judge ourselves by what we feel capable of doing, while others judge us by what we have already done.
> —LONGFELLOW

Absence
The same wind snuffs candles yet kindles fires; so, where absence kills a little love, it fans a great one.
> —LA ROCHEFOUCAULD

Accent
I once knew a fellow who spoke a dialect with an accent.
> —IRVIN COBB

Accomplishment
Be ashamed to die until you have achieved some victory for humanity.   —HORACE MANN

Accidents
The way some people drive you'd think they were late for their accident.   —EDDIE CANTOR

Acting

The art of acting consists in keeping people from coughing.   —SIR RALPH RICHARDSON

I don't act—I react.   —JOHN WAYNE

Action

Action may not always bring happiness; but there is no happiness without action.   —DISRAELI

You will recall what Senator Dirksen said about the rocking chair—it gives you a sense of motion without any sense of danger.   —JOHN F. KENNEDY

Actions

All our actions take their hue from the complexion of the heart, as landscapes their variety from light.

—FRANCIS BACON

Adversity

Adversity introduces a man to himself.

—ANONYMOUS

There is no education like adversity.   —DISRAELI

What on earth would a man do with himself if something did not stand in his way.   —H. G. WELLS

Advertising

Doing business without advertising is like winking at a girl in the dark; you know what you're doing, but nobody else does.   —STEWART H. BRITT

Advertising is nothing more than the arts of persuasion practiced in mass media.   —ARTHUR E. MEYERHOFF

You can tell the ideals of a nation by its advertisements.

—NORMAN DOUGLAS

Advice

Advice is like castor oil, easy enough to give but dreadful uneasy to take.   —JOSH BILLINGS

To profit from good advice requires more wisdom than to give it.   —JOHN CHURTON COLLINS

I am glad that I paid so little attention to good advice;

had I abided by it I might have been saved from some of my most valuable mistakes.   —GENE FOWLER

A bad cold wouldn't be so annoying if it weren't for the advice of our friends.   —KIN HUBBARD

If you can tell the difference between good advice and bad advice, you don't need advice.
                          —OKMULGEE (Okla.) Rotary Club Bulletin

I sometimes give myself admirable advice, but I am incapable of taking it.   —MARY WORTLEY MONTAGU

Old men are fond of giving good advice, to console themselves for being no longer in a position to give bad examples.   —LA ROCHEFOUCAULD

How is it possible to expect that mankind will take advice when they will not so much as take warning?
                                              —JONATHAN SWIFT

Age

Middle age occurs when you are too young to take up golf and too old to rush up to the net.
                                        —FRANKLIN PIERCE ADAMS

To me, old age is always fifteen years older than I am.
                                              —BERNARD BARUCH

Middle age is when you have a choice of two temptations and choose the one that will get you home earlier.
                                                —DAN BENNETT

In youth we run into difficulties, in old age difficulties run into us.   —JOSH BILLINGS

Middle age is the time when you begin to exchange your emotions for symptoms.   —JACOB BRAUDE

Many people's tombstones should read: "Died at 30. Buried at 60."   —NICHOLAS MURRAY BUTLER

Old age isn't so bad when you consider the alternative.
                                          —MAURICE CHEVALIER

Everything I know I learned after I was thirty.
                                        —GEORGES CLEMENCEAU

No matter how young I think, I can't get under sixty.
                                              —BILL COPELAND

Youth is a blunder, manhood a struggle, old age a regret.   —DISRAELI

It's not how old you are but how you are old.

— MARIE DRESSLER

Growing old is an emotion which comes over us at almost any age; I had it myself between the ages of 25 and 30.   — E. M. FORSTER

Middle age is when your age starts to show around your middle.   — BOB HOPE

You've reached middle age when all you exercise is caution.   — FRANKLIN P. JONES

Forty is the old age of youth, fifty is the youth of old age.   — VICTOR HUGO

Senescence begins and middle age ends the day your descendants outnumber your friends.   — OGDEN NASH

A man loses his illusions first, his teeth second, and his follies last.   — HELEN ROWLAND

The first forty years of life give us the text; the next thirty supply the commentary on it.   — SCHOPENHAUER

It's not like running out of gas; it's more like burning out your bearings.   — DR. ELVIS STAHR

Agnostic

Don't be an agnostic. Be *something*.

— ROBERT FROST

Alimony

Alimony is like buying oats for a dead horse.

— ARTHUR (BUGS) BAER

You never realize how short a month is until you pay alimony.   — JOHN BARRYMORE

Billing minus cooing.   — MARY C. DORSEY

A man's cash surrender value.

— TOASTER'S HANDBOOK

Ambition

Ambition raises a secret tumult in the soul; it inflames the mind, and puts it into a violent hurry of thought.

— JOSEPH ADDISON

All ambitions are lawful except those which climb upward on the miseries or credulities of mankind.

— JOSEPH CONRAD

America

We must dream of an aristocracy of achievement arising out of a democracy of opportunity.

—THOMAS JEFFERSON

Ours is the only country deliberately founded on a good idea. —JOHN GUNTHER

Intellectually I know that America is no better than any other country; emotionally I know she is better than every other country. —SINCLAIR LEWIS

The American dream does not come to those who fall asleep. —RICHARD M. NIXON

Anger

Two things a man should never be angry at; what he can help and what he cannot help. —THOMAS FULLER

When angry, count four; when very angry, swear.

—MARK TWAIN

The size of a man can be measured by the size of the thing that makes him angry. —J. KENFIELD MORLEY

Apology

Nine times out of ten, the first thing a man's companion knows of his shortcoming is from his apology.

—OLIVER WENDELL HOLMES

Architects

A doctor can bury his mistakes, but an architect can only advise his client to plant vines.

—FRANK LLOYD WRIGHT

Argument

Never argue with a woman when she's tired—or rested.

—H. C. DIEFENBACH

You raise your voice when you should reinforce your argument. —SAMUEL JOHNSON

In most instances, all an argument proves is that two people are present. —TONY PETTITO

Art

Art, like morality consists in drawing the line somewhere.   —G. K. Chesterton

A man who works with his hands is a laborer; a man who works with his hands and his brain is a craftsman; but a man who works with his hands and his brain and his heart is an artist.   —Louis Nizer

When love and skill work together expect a masterpiece.
—John Ruskin

In life beauty perishes, but not in art.
—Leonardo Da Vinci

Automation

The real danger of our technological age is not so much that machines will begin to think like men, but that men will begin to think like machines.   —Sidney J. Harris

It's going to be a tough decision when the purchasing agent starts negotiating to buy the machine that's to replace him.   —Dave Murray

Babies

Babies do not want to hear about babies; they like to be told of giants and castles.   —Samuel Johnson

Baldness

There's one thing about baldness: it's neat.
—Don Herold

Baldness may indicate masculinity, but it diminishes one's opportunity to find out.
—Sir Cedric Hardwicke

Banking

Bank accounts are like toothpaste; easy to take out but hard to put back.   —Robert Ackerstrom

Beauty

Beauty is not caused. It is.   —Emily Dickinson

Beauty is all very well at sight, but who can look at it when it has been in the house three days?
—George Bernard Shaw

Beginning

A journey of a thousand leagues begins with a single step.   —CHINESE PROVERB

Behavior

Manners are the happy ways of doing things.
                    —RALPH WALDO EMERSON
Some people take everything on a vacation but their manners.
                    —MARSHALLTOWN, IOWA, TIMES-REPUBLICAN
We have committed the Golden Rule to memory; let us now commit it to life.   —EDWIN MARKHAM
One of the very best of all earthly possessions is self-possession.   —GEORGE D. PRENTICE

Belief

Some things have to be believed to be seen.
                    —RALPH HODGSON
Some men like to understand what they believe in. Others like to believe in what they understand.
                    —ANONYMOUS

Bigamy

The only crime on the books where two rites make a wrong.   —BOB HOPE

Birth Control

It may boil down to a little pill whether or not the world comes to its right census.   —CURRENT COMEDY

Books

On how many people's libraries, as on bottles from the drugstore, one might write: "For external use only."
                    —ALPHONSE DAUDET

Bore

He is not only dull himself but the cause of dullness in others.   —SAMUEL FOOTE

A bore is a man who deprives you of solitude without providing you with company.

—GIAN VINCENZO GRAVINA

The secret of being a bore is to tell everything.

—VOLTAIRE

Boredom

Some people can stay longer in an hour than others can in a week.   —WILLIAM DEAN HOWELLS

A yawn is a silent shout.   —G. K. CHESTERTON

Borrowing

A moneylender serves you in the present tense, lends you in the conditional mood, keeps you in the subjunctive, and ruins you in the future.   —JOSEPH ADDISON

Before borrowing money from a friend, decide which you need more.   —ADDISON H. HALLOCK

Brevity

All pleasantries ought to be short—and for that matter, gravities too.   —VOLTAIRE

Business

Few people do business well who do nothing else.

—LORD CHESTERFIELD

The business of America is business.

—CALVIN COOLIDGE

Competition is getting keener all the time; are you?

—ELMER LETERMAN

Good will is the one and only asset that competition cannot undersell or destroy.   —MARSHALL FIELD

I don't meet competition. I crush it.

—CHARLES REVSON

Next to knowing all about your own business, the best thing is to know all about the other fellow's.

—JOHN D. ROCKEFELLER

Business World

A company is known by the men it keeps.

—MELLON INSTITUTE NEWS

Busy

Bees are not as busy as we think they are. They just can't buzz any slower.   —KIN HUBBARD

Buying

People will buy anything that's one to a customer.
—SINCLAIR LEWIS

Camping

He who believes that where there's smoke there's fire hasn't tried cooking on a camping trip.
—CHANGING TIMES

Capability

If there's a job to be done, I always ask the busiest man in my parish to take it on and it gets done.
—HENRY WARD BEECHER

Celebrity

Someone who works hard to become well known and then wears dark glasses to avoid being recognized.
—HAPPY VARIETY

Challenge

The Difficult is that which can be done immediately; the Impossible that which takes a little longer.
—GEORGE SANTAYANA

Prosperity is a great teacher; adversity is a greater; possession pampers the mind; privation trains and strengthens it.   —WILLIAM HAZLITT

Chance

He that leaveth nothing to chance will do few things ill, but he will do very few things.
—MARQUIS OF HALIFAX

Character

You must look into people as well as at them.
—LORD CHESTERFIELD

Every man has three characters—that which he exhibits, that which he has, and that which he thinks he has.

—ALPHONSE KARR

The shortest and surest way to live with honor in the world is to be in reality what we appear to be.

—SOCRATES

Charity

Charity begins at home, and justice begins next door.

—CHARLES DICKENS

Our charity begins at home, and mostly ends where it begins.   —HORACE SMITH

Charm

If you have charm, you don't need to have anything else; and if you don't have it, it doesn't matter what else you have.   —J. M. BARRIE

Cheerfulness

Cheerfulness keeps up a kind of daylight in the mind, and fills it with a steady and perpetual serenity.

—JOSEPH ADDISON

A cheerful face is nearly as good for an invalid as healthy weather.   —BENJAMIN FRANKLIN

A cheerful look makes a dish a feast.

—A. P. HERBERT

Children

For adult education nothing beats children.

—BANKING

Diogenes struck the father when the son swore.

—ROBERT BURTON

You can tell that a child is growing up when he stops asking where he came from and starts refusing to tell where he's going.   —CHANGING TIMES

Hooky is when a small boy lets his mind wander—and then follows it.   —CIRCLE ARROW RETAILER

We have not passed that subtle line between childhood and adulthood until we have stopped saying, "It got lost," and say, "I lost it."   —SYDNEY J. HARRIS

There is little use to talk about your child to anyone; other people either have one or haven't.

—Don Herold

Children have more need of models than of critics.

—Joseph Joubert

Insanity is hereditary. You can get it from your children.

—Sam Levenson

Children aren't happy with nothing to ignore,
And that's what parents were created for.

—Ogden Nash

The surest way to make it hard for children is to make it easy for them.   —Eleanor Roosevelt

Circumstance

Man is not the creature of circumstances,
Circumstances are the creatures of men.   —Disraeli

Citizens

Whatever makes good Christians, makes them good citizens.   —Daniel Webster

City

If you would be known, and not know, vegetate in a village; if you would know, and not be known, live in a city.   —Charles Caleb Colton

City Life

City life: millions of people being lonesome together.

—Henry David Thoreau

Civilization

The end of the human race will be that it will eventually die of civilization.   —Ralph Waldo Emerson

The path of civilization is paved with tin cans.

—Elbert Hubbard

It wouldn't be so bad if civilization were only at the crossroads, but this is one of those cloverleaf jobs.

—"Senator Soaper"

Civilization is a movement and not a condition, a voyage and not a harbor.   —Arnold Toynbee

Classes

There may be said to be two classes of people in the world; those who constantly divide the people of the world into two classes, and those who do not.

—ROBERT BENCHLEY

Clothes

It is an interesting question how far men would retain their relative rank if they were divested of their clothes.

—HENRY DAVID THOREAU

She looked as if she had been poured into her clothes and had forgotten to say "when."   —P. G. WODEHOUSE

Cold

A cold is both positive and negative; sometimes the Eyes have it and sometimes the Nose.

—WILLIAM LYON PHELPS

Committee

A committee is a group that keeps minutes and loses hours.   —MILTON BERLE

Common Sense

Common sense is, of all kinds, the most uncommon. It implies good judgment, sound discretion, and true and practical wisdom applied to common life.

—TRYON EDWARDS

Common sense is not so common.   —VOLTAIRE

Company

Misery loves company, but company does not reciprocate.   —ADDISON MIZNER

Compliment

Every day you look lovelier and lovelier and today you look like tomorrow.   —CHARLIE MCCARTHY

I can live for two months on a good compliment.

—MARK TWAIN

Some people pay a compliment as if they expected a receipt.   —KIN HUBBARD

Computer

To err is human; to really foul things up requires a computer.   —BILL VAUGHAN

Conference

A conference is a gathering of important people who singly can do nothing, but together can decide that nothing can be done.   —FRED ALLEN

A meeting of the bored.   —RUSSELL' NEWBOLD

Confessions

Confessions may be good for the soul but they are bad for the reputation.   —THOMAS ROBERT DEWAR

Connections

Many a live wire would be a dead one except for his connections.   —WILSON MIZNER

Conscience

Conscience and reputation are two things. Conscience is due to yourself, reputation to your neighbor.

—ST. AUGUSTINE

Reason often makes mistakes, but conscience never does.

—JOSH BILLINGS

Conscience is thoroughly well bred and soon leaves off talking to those who do not wish to hear it.

—SAMUEL BUTLER

Once we assuage our conscience by calling something a "necessary evil," it begins to look more and more necessary and less and less evil.   —SYDNEY J. HARRIS

Conscience: the inner voice which warns us that someone may be looking.   —H. L. MENCKEN

Conservatism

What is conservatism? Is it not adherence to the old and tried, against the new and untried?

—ABRAHAM LINCOLN

Conservative

I never dared to be a radical when young
For fear it would make me conservative when old.
—ROBERT FROST

Consideration

Be kind and considerate to others, depending somewhat
upon who they are.   —DON HEROLD

Contentment

Enjoy your own life without comparing it with that of
another.   —CONDORCET

When we cannot find contentment in ourselves it is use-
less to seek it elsewhere.   —LA ROCHEFOUCAULD

Control

In the order named, these are the hardest to control:
Wine, Women, and Song.   —FRANKLIN PIERCE ADAMS

Conversation

The true spirit of conversation consists in building on
another man's observation, not overturning it.
—EDWARD BULWER-LYTTON

His conversation does not show the minute hand, but
he strikes the hour very correctly.
—BENJAMIN FRANKLIN

Conversation is the slowest form of human communication.   —DON HEROLD

Conversation should be fired in short bursts; anybody
who talks steadily for more than a minute is in danger of
boring somebody.   —HARLAN MILLER

The less men think, the more they talk.
—MONTESQUIEU

I often quote myself; it adds spice to my conversation.
—GEORGE BERNARD SHAW

Conceit causes more conversation than wit.
—LA ROCHEFOUCAULD

It is better to ask some of the questions than to know
all the answers.   —JAMES THURBER

Cooking

Fish, to taste right, must swim three times—in water, in butter, and in wine.   —POLISH PROVERB

Let the salad-maker be a spendthrift for oil—a miser for vinegar—a statesman for salt—and a madman for mixing.   —SPANISH PROVERB

Courage

Fear gives sudden instincts of skill.
                              —SAMUEL TAYLOR COLERIDGE

Fortune favors the audacious.   —ERASMUS

Nature reacts only to physical disease, but also to moral weakness; when the danger increases, she gives us greater courage.   —GOETHE

I have never thought much of the courage of the lion-tamer; inside the cage he is, at least, safe from other men.
                              —GEORGE BERNARD SHAW

Courtesy

True politeness consists in being easy with one's self, and making every one about one as easy as one can.
                              —ALEXANDER POPE

We cannot always oblige, but we can always speak obligingly.   —VOLTAIRE

Courtship

The word "engagement" has two meanings: in war it's a battle, in courtship it's a surrender.
                              —GENERAL FEATURES CORPORATION

Coward

To sin by silence when they should protest makes cowards out of men.   —ABRAHAM LINCOLN

Crime

If you do big things they print your face, and if you do little things they only print your thumbs.
                              —ARTHUR (BUGS) BAER

We enact many laws that manufacture criminals, and then a few that punish them.   —JOSIAH TUCKER

Critic

A drama critic is a man who leaves no turn unstoned.
—GEORGE BERNARD SHAW

Criticism

There is always something wrong with a man, as there is with a motor, when he knocks continually.
—COLUMBIA RECORD

Clean your finger before you point at my spots.
—BENJAMIN FRANKLIN

The actor who took the role of King Lear played the King as though he expected someone to play the ace.
—EUGENE FIELD

Even the lion has to defend himself against flies.
—GERMAN PROVERB

I don't like yes men. I want you to tell me what you really think—even if it costs you your job.
—SAM GOLDWYN

The trouble with most of us is that we would rather be ruined by praise than saved by criticism.
—NORMAN VINCENT PEALE

Critic: One who finds a little bad in the best of things.
—JOSEPH P. RITZ

When you point your finger at someone else, you have three fingers pointed at yourself.   —LOUIS NIZER

The scenery in the play was beautiful, but the actors got in front of it.   —ALEXANDER WOOLLCOTT

Cures

There's something alive about a kitchen, the way it smells and sounds and feels. Maybe sick people would all live longer if they sat in kitchens.
—CHRISTOPHER MORLEY

Curiosity

Curiosity is the only intelligence test which tells what one may become as well as what one is.
—SATURDAY REVIEW

Why do they call it idle curiosity when it's pretty close to the one thing never idle?   —MARION STAR

Debt

The house was more covered with mortgages than with paint.   —GEORGE ADE

Debt is a trap which a man sets and baits himself—and catches himself.   —JOSH BILLINGS

Deception

Nothing is so easy as to deceive one's self, for what we wish, that we readily believe.   —DEMOSTHENES

Necessity is the mother of deception.
   —BELLE SARNOFF

Decision

When a decision has been made and the die is cast, then murder the alternatives.   —MRS. EMORY S. ADAMS, JR.

Making up your mind is like making a bed; it usually helps to have someone on the other side.
   —GERALD HORTON BATH

A woman's final decision is not necessarily the same as the one she makes later.   —H. N. FERGUSON

Deeds

One good deed has many claimants.
   —YIDDISH PROVERB

Democracy

The tyranny of the multitude is a multiplied tyranny.
   —EDMUND BURKE

. Democracy is based upon the conviction that there are extraordinary possibilities in the ordinary people.
   —HARRY EMERSON FOSDICK

Republics end through luxury; monarchies through poverty.   —MONTESQUIEU

Democracy is a form of government in which it is permitted to wonder aloud what the country could do under first-class management.   —"SENATOR SOAPER"

Dentist

A dentist at work in his vocation always looks down in the mouth.   —GEORGE D. PRENTICE

Depressions

Depressions may bring people closer to the church, but so do funerals.　—CLARENCE DARROW

Description

When something defies description, let it.

—ARNOLD H. GLASOW

Diet

She used to diet on any kind of food she could lay her hands on.　—ARTHUR (BUGS) BAER

Eat breakfast like a king, eat lunch like a prince, but eat dinner like a pauper.　—ADELLE DAVIS

The sad thing about most diets is they do so much for the will power and so little for the waistline.

—"GRAND OLE OPRY"

Another good reducing exercise consists in placing both hands against the table edge and pushing back.

—ROBERT QUILLEN

Differences

People differ. Some object to the fan dancer, and others to the fan.　—ELIZABETH W. SPALDING

Diligence

Everything yields to diligence.　—ANTIPHANES

Diplomacy

Diplomacy: lying in state.　—OLIVER HERFORD

Diplomacy is to do and say the nastiest thing in the nicest way.　—ISAAC GOLDBERG

A diplomat is a man who remembers a lady's birthday but forgets her age.　—AUTHOR UNKNOWN

Discipline

Say what you will about the Ten Commandments, you must always come back to the pleasant fact that there are only ten of them.　—H. L. MENCKEN

Discretion

There's a time to wink as well as to see.

—BENJAMIN FRANKLIN

Discussion

I'll discuss anything. I like to go perhaps-ing around on all subjects. —ROBERT FROST

Dissatisfaction

It's when you're safe at home that you wish you were having an adventure. When you're having an adventure you wish you were safe at home. —THORNTON WILDER

Divorce

Divorce is what happens when the marriage you thought was a merger turns out to be a conglomerate.

—"HOT LINES"

People wouldn't get divorced for such trivial reasons if they didn't get married for such trivial reasons.

—BRIDGEPORT STAR

Doctor

A man who tells you if you don't cut something out, he will. —FRANK ROSSITER

Dogs

If dogs could talk, perhaps we'd find it just as hard to get along with them as we do with people.

—KAREL ČAPEK

Doubt

To believe with certainty we must begin with doubting.

—STANISLAUS LESCYNSKI

I respect faith, but doubting is what gets you an education. —WILLIAM MIZNER

Drinking

Some men are like musical glasses; to produce their finest tones you must keep them wet.

—SAMUEL TAYLOR COLERIDGE

Bacchus has drowned more men than Neptune.

—GARIBALDI

Wine makes a man better pleased with himself; I do not say that it makes him more pleasing to others.

—SAMUEL JOHNSON

There is a devil in every berry of the grape.

—THE KORAN

Liquor talks mighty loud when it gets loose from the jug. —JOEL CHANDLER HARRIS

I drink to make other people interesting.

—GEORGE JEAN NATHAN

I'm not willing to sacrifice the control of physical and mental ability that drinking and smoking take away for what they give in return. —PIERRE TRUDEAU

I must get out of these wet clothes and into a dry martini. —ALEXANDER WOOLLCOTT

Driving

Drive carefully! Remember: it's not only a car that can be recalled by its maker. —CONSUMERS DIGEST

Duty

One trouble with the world is that so many people who stand up vigorously for their rights fall down miserably on their duties. —GRIT

A sense of duty is useful in work but offensive in personal relations. —BERTRAND RUSSELL

He who eats the fruit should at least plant the seed.

—HENRY DAVID THOREAU

Earnestness

Earnest people are often people who habitually look on the serious side of things that have no serious side.

—VAN WYCK BROOKS

Economy

So often we rob tomorrow's memories by today's economies. —JOHN MASON BROWN

Editing

I have made this a rather long letter because I haven't had time to make it shorter.   —PASCAL

The hardest thing for some people to say in 25 words or less is "Good-by."   —TONY PETTITO

Education

I find that a great part of the information I have was acquired by looking up something and finding something else on the way.   —FRANKLIN P. ADAMS

The primary purpose of education is not to teach you to earn your bread, but to make every mouthful sweeter.
—JAMES ANGELL

I have never let my schooling interfere with my education.   —MARK TWAIN

There is nothing so stupid as an educated man, if you get off the thing that he was educated in.
—WILL ROGERS

Universities are full of knowledge; the freshman brings a little in and the seniors take none away, and knowledge accumulates.   —ABBOT LAWRENCE LOWELL

Education is what remains when we have forgotten all that we have been taught.
—GEORGE SAVILE, MARQUIS OF HALIFAX

A man who has never gone to school may steal from a freight car; but if he has a university education, he may steal the whole railroad.   —THEODORE ROOSEVELT

Ego

Most men are like eggs, too full of themselves to hold anything else.   —JOSH BILLINGS

The personal pronoun "I" should be the coat of arms of some individuals.   —COMTE DE RIVAROL

When a man is wrapped up in himself he makes a pretty small package.   —JOHN RUSKIN

Eloquence

Eloquence is logic on fire.   —LYMAN BEECHER

Emotions

This is the greatest paradox; the emotions cannot be trusted, yet it is they that tell us the greatest truths.

—DON HEROLD

Encouragement

Correction does much, but encouragement does more; encouragement after censure is as the sun after a shower.

—GOETHE

Entertainment

Nightclub: A place where they take the rest out of restaurant and put the din in dinner.   —READER'S DIGEST

Enthusiasm

Every production of genius must be the production of enthusiasm.   —DISRAELI

He came to his job fired with enthusiasm and left it the same way.   —MAX RUBIN

Equality

Though all men are made of one metal, yet they were not cast all in the same mold.   —THOMAS FULLER

Men are made by nature unequal. It is vain, therefore, to treat them as if they were equal.

—JAMES ANTHONY FROUDE

The only real equality is in the cemetery.

—GERMAN PROVERB

Evaluation

The injury we do and the one we suffer are not weighed in the same scales.   —AESOP

Executive

The mark of a true executive is usually illegible.

—LEO J. FARRELL, JR.

Exercise

Whenever I feel like exercise, I lie down until the feeling passes.   —ROBERT M. HUTCHINS

The only exercise I get is when I take the studs out of one shirt and put them in another.   —RING LARDNER

Experience

Experience increases our wisdom but doesn't reduce our follies.   —JOSH BILLINGS

To stumble twice against the same stone, is a proverbial disgrace.   —CICERO

I believe in getting into hot water; it keeps you clean.
—G. K. CHESTERTON

Experience is not what happens to a man. It is what a man does with what happens to him.
—ALDOUS HUXLEY

Experience is the name everyone gives to his mistakes.
—OSCAR WILDE

Eyes

The eyes of the dead are closed gently; we also have to open gently the eyes of the living.   —JEAN COCTEAU

The sky is the daily bread of the eyes.
—RALPH WALDO EMERSON

There's so much to say but your eyes keep interrupting me.   —CHRISTOPHER MORLEY

Face

There are people who think that everything one does with a serious face is sensible.   —G. C. LICHTENBERG

He had the sort of face that, once seen, is never remembered.   —OSCAR WILDE

Facts

Every man has a right to his opinion, but no man has a right to be wrong in his facts.   —BERNARD BARUCH

Faith

All I have seen teaches me to trust the Creator for all I have not seen.   —RALPH WALDO EMERSON

I have no faith, very little hope, and as much charity as I can afford.   —T. H. HUXLEY

Let us have faith that right makes might; and in that faith, let us, to the end, dare to do our duty as we understand it.   —ABRAHAM LINCOLN

I can see how it might be possible for a man to look down upon the earth and be an atheist, but I cannot conceive how he could look up into the heavens and say there is no God.   —ABRAHAM LINCOLN

Faith is the force of life.   —TOLSTOY

I can believe anything, provided it is incredible.

—OSCAR WILDE

Fame

Fame is the perfume of heroic deeds.   —SOCRATES

Familiarity

Though familiarity may not breed contempt, it takes off the edge of admiration.   —WILLIAM HAZLITT

Family

The first half of our lives is ruined by our parents and the second half by our children.   —CLARENCE DARROW

Most parents don't worry about a daughter till she fails to show up for breakfast, and then it's too late.

—KIN HUBBARD

All happy families are alike, but each unhappy family is unhappy in its own way.   —TOLSTOY

There is little less trouble in governing a private family than a whole kingdom.   —MONTAIGNE

Fashion

Fashion is made to become unfashionable.

—GABRIELLE CHANEL

Fashion is gentility running away from vulgarity, and afraid of being overtaken.   —WILLIAM HAZLITT

She had a passion for hats, none of which returned her affection.   —STORM JAMESON

High heels were invented by a woman who had been kissed on the forehead.   —CHRISTOPHER MORLEY

I see that the fashion wears out more apparel than the man.   —SHAKESPEARE

A fashion is nothing but an induced epidemic.

—GEORGE BERNARD SHAW

Women's styles may change but the designs remain the same. —OSCAR WILDE

Fashion is a form of ugliness so intolerable that we have to alter it every six months. —OSCAR WILDE

All women's dresses are merely variations on the eternal struggle between the admitted desire to dress and the unadmitted desire to undress. —LIN YUTANG

Fault

She is intolerable, but that is her only fault.

—TALLEYRAND

Fear

If a man harbors any sort of fear, it percolates through all his thinking, damages his personality, makes him landlord to a ghost. —LLOYD C. DOUGLAS

There's nothing I'm afraid of like scared people.

—ROBERT FROST

The misfortunes hardest to bear are those which never happen. —JAMES RUSSELL LOWELL

Of all the liars in the world, sometimes the worst are your own fears. —RUDYARD KIPLING

In this world, there is always danger for those who are afraid of it. —GEORGE BERNARD SHAW

To him who is in fear everything rustles.

—SOPHOCLES

It takes up too much time, being afraid.

—PIERRE TRUDEAU

Feeling

Half our mistakes in life arise from feeling where we ought to think, and thinking where we ought to feel.

—JOHN CHURTON COLLINS

Figures

She had a lot of fat that did not fit.

—HERBERT GEORGE WELLS

Nothing is so fallacious as facts, except figures.

—GEORGE CANNING

Flattery

He soft-soaped her until she couldn't see for the suds.

—MARY ROBERTS RINEHART

The art of telling another person exactly what he thinks of himself.   —PAUL H. GILBERT

Flattery never hurts a man unless he inhales.

—HARRY EMERSON FOSDICK

Men are like stone jugs—you may lug them where you like by the ears.   —SAMUEL JOHNSON

Flirtation

Flirtation, attention without intention.

—MAX O'RELL

Folly

A good folly is worth whatever you pay for it.

—GEORGE ADE

If fifty million say a foolish thing it is still a foolish thing.   —ANATOLE FRANCE

Food

No man is lonely while eating spaghetti—it requires so much attention.   —CHRISTOPHER MORLEY

Fools

A learned fool is more foolish than an ignorant fool.

—MOLIÈRE

Forgiveness

Forgive others often, yourself never.

—PUBLILIUS SYRUS

Freedom

In free countries, every man is entitled to express his opinions—and every other man is entitled not to listen.

—G. NORMAN COLLIE

All men are born free and unequal.   —GRANT ALLEN

A man's worst difficulties begin when he is able to do as he likes.   —T. H. HUXLEY

We must be willing to pay a price for freedom, for no price that is ever asked for it is half the cost of doing without it.   —H. L. MENCKEN

Liberty means responsibility. That is why most men dread it.   —GEORGE BERNARD SHAW

Friends

A true friend is one soul in two bodies.   —ARISTOTLE

Friend: one who knows all about you and loves you just the same.   —ELBERT HUBBARD

Friendship

Love is blind; friendship tries not to notice.
—OTTO VON BISMARCK

The only way to have a friend is to be one.
—RALPH WALDO EMERSON

Friendship is the best gift you can give yourself.
—ELMER LETERMAN

Fun

Fun is like life insurance; the older you get, the more it costs.   —KIN HUBBARD

Future

I try to be as philosophical as the old lady from Vermont who said that the best thing about the future is that it only comes one day at a time.   —DEAN ACHESON

My interest is in the future because I am going to spend the rest of my life there.
—CHARLES FRANKLIN KETTERING

The trouble with our times is that the future is not what it used to be.   —PAUL VALÉRY

Giving

The world is composed of takers and givers. The takers may eat better, but the givers sleep better.
—BYRON FREDERICK in *Ohio State Grange Monthly*

Golf

A game where the ball always lies poorly and the player well.   —READER'S DIGEST

I play Civil War golf—out in 61—back in 65.

—DOROTHY SARNOFF

Golf is a good walk spoiled.   —MARK TWAIN

Gossip

Too often when you tell a secret it goes in one ear and in another.   —LESLIE E. DUNKIN

Rare is the person who can weigh the faults of others without putting his thumb on the scales.

—BYRON J. LANGENFELD

She poured a little social sewage into his ears.

—GEORGE MEREDITH

Busy souls have no time to be busybodies.

—AUSTIN O'MALLEY

Government

We sometimes wonder whether the members of Congress would have to mend their fences so often if they had not sat on them so much.   —CHRISTIAN SCIENCE MONITOR

Isn't it a shame that future generations can't be here to see all the wonderful things we're doing with their money?   —EARL WILSON

Graduation

Some men are graduated from college cum laude, some are graduated summa cum laude, and some are graduated mirabile dictu.   —WILLIAM HOWARD TAFT

Grammar

Grammar school never taught me anything about grammar.   —ISAAC GOLDBERG

Grief

The busy have no time for tears.   —LORD BYRON

The swallows of sorrow may fly overhead, but don't let them nest in your hair.   —CHINESE PROVERB

Sorrows are like thunderclouds—in the distance they look black, over our heads scarcely gray.

—JEAN PAUL RICHTER

Guest

No one can be so welcome a guest that he will not annoy his host after three days.   —PLAUTUS

Habit

Cultivate good habits—the bad ones all grow wild.

—DETROIT HOME GAZETTE

The unfortunate thing about this world is that good habits are so much easier to get out of than bad ones.

—W. SOMERSET MAUGHAM

Habits are at first cobwebs, then cables.

—SPANISH PROVERB

Hair

What's on the head is not as important as what's in it.

—MILTON RAYMOND

Happiness

Not in doing what you like but in liking what you do is the secret of happiness.   —J. M. BARRIE

There is no cosmetic for beauty like happiness.

—LADY MARGUERITE BLESSINGTON

Action may not always bring happiness, but there is no happiness without action.   —DISRAELI

Though we travel the world over to find the beautiful, we must carry it with us or we find it not.

—RALPH WALDO EMERSON

Human felicity is produced not so much by great pieces of good fortune that seldom happen, as by little advantages that occur every day.

—BENJAMIN FRANKLIN

Happiness makes up in height for what it lacks in length.

—ROBERT FROST

We act as though comfort and luxury were the chief requirements of life when all that we need to make us really happy is something to be enthusiastic about.

—CHARLES KINGSLEY

Most folks are about as happy as they make up their minds to be.   —ABRAHAM LINCOLN

Hate

Hating people is like burning down your own house to get rid of a rat.   —HARRY EMERSON FOSDICK

People hate, as they love, unreasonably.

—THACKERAY

Health

He who has health has hope, and he who has hope has everything.   —ARABIAN PROVERB

My constitution was destroyed long ago; now I'm living under the bylaws.   —CLARENCE DARROW

Help

The best place to find a helping hand is at the end of your arm.   —ELMER LETERMAN

Hesitation

He who hesitates is sometimes saved.

—JAMES THURBER

Hindsight

Ah, the insight of hindsight!   —THURSTON N. DAVIS

Hobby

Hard work that you would be ashamed to do for a living.   —GILBERT NORWOOD

Honor

Our own heart, and not other men's opinion, forms our true honor.   —SAMUEL TAYLOR COLERIDGE

Hope

Appetite, with an opinion of attaining, is called hope; the same without such opinion, despair.

—THOMAS HOBBES

Hosts

People are either born hosts or born guests.

—MAX BEERBOHM

Hotels

Where you give up good dollars for bad quarters.

—BILLY ROSE

Sign outside a small hotel: "Have your next affair here."

—SPEAKER'S ENCYCLOPEDIA

Houses

A man's dignity may be enhanced by the house he lives in, but not wholly secure by it; the owner should bring honor to the house, not the house to its owner.

—CICERO

Humanity

I love my country better than my family; but I love humanity better than my country.   —FÉNELON

You must not lose faith in humanity. Humanity is an ocean; if a few drops of the ocean are dirty, the ocean does not become dirty.   —GANDHI

After all there is but one race—humanity.

—GEORGE MOORE

Humor

Humor is the good-natured side of truth.

—MARK TWAIN

Ideas

Great ideas need landing gear as well as wings.

—ADOLPH A. BERLE, JR.

Ignorance

Everybody is ignorant, only on different subjects.

—WILL ROGERS

Illusion

Illusion is the first of all pleasures.   —VOLTAIRE

Image

To know oneself is to foresee oneself; to foresee oneself amounts to playing a part.   —PAUL VALÉRY

Imagination

A man's life is dyed the color of his imagination.
                                                            —MARCUS AURELIUS
Imagination is more important than knowledge.
                                                            —ALBERT EINSTEIN
Anything one man can imagine, other men can make real.   —JULES VERNE
Imagination is the eye of the soul.   —JOUBERT

Impossibility

You cannot make a crab walk straight.
                                                            —ARISTOPHANES
The airplane, the atomic bomb, and the zipper have cured me of any tendency to state that a thing can't be done.   —R. L. DUFFUS

Improbable

The improbable happens just often enough to make life either disturbing or delightful.
                                                            —WILLIAM FEATHER

Improvement

It is necessary to try to surpass one's self always; this occupation ought to last as long as life.
                                                            —QUEEN CHRISTINA

Indecision

There is grief in indecision.   —CICERO

Inferiority

No one can make you feel inferior without your consent.
                                                            —ELEANOR ROOSEVELT

Infidelity

The plural of spouse is spice.
                                                            —CHRISTOPHER MORLEY

Inflation

A little inflation is like a little pregnancy—it keeps on growing.　—LEON HENDERSON

Influence

Goethe said there would be little left of him if he were to discard what he owed to others.

—CHARLOTTE CUSHMAN

It is only the people with push who have a pull.

—THOMAS ROBERT DEWAR

I am a part of all that I have met.

—ALFRED LORD TENNYSON

Interest

You must learn day by day, year by year, to broaden your horizon. The more things you love, the more you are interested in, the more you enjoy.

—ETHEL BARRYMORE

Intolerance

If the bell of intolerance tolls for one, it tolls for all.

—HENRY SEIDEL CANBY

Intuition

Intuition is reason in a hurry.　—HOLBROOK JACKSON

A woman's guess is much more accurate than a man's certainty.　—RUDYARD KIPLING

Invention

How come, if necessity is the mother of invention, all this unnecessary stuff gets invented?

—GENERAL FEATURES CORPORATION

Italy

The Creator made Italy from designs by Michelangelo.

—MARK TWAIN

Joy

Real joy comes not from ease or riches or from the praise of men, but from doing something worthwhile.

—Sir Wilfred Grenfell

Grief can take care of itself; but to get the full value of joy you must have somebody to divide it with.

—Mark Twain

Judgment

Next to knowing when to seize an opportunity, the most important thing in life is to forgo an advantage.

—Disraeli

Jury

A jury consists of twelve persons chosen to decide who has the better lawyer.   —Robert Frost

Justice

By the just we mean that which is lawful and that which is fair and equitable.   —Aristotle

Justice is too good for some people, and not good enough for the rest.   —Norman Douglas

Justice is the constant desire and effort to render to every man his due.   —Justinian

Justice is spontaneous respect, mutually guaranteed, for human dignity, in whatever person it may be compromised and under whatever circumstances, and to whatever risk its defense may expose us.   —P. J. Proudhon

Kindness

The kindness planned for tomorrow doesn't count today.

—Newark (Del.) Post

Loving kindness is greater than laws; and the charities of life are more than all ceremonies.   —The Talmud

Knowledge

Strange how much you've got to know before you know how little you know.   —Best Quotations

To be conscious that you are ignorant is a great step to knowledge.   —Disraeli

There are two great boosters which propel a man into the upper spaces of society and accomplishment—knowledge and wisdom. —SELIG EDELMAN

Our knowledge is the amassed thought and experience of innumerable minds. —RALPH WALDO EMERSON

He was not made for climbing the tree of knowledge.
—SIGRID UNDSET

Lady

A lady is a woman in whose presence a man is a gentleman. —PEG BRACKEN

Land

If a man owns land, the land owns him.
—RALPH WALDO EMERSON

Language

Slang is language that takes off its coat, spits on its hands, and goes to work. —CARL SANDBURG

England and America are two countries separated by the same language. —GEORGE BERNARD SHAW

Laughter

Laughing is the sensation of feeling good all over, and showing it principally in one spot. —JOSH BILLINGS

Men show their character in nothing more clearly than by what they think laughable. —GOETHE

Law

Laws too gentle are seldom obeyed; too severe, seldom executed. —BENJAMIN FRANKLIN

A successful lawsuit is the one worn by a policeman.
—ROBERT FROST

Be you never so high, the law is above you.
—THOMAS FULLER

Law is experience developed by reason and applied continually to further experience.
—ROSCOE POUND, *Time*, May 5, 1958

The execution of the laws is more important than the making of them. —JEFFERSON

Innocence finds not near so much protection as guilt.
—LA ROCHEFOUCAULD

Leadership

One of the tests of leadership is the ability to recognize a problem before it becomes an emergency.
—ARNOLD H. GLASOW

We don't want to be like the leader in the French Revolution who said, "There go my people. I must find out where they are going so I can lead them."
—THE KENNEDY WIT

The shepherd always tries to persuade the sheep that their interests and his own are the same.   —STENDHAL

Learning

Histories make men wise; poets, witty; mathematics, subtile; natural philosophy, deep; morals, grave; logic and rhetoric, able to contend.   —BACON

There are more men ennobled by study than by nature.
—CICERO

We can easily forgive a child who is afraid of the dark; the real tragedy of life is when men are afraid of the light.
—PLATO

Iron sharpens iron; scholar, the scholar.
—THE TALMUD

Lecturer

Lecturer: one with his hand in your pocket, his tongue in your ear, and his faith in your patience.
—AMBROSE BIERCE

Leisure

The secret of being miserable is to have leisure to bother about whether you are happy or not.
—GEORGE BERNARD SHAW

Liberal

I can remember way back when a liberal was one who was generous with his own money.   —WILL ROGERS

Life

Life is a long lesson in humility.   —J. M. BARRIE

Life is like playing a violin solo in public and learning the instrument as one goes on.   —SAMUEL BUTLER

The tragedy of life is not so much what men suffer, but rather what they miss.   —THOMAS CARLYLE

Life is too short to be small.   —DISRAELI

You've got to love people, places, ideas; you've got to live with mind, body, soul; you've got to be committed; there is no life on the side-lines.

—BESS MYERSON GRANT

It is but a few short years from diapers to dignity and from dignity to decomposition.   —DON HEROLD

Life can only be understood backwards, but it must be lived forwards.   —SØREN KIERKEGAARD

Life is easier to take than you'd think; all that is necessary is to accept the impossible, do without the indispensable, and bear the tolerable.   —KATHLEEN NORRIS

Life is not a spectacle or a feast; it is a predicament.

—GEORGE SANTAYANA

The process of living is the process of reacting to stress.

—STANLEY J. SARNOFF, *Time*, November 29, 1963

Begin at once to live, and count each day as a separate life.   —SENECA

As is a tale, so is life: not how long it is, but how good it is, is what matters.   —SENECA

Simply the thing I am shall make me live.

—SHAKESPEARE

Life is no brief candle to me; it is a sort of splendid torch which I have got hold of for the moment, and I want to make it burn as brightly as possible before handing it on to future generations.

—GEORGE BERNARD SHAW

It is better to burn the candle at both ends, and in the middle, too, than to put it away in the closet and let the mice eat it.   —HENRY VAN DYKE

Listening

We have two ears and only one tongue in order that we may hear more and speak less.   —DIOGENES

No man would listen to you talk if he didn't know it was his turn next.   —EDGAR WATSON HOWE

A good listener is not only popular everywhere, but after a while he knows something.   —WILSON MIZNER

Love

When a couple of young people strongly devoted to each other commence to eat onions, it is safe to pronounce them engaged.   —JAMES MONTGOMERY BAILEY

Love is the delightful interval between meeting a beautiful girl and discovering that she looks like a haddock.
—JOHN BARRYMORE

Love is said to be blind, but I know lots of fellows in love who can see twice as much in their sweethearts as I can.   —JOSH BILLINGS

The way to love anything is to realize that it might be lost.   —G. K. CHESTERTON

Love is an ocean of emotions, entirely surrounded by expenses.   —THOMAS ROBERT DEWAR

If you would be loved, love and be lovable.
—BENJAMIN FRANKLIN

As soon as you cannot keep anything from a woman, you love her.   —PAUL GERALDY

No one knows the worth of woman's love till he sues for alienation.   —OLIVER HERFORD

He gave her a look that you could have poured on a waffle.   —RING LARDNER

Come live in my heart and pay no rent.
—SAMUEL LOVER

Love has the power of making you believe what you would normally treat with the deepest suspicion.
—PIERRE MARIVAUX

Love is the triumph of imagination over intelligence.
—H. L. MENCKEN

Most of these love triangles are wreck tangles.
—JACOB BRAUDE

Love is a gross exaggeration of the difference between one person and everybody else.
—GEORGE BERNARD SHAW

To love her was a liberal education

—WILBUR DANIEL STEELE

Luck

I am a great believer in luck, and I find the harder I work the more I have of it.   —STEPHEN LEACOCK

He is so unlucky that he runs into accidents which started out to happen to somebody else.

—DON MARQUIS

The only good luck many great men ever had was being born with the ability and determination to overcome bad luck.   —CHANNING POLLOCK

Luxury

Give me the luxuries in life and I will willingly do without the necessities.   —FRANK LLOYD WRIGHT

Any bare necessity—with taxes added.

—DAVID CROWN

Lying

I can't tell a lie—even when I hear one.

—JOHN KENDRICK BANGS

No man has a good enough memory to make a successful liar.   —ABRAHAM LINCOLN

The tombstone is about the only thing that can stand upright and lie on its face at the same time.

—MARY WILSON LITTLE

Man

Every man is a volume, if you know how to read him.

—WILLIAM ELLERY CHANNING

It is easier to know mankind in general than man individually.   —LA ROCHEFOUCAULD

Man is the greatest miracle and greatest problem on earth.   —DAVID SARNOFF

Man was made at the end of the week's work when God was tired.   —MARK TWAIN

Mankind

One small step for a man, one giant leap for mankind.
—NEIL ARMSTRONG

The human race is in jeopardy whenever power, insensitivity and ignorance are joined together whatever the national banner.   —NORMAN COUSINS

Man-Woman

The test of a man is how well he is able to feel about what he thinks. The test of a woman is how well she is able to think about what she feels.

—MARY McDOWELL

Dancing is wonderful training for girls, it's the first way you learn to guess what a man is going to do before he does it.   —CHRISTOPHER MORLEY

Most men hope that their lean years are behind them; women hope that theirs are ahead.   —READER'S DIGEST

A woman is perturbed by what a man forgets—a man by what a woman remembers.   —ARCH WARD

I like men who have a future and women who have a past.   —OSCAR WILDE

To a smart girl, men are no problem—they're the answer.   —ZSA ZSA GABOR

Manners

When Civil Service was a commodity obtainable in restaurants.   —JACOB BRAUDE

Men make laws; women make manners.

—DE SÉGUR

Happiness is the best teacher of good manners; only the unhappy are churlish.   —CHRISTOPHER MORLEY

Good breeding consists in concealing how much we think of ourselves and how little we think of the other person.   —MARK TWAIN

Marriage

Some women work so hard to make good husbands that they never quite manage to make good wives.

—MARY ALKUS

If you are afraid of loneliness do not marry.
—CHEKHOV

Marriage is a feast where the grace is sometimes better than the dinner. —CHARLES CALEB COLTON

Don't think because there's a ring on your finger you don't have to try anymore.
—HAL DAVID, *Wives and Lovers*

It destroys one's nerves to be amiable every day to the same human being. —DISRAELI

The chain of wedlock is so heavy that it takes two to carry it, sometimes three. —ALEXANDRE DUMAS

Keep your eyes wide open before marriage, and half-shut afterwards. —BENJAMIN FRANKLIN

There is nothing stronger
and nobler than when man and wife
are of one heart and mind in a house,
A grief to their foes,
and to their friends great joy,
but their own hearts know it best. —HOMER

Many a man in love with a dimple makes the mistake of marrying the whole girl. —STEPHEN LEACOCK

The trouble with marriage is that while every woman is at heart a mother, every man is at heart a bachelor.
—E. V. LUCAS (*Reader's Digest*)

In modern wedlock, too many misplace the key.
—TOM MASSON

The great secret of successful marriage is to treat all disasters as incidents and none of the incidents as disasters.
—HAROLD NICOLSON

A husband is one who stands by you in troubles you wouldn't have had if you hadn't married him.
—READER'S DIGEST

In olden times sacrifices were made at the altar—a custom which is still continued. —HELEN ROWLAND

Matrimony was probably the first union to defy management. —CHARLES RUFFING

Why does "I do" turn into "I don't," "I won't," "I want"?
—MARILYN SCHUSTRIN

If we take matrimony at its lowest, we regard it as a sort of friendship recognized by the police.

—ROBERT LOUIS STEVENSON

Medicine

The trouble with being a hypochondriac these days is that antibiotics have cured all the good diseases.

—CASKIE STINNETT

Men

Boys will be boys, and so will a lot of middle-aged men.

—KIN HUBBARD

In relation to each other men are like irregular verbs in different languages; nearly all verbs are slightly irregular.

—SØREN KIERKEGAARD

Mind

It is well for people who think to change their minds occasionally in order to keep them clean.

—LUTHER BURBANK

Minds are like parachutes: they only function when open.

—THOMAS ROBERT DEWAR

Man's mind stretched to a new idea never goes back to its original dimensions.   —OLIVER WENDELL HOLMES

Mistakes

I can pardon everyone's mistakes except my own.

—MARCUS CATO

Moderation

I believe in moderation in all things including moderation.   —J. F. CARTER

I have not been afraid of excess: excess on occasion is exhilarating. It prevents moderation from acquiring the deadening effect of a habit.   —SOMERSET MAUGHAM

Money

Money often costs too much.

—RALPH WALDO EMERSON

The safest way to double your money is to fold it over once and put it in your pocket.   —KIN HUBBARD

I'm living so far beyond my income that we may almost be said to be living apart.   —H. H. MUNRO

When I was young I used to think that money was the most important thing in life; now that I am old, I know it is.   —OSCAR WILDE

Morals

What is moral is what you feel good after and what is immoral is what you feel bad after.

—ERNEST HEMINGWAY

A moral being is one who is capable of reflecting on his past actions and their motives—of approving of some and disapproving of others.   —CHARLES DARWIN

The state has no place in the bedrooms of the nation.

—PIERRE TRUDEAU

Motivation

The one sacred thing is the dissatisfaction of man with himself and his striving to be better than he is.

—MAXIM GORKY

The world is divided into people who do things and people who get the credit. Try, if you can, to belong to the first class. There's far less competition.

—DWIGHT MORROW

When I was a young man I observed that nine out of ten things I did were failures. I didn't want to be a failure, so I did ten times more work.

—GEORGE BERNARD SHAW

Movies

A wide screen just makes a bad film twice as bad.

—SAMUEL GOLDWYN

Music

Of all noises, I think music is the least disagreeable.

—SAMUEL JOHNSON

Wagner has beautiful moments but awful quarter hours.

—GIOACCHINO A. ROSSINI

How wonderful opera would be if there were no singers.
—GIOACCHINO A. ROSSINI

Nation

A nation can be only as great as its people want it to be.
A nation can be only as free as its people insist that it be.
A nation's laws are only as strong as its people's will to
see them enforced.   —RICHARD M. NIXON

Need

The entire sum of existence is the magic of being needed
by just one person.   —VII PUTNAM

Nerves

As nervous as a topless waitress at a candlelight dinner.
—BOB HOPE
As nervous as a tree on the Lassie program.

—FERRIS MACK

Neurotic

A person who, when you ask how she is, tells you.
—ELEANOR CLARAGE (*Reader's Digest*)

Nudity

I never expected to see the day when girls get sunburned
in the places they now do.   —WILL ROGERS

Obedience

One of the first things a man notices in a backward
country is that the children are still obeying their parents.
—CLAUDE CALLAN (*Reader's Digest*)

Obsolescence

The danger of personal obsolescence has never been
greater.   —LOUIS R. RADER

Opinion

He thinks by infection, catching an opinion like a cold.
—JOHN RUSKIN

He never chooses an opinion; he just wears whatever happens to be in style.   —LEO TOLSTOY

Opportunity

A wise man will make more opportunities than he finds.
                                                      —FRANCIS BACON

There is an hour in each man's life appointed to make his happiness, if then he seize it.
                                            —BEAUMONT AND FLETCHER

Many are called but few get up.
                                                    —OLIVER HERFORD

Equality of opportunity is an equal opportunity to prove unequal talents.   —VISCOUNT SAMUEL

Optimism

I am an optimist. It does not seem too much use being anything else.   —WINSTON CHURCHILL

A pinch of probably is worth a pound of perhaps.
                                                      —JAMES THURBER

Parents

The two most difficult careers are entrusted to amateurs —citizenship and parenthood.
                                        —ST. JOHN'S (Newfoundland) HERALD

Parties

Disarmament is like a party. Nobody wants to arrive until everyone else is there.   —CHANGING TIMES

Patience

Laziness is often mistaken for patience.
                                                    —FRENCH PROVERB

Patience is the art of hoping.   —VAUVENARGUES

Patriotism

"My country, right or wrong" is like saying, "My mother, drunk or sober".   —G. K. CHESTERTON

I venture to suggest that patriotism is not a short and frenzied outburst of emotion but the tranquil and steady dedication of a lifetime.   —ADLAI STEVENSON

People

There are two kinds of men who never amount to much: those who cannot do what they are told, and those who can do nothing else.   —CYRUS H. K. CURTIS

God must have loved the plain people: He made so many of them.   —ABRAHAM LINCOLN

Everyone is a moon, and has a dark side which he never shows to anybody.   —MARK TWAIN

The two kinds of people on earth that I mean are the people who lift and the people who lean.

—ELLA WHEELER WILCOX

Perfection

The nearest to perfection most people ever come is when filling out an employment application.   —KEN KRAFT

Persistence

Consider the postage stamp: its usefulness consists in the ability to stick to one thing till it gets there.

—JOSH BILLINGS

Everything comes to him who hustles while he waits.

—THOMAS A. EDISON

Keep on going; I have never heard of anyone stumbling on anything sitting down.   —CHARLES KETTERING

I must recommend to you what I endeavor to practice for myself, patience and perseverance.

—GEORGE WASHINGTON

Playboy

He had heard that one is permitted a certain latitude with widows, and went in for the whole 180 degrees.

—GEORGE ADE

Pleasure

The great pleasure in life is doing what people say you cannot do.   —WALTER BAGEHOT

Poise

Always behave like a duck—keep calm and unruffled on the surface but paddle like the devil underneath.

—JACOB BRAUDE

Politicians

The world is weary of statesmen whom democracy has degraded into politicians.   —DISRAELI

Trouble is there are too many Democratic and Republican Senators and not enough United States Senators.

—SENATOR FORD

The mistake a lot of politicians make is in forgetting they've been appointed and thinking they've been anointed.

—MRS. CLAUDE PEPPER

Politicians and wives agree on one thing—if you postpone payment until some time in the future, it's not really spending.   —BILL VAUGHAN

Politics

Vote for the man who promises least; he'll be the least disappointing.   —BERNARD BARUCH

A politician is an animal who can sit on a fence and yet keep both ears to the ground.   —BEST QUOTATIONS

A politician thinks of the next election; a statesman, of the next generation.   —JAMES FREEMAN CLARKE

In politics, nothing is contemptible.   DISRAELI

Politics makes strange postmasters.   —KIN HUBBARD

The politicians were talking themselves red, white, and blue in the face.   —CLARE BOOTHE LUCE

Bad officials are elected by good citizens who do not vote.   —GEORGE JEAN NATHAN

Nothing is politically right which is morally wrong.

—DANIEL O'CONNELL

There is no more independence in politics than there is in jail.   —WILL ROGERS

Democracy substitutes election by the incompetent many for appointment by the corrupt few.

—GEORGE BERNARD SHAW

Every man who takes office in Washington either grows or swells.   —WOODROW WILSON

Pollution

Can pollution be a result of all that trash we've been
burning in our TV sets?   —GOODMAN ACE

Industries seem to find it as hard to give up smoking
as people do.   —BILL VAUGHAN

Poverty

For every talent that poverty has stimulated it has
blighted a hundred.   —JOHN W. GARDNER

Power

Nearly all men can stand adversity, but if you want to
test a man's character, give him power.

—ABRAHAM LINCOLN

In international affairs the weak can be rash, the powerful must be restrained.   —WILLIAM P. ROGERS

Praise

I praise loudly; I blame softly.

—CATHERINE II OF RUSSIA

Preaching

There is not the least use in preaching to anyone unless
you chance to catch them ill.   —SYDNEY SMITH

Prejudice

The difference between a conviction and a prejudice is
that you can explain a conviction without getting angry.

—READER'S DIGEST

President

When I was a boy I was told that anybody could become President; I'm beginning to believe it.

—CLARENCE DARROW

There's some folks standing behind the President that
ought to get around where he can watch 'em.

—KIN HUBBARD

No man will ever bring out of the Presidency the reputation which carries him into it.   —THOMAS JEFFERSON

Problems

The best way out is always through.

—ROBERT FROST

Any man who is worth his salt has by the time he is 45 accumulated a crown of thorns, and the problem is to learn how to wear it over one ear.

—CHRISTOPHER MORLEY

Progress

No army can withstand the strength of an idea whose time has come.   —VICTOR HUGO

What we call progress is the exchange of one Nuisance for another Nuisance.   —HAVELOCK ELLIS

The longer I live the more keenly I feel that whatever was good enough for our fathers is not good enough for us.   —OSCAR WILDE

Psychoanalysis

Freud had it just backward. The task is not to make people conscious of their unconscious but to make them unconscious of their conscious.   —ROBERT M. HUTCHINS

Public Speaking

Accustomed as I am to public speaking, I know the futility of it.   —FRANKLIN PIERCE ADAMS

You can't usually tell whether a man is a finished speaker until he sits down.   —JACOB BRAUDE

A speaker who does not strike oil in ten minutes should stop boring.   —JACOB BRAUDE

Why doesn't the fellow who says, "I'm no speechmaker," let it go at that instead of giving a demonstration.

—FRANK MCKINNEY HUBBARD

Three things matter in a speech: who says it, how he says it, and what he says—and of the three, the last matters the least.   —JOHN MORLEY

Rhetoric is the art of ruling the minds of men.

—PLATO

Punctuality

The only way of catching a train I ever discovered is to miss the train before.   —G. K. CHESTERTON

People who are late are often so much jollier than the people who have to wait for them.

—EDWARD VERRALL LUCAS

I am a believer in punctuality though it makes me very lonely.   —EDWARD VERRALL LUCAS

I've been on a calendar, but never on time.

—MARILYN MONROE

Questions

No question is so difficult to answer as that to which the answer is obvious.   —GEORGE BERNARD SHAW

Reading

Reading means borrowing.   —G. C. LICHTENBERG

Knowing you'll have something good to read before bed is among the most pleasurable of sensations.

—VLADIMIR NABOKOV

Reason

It is the triumph of reason to get on well with those who possess none.   —VOLTAIRE

Recognition

I don't recall your name, but your manners are familiar.

—OLIVER HERFORD

Regret

What cannot be repaired is not to be regretted.

—SAMUEL JOHNSON

Regret is an appalling waste of energy; you can't build on it; it's only good for wallowing in.

—KATHERINE MANSFIELD

Religion

If men are so wicked with religion, what would they be without it?   —BENJAMIN FRANKLIN

God will forgive me; that's his business.

—HEINRICH HEINE

I feel that Simon and Garfunkel have done more to articulate a deep religious hunger in young people than Norman Vincent Peale, Billy Graham and Fulton Sheen all put together. —JOHN P. LEAHY

The half-baked sermon causes spiritual indigestion.

—AUSTIN O'MALLEY

There's too much churchianity and not enough christianity. —ADAM CLAYTON POWELL

My teachers used to say that for a Catholic I was pretty much of a Protestant. —PIERRE TRUDEAU

Research

When you take stuff from one writer, it's plagiarism; but when you take it from many writers, it's research.

—WILSON MIZNER

Reward

The reward of a thing well done is to have done it.

—RALPH WALDO EMERSON

Right

Always do right; this will gratify some people and astonish the rest. —MARK TWAIN

Rumor

Nobody believes a rumor here until it's officially denied.

—EDWARD CHEYFITZ

Nothing ever happens in a small town, but what you hear makes up for it. —VIRGINIA SAFFORD

Science

Science has promised us truth. It has never promised us either peace or happiness. —GUSTAVE LE BON

The most incomprehensible thing about the world is that it is comprehensible. —ALBERT EINSTEIN

Seeing

When indifferent, the eye takes still photographs; when interested, movies.   —AUTHOR UNKNOWN

Self-Esteem

No man can be happy unless he feels his life in some way important.   —BERTRAND RUSSELL

Silence

Blessed are they who have nothing to say, and who cannot be persuaded to say it.

—JAMES RUSSELL LOWELL

Sin

There are many people who think that Sunday is a sponge to wipe out all the sins of the week.

—HENRY WARD BEECHER

Pleasure's a sin, and sometimes sin's a pleasure.

—LORD BYRON

God may forgive your sins, but your nervous system won't.   —ALFRED KORZYBSKI

Singing

She was a town-and-country soprano of the kind often used for augmenting the grief at a funeral.

—GEORGE ADE

She was a singer who had to take any note above A with her eyebrows.   —MONTAGUE GLASS

Skill

A skill, like an appetite, demands to be used; once you have a skill you are absolutely energized.

—ERIC HOFFER

Sky

The sky is the daily bread of the eyes.

—RALPH WALDO EMERSON

Smile

They gave each other a smile with a future in it.

—RING LARDNER

Smiles

Wrinkles should merely indicate where smiles have been.

—MARK TWAIN

Smoking

Having read so much about the bad effects of smoking he decided to give up reading.   —JACOB BRAUDE

It is now proved beyond doubt that smoking is one of the leading causes of statistics.   —FLETCHER KNEBEL

What doctors seem to say in their reports on cigarette smoking is that Tobacco Road runs into a dead end.

—NATHAN NIELSEN

More than one cigar at a time is excessive smoking.

—MARK TWAIN

Snobbishness

He walks as if balancing the family tree on his nose.

—RAYMOND MOLEY

Solitude

Solitude is as needful to the imagination as society is wholesome for the character.

—JAMES RUSSELL LOWELL

Solutions

Some people think in terms of problems and some in terms of solutions.   —THEODORE KHEEL

Soul

Self is the only prison that can ever bind the soul.

—HENRY VAN DYKE

Speech

He talks like a watch which ticks away minutes, but never strikes the hour.   —SAMUEL JOHNSON

Nature, which gave us two eyes to see and two ears to hear, has given us but one tongue to speak.

—JONATHAN SWIFT

Noise proves nothing. Often a hen who has merely laid an egg cackles as if she laid an asteroid.

—MARK TWAIN

The reason there are so few good talkers in public is that there are so few thinkers in private.

—WOMAN'S HOME COMPANION

Speechmaker's Prayer

"Oh Lord," he says, "let my words be tender and sweet, for tomorrow I may have to eat them."

—NORMAN VINCENT PEALE

Statesmanship

In statesmanship, get the formalities right; never mind about the moralities.   —MARK TWAIN

Statistics

There are three kinds of lies; lies, damned lies, and statistics.   —DISRAELI

Study

He who devotes sixteen hours a day to hard study may become as wise at sixty as he thought himself at twenty.

—MARY WILSON LITTLE

Success

I had rather men should ask why no statue has been erected in my honor, than why one has.

—MARCUS PORCIUS CATO

The man who rests on his laurels is wearing them in the wrong place.   —HAROLD COFFIN

Everyone who got where he is had to begin where he was.   —ROBERT L. EVANS

Enthusiasm is the propelling force that is necessary for climbing the ladder of success.   —B. C. FORBES

The eminently successful man should beware of the tendency of wealth to chill and isolate.

—OTTO H. KAHN

The gent who wakes up and finds himself a success hasn't been asleep.   —WILSON MIZNER

The secret of business success is when you've got a lemon, make a lemonade out of it.

—JULIUS ROSENWALD

Superiority

I love being superior to myself better than [to] my equals.   —SAMUEL TAYLOR COLERIDGE

Superstition

Superstition is the religion of feeble minds.

—EDMUND BURKE

Suspicion

Suspicion is far more apt to be wrong than right; oftener unjust than just. It is no friend to virtue, and always an enemy to happiness.   —HOSEA BALLOU

Tact

Tact consists of knowing how far we may go too far.

—JEAN COCTEAU

Without tact you can learn nothing.   —DISRAELI

To speak kindly does not hurt the tongue.

—FRENCH PROVERB

Talent

It took me fifteen years to discover I had no talent for writing, but I couldn't give it up because by that time I was too famous.   —ROBERT BENCHLEY

Natural gifts without education have more often attained to glory and virtue than education without natural gifts.

—CICERO

Every natural power exhilarates; a true talent delights the possessor first.   —RALPH WALDO EMERSON

Talk

Half the world is composed of people who have something to say and can't, and the other half who have nothing to say and keep on saying it.   —ROBERT FROST

Every time I read where some woman gave a short talk I wonder how she stopped.   —KIN HUBBARD

He can compress the most words into the smallest ideas of any man I ever met.   —ABRAHAM LINCOLN

Wise men talk because they have something to say; fools, because they have to say something.   —PLATO

His mouth works faster than his brain—he says things he hasn't thought of yet.   —READER'S DIGEST

Taste

There's no accounting for tastes, as the woman said when somebody told her her son was wanted by the police.
                                        —FRANKLIN PIERCE ADAMS

Vulgarity is the garlic in the salad of taste.
                                        —MARC CONNOLLY

My tastes are aristocratic; my actions democratic.
                                        —VICTOR HUGO

Taxes

An income-tax form is like a laundry list—either way you lose your shirt.   —FRED ALLEN

The United States is the only country where it takes more brains to figure your tax than to earn the money to pay it.   —EDWARD J. GURNEY

Tears

The most effective water power in the world—women's tears.   —WILSON MIZNER

Tears are the silent language of grief.   —VOLTAIRE

Teaching

I had, out of my sixty teachers, a scant half dozen who couldn't have been supplanted by phonographs.
                                        —DON HEROLD

Technology

The concern for man and his destiny must always be the chief interest of all technical effort.

—ALBERT EINSTEIN

Telephone

Average woman: One who can stay on the telephone longer than on a diet.　—HUGH ALLEN

The telephone has been described by a sociologist as "the greatest nuisance among conveniences and the greatest convenience among nuisances."　—ORTHODONTIPS

Temper

A perverse temper and fretful disposition will make any state of life whatsoever unhappy.　—CICERO

We boil at different degrees.

—RALPH WALDO EMERSON

People who fly into a rage always make a bad landing.

—WILL ROGERS

Temptation

The devil's boots don't creak.　—SCOTTISH PROVERB

I can resist everything except temptation.

—OSCAR WILDE

Thanks

As the cow said to the Maine farmer, "Thank you for a warm hand on a cold morning."

—THE KENNEDY WIT

Theater

A good musical comedy consists largely of disorderly conduct occasionally interrupted by talk.

—GEORGE ADE

It was one of those plays in which all the actors unfortunately enunciated very clearly.

—ROBERT BENCHLEY

Time

Americans have more timesaving devices and less time than any other group of people in the world.

—DUNCAN CALDWELL

I recommend you to take care of the minutes, for the hours will take care of themselves.

—LORD CHESTERFIELD

There is no time like the pleasant.

—OLIVER HERFORD

It's not the hours you put in; it's what you put in the hours.   —ELMER LETERMAN

Toasts

May you live all the days of your life.

—JONATHAN SWIFT

Transportation

Leisure time is no longer a problem; thanks to modern methods of transportation, you use it all up getting to and from work.   —FLETCHER KNEBEL

Travel

Tourists taking countries like vitamin pills—one a day.

—HELEN MACINNES

I dislike feeling at home when I'm abroad.

—GEORGE BERNARD SHAW

Troubles

Troubles, like babies, grow larger by nursing.

—LADY HOLLAND

Trust

Public office is a public trust.   —DAN S. LAMONT

Truth

As scarce as truth is, the supply has always been in excess of the demand.   —JOSH BILLINGS

The course of true anything never does run smooth.

—SAMUEL BUTLER

Men occasionally stumble over the truth, but most of them pick themselves up and hurry off as if nothing had happened.   —WINSTON CHURCHILL

The terrible thing about the quest for truth is that you find it.   —REMY DE GOURMONT

Pretty much all the honest truth-telling there is in the world is done by children.

—OLIVER WENDELL HOLMES

It is always the best policy to speak the truth, unless of course you are an exceptionally good liar.

—JEROME K. JEROME

He who is not very strong in memory should not meddle with lying.   —MONTAIGNE

Because I have confidence in the power of truth and of the spirit, I believe in the future of mankind.

—ALBERT SCHWEITZER

Ugliness

There are no ugly women; there are only women who do not know how to look pretty.

—JEAN DE LA BRUYÈRE

Better an ugly face than an ugly mind.

—JAMES ELLIS

Ugliness is a point of view: an ulcer is wonderful to a pathologist.   —AUSTIN O'MALLEY

Absolute and entire ugliness is rare.

—JOHN RUSKIN

Unselfishness

If I were a godfather wishing a gift on a child, it would be that he should always be more interested in other people than in himself. That's a real gift.

—COMPTON MACKENZIE

Real unselfishness consists in sharing the interests of others.   —GEORGE SANTAYANA

Vacation

No man needs a vacation so much as the person who has just had one.   —ELBERT HUBBARD

Value

I have received no more than one or two letters in my life that were worth the postage.

—HENRY DAVID THOREAU

Values

The longer one lives, the less importance one attaches to things, and also the less importance to importance.

—JEAN ROSTAND

Virtue

Recommend to your children virtue; that alone can make them happy, not gold. —BEETHOVEN
The only reward of virtue is virtue.

—RALPH WALDO EMERSON

Only the young die good. —OLIVER HERFORD
Men's virtues have their seasons even as fruits have.

—LA ROCHEFOUCAULD

I prefer an accommodation vice to an obstinate virtue.

—MOLIÈRE

Voice

Three things you can be judged by, your voice, your face and your disposition. —IGNAS BERNSTEIN

Weather

If you don't like the weather in New England, just wait a few minutes. —MARK TWAIN

Weight

He must have had a magnificent build before his stomach went in for a career of its own.

—MARGARET HALSEY

Welfare

You cannot help men permanently by doing for them what they could and should do for themselves.

—ABRAHAM LINCOLN

Wife

Of all the home remedies, a good wife is the best.

—KIN HUBBARD

Bigamy is having one wife too many. Monogamy is the same.   —H. L. MENCKEN

A loving wife will do anything for her husband except stop criticizing and trying to improve him.

—J. B. PRIESTLEY

Will

In her single person she managed to produce the effect of a majority.   —ELLEN GLASGOW

Where there's a will, there's a lawsuit.

—ADDISON MIZNER

Wisdom

It is easy to be wise after the event.

—ENGLISH PROVERB

Some are weather-wise, some are otherwise.

—BENJAMIN FRANKLIN

Gray hair is a sign of age, not of wisdom.

—GREEK PROVERB

The heart is wiser than the intellect.

—J. G. HOLLAND

Nine-tenths of wisdom consists in being wise in time.

—THEODORE ROOSEVELT

Wishing

A man will sometimes devote all his life to the development of one part of his body—the wishbone.

—ROBERT FROST

Wit

Sharp wits, like sharp knives, do often cut their owner's fingers.   —SINCLAIR LEWIS, *Arrowsmith*

A wise man will live as much within his wit as his income.   —LORD CHESTERFIELD

Wit is the salt of conversation, not the food.

—WILLIAM HAZLITT

Woman

Her features did not seem to know the value of teamwork.   —GEORGE ADE

I have never seen a pair of slacks that had very much slack in them.   —FRED ALLEN

She never quite leaves her children at home, even when she doesn't take them along.

—MARGARET CULKIN BANNING

She was a large woman who seemed not so much dressed as upholstered.   —J. M. BARRIE

My wife was too beautiful for words, but not for arguments.   —JOHN BARRYMORE

I wish Adam had died with all his ribs in his body.

—DION BOUCICAULT

Most women are not so young as they are painted.

—MAX BEERBOHM

With a man, a lie is a last resort; with women, it's First Aid.   —GELETT BURGESS

There are only three things in the world that women do not understand, and they are Liberty, Equality, and Fraternity.   —G. K. CHESTERTON

A mother takes twenty years to make a man of her boy, and another woman makes a fool of him in twenty minutes.

—ROBERT FROST

Despite my 30 years of research into the feminine soul, I have not yet been able to answer . . . the great question that has never been answered: What does a woman want?

—SIGMUND FREUD

Every woman is wrong until she cries, and then she is right, instantly.

—THOMAS CHANDLER HALIBURTON

A woman's mind is cleaner than a man's; she changes it more often.   —OLIVER HERFORD

Man has his will, but woman has her way.

—OLIVER WENDELL HOLMES

Women are unpredictable. You never know how they are going to manage to get their own way.

—FRANKLIN P. JONES

A perpetual emotion machine.   —FRANK LOESSER

The only time a woman wishes she were a year older is when she is expecting a baby.   —MARY MARSH

A woman is never too old to yearn.

—ADDISON MIZNER

Your mind needs an uplift as well as your bust.

—CHRISTOPHER MORLEY

Why is the word "tongue" feminine in Greek, Latin, Italian, Spanish, French, and German?

—AUSTIN O'MALLEY

Every woman should have a three-way mirror in her life to see herself as others do.   —MITZI NEWHOUSE

Words

Man does not live by words alone, despite the fact that sometimes he has to eat them.   —ADLAI STEVENSON

The difference between the right word and the almost right word is the difference between lightning and the lightning bug.   —MARK TWAIN

Work

I always live by this code: You can't have bread—and loaf.   —LOUIS ARMSTRONG

I do most of my work sitting down; that's where I shine.   —ROBERT BENCHLEY

Doing a woman's work is like walking down a railroad track; the end seems in sight but never is.

—MARCELENE COX

The world is full of willing people; some willing to work, the rest willing to let them.   —ROBERT FROST

The brain is a wonderful organ; it starts working the moment you get up in the morning, and does not stop until you get into the office.   —ROBERT FROST

By working faithfully eight hours a day, you may eventually get to be a boss and work twelve hours a day.

—ROBERT FROST

I am a great believer in luck, and I find the harder I work the more I have of it.   —STEPHEN LEACOCK

My father taught me to work; he did not teach me to love it.   —ABRAHAM LINCOLN

The highest reward for man's toil is not what he gets for it but what he becomes by it.   —JOHN RUSKIN

The test of a vocation is the love of the drudgery it involves.   —LOGAN P. SMITH

Work keeps at bay three great evils: boredom, vice and need.   —VOLTAIRE

World

You'll never have a quiet world till you knock the patriotism out of the human race.

—GEORGE BERNARD SHAW

Worry

The reason why worry kills more people than work is that more people worry than work.   —ROBERT FROST

Worry is interest paid on trouble before it falls due.

—WILLIAM RALPH INGE

Life is too short for mean anxieties.

—CHARLES KINGSLEY

He who foresees calamities, suffers them twice over.

—PORTEUS

Writing

It has always been much like writing a check—it is easy to write a check if you have enough money in the bank, and writing comes more easily if you have something to say.   —SHOLEM ASCH

Sometimes it sounds like I walked out of the room and left the typewriter running.   —GENE FOWLER

With sixty staring me in the face, I have developed inflammation of the sentence structure and a definite hardening of the paragraph.   —JAMES THURBER

Youth

The young can bear solitude better than the old, for their passions occupy their thoughts.

—JEAN DE LA BRUYÈRE

In youth we learn; in age we understand.

—MARIE EBNER-ESCHENBACH

Adolescence: That period when a boy refuses to believe that someday he'll be as dumb as his father.

—HAWLEY R. EVERHART

The first years of man must make provision for the last.

—SAMUEL JOHNSON

All sorts of allowances are made for the illusions of youth; and none, or almost none, for the disenchantments of age.   —ROBERT LOUIS STEVENSON

Snow and adolescence are the only problems that disappear if you ignore them long enough.

—EARL WILSON

D. Suggested References

Excellent Inexpensive Paperbacks

FOR THE PUBLIC SPEAKER:

2500 Anecdotes for all Occasions—Fuller (Dolphin)
The Great Quotations—Seldes (Pocketbooks)
Best Quotations—Henry (Premier)
Viking Dictionary of Aphorisms
Dictionary of Humorous Quotations—Esar (Paperback)
Left Handed Dictionary—Levinson (Collier)
Reader's Digest Dictionary of Quotations

Periodicals: *Forbes Magazine,* "Thoughts on the Business
of Life," monthly feature.
Vital Speeches of the Day (City News Publishing, Box 606, Southold, New York.)

FOR ADDING TO WORDROBES:

Dictionary of Synonyms and Antonyms—Devlin (Popular
Special)
New Pocket Roget's Thesaurus (Washington Square Press)
Barron's Vocabulary Builder
30 Days to a Better Vocabulary—Funk & Lewis (Wash-
ington Square Press)

FOR PRONUNCIATION:

Pronunciation Dictionary of Troublesome Words—Colby (Apollo)
Better English (grammar, pronunciation, spelling)—Lewis (Dell)
Pronunciation Exercises in English—Clarey-Dixon (Regents)

Hard Cover

FOR SPEAKERS:

The International Dictionary of Thoughts (Doubleday)
Contemporary Quotations—Simpson (Crowell)
Speaker's Encyclopedia—Braude (Prentice-Hall)
Funk & Wagnall's Standard Encyclopedic Dictionary (See Quotation section)
The Complete Rhyming Dictionary—Wood (Garden City)
NBC Handbook of Pronunciation—Crowell (Crowell)

TEXTBOOKS FOR THE STUDENT:

Basic Principles of Speech—Sarett (Houghton-Mifflin)
Training the Speaking Voice—Anderson (Oxford)
Your Voice and Speech—Raubichek (Prentice-Hall)
Guide to Speech Training—Hibbitt-Norman (Ronald)

Index